Korean Pansori as Voice Theatre

FORMS OF DRAMA

Forms of Drama meets the need for accessible, mid-length volumes that offer undergraduate readers authoritative guides to the distinct forms of global drama. From classical Greek tragedy to Chinese pear garden theatre, cabaret to *kathakali*, the series equips readers with models and methodologies for analysing a wide range of performance practices and engaging with these as 'craft'.

SERIES EDITOR: SIMON SHEPHERD

Badhai: Hijra-Khwaja Sira-Trans *Performance across Borders in South Asia*
978-1-3501-7453-5
Adnan Hossain, Claire Pamment and Jeff Roy

Cabaret
978-1-3501-4025-7
William Grange

Classical Greek Tragedy
978-1-3501-4456-9
Judith Fletcher

The Commedia dell'Arte
978-1-3501-4418-7
Domenico Pietropaolo

Kaṭṭaikkūttu: A Rural Theatre Tradition in South India
978-1-3502-3660-8
Hanne M. de Bruin

Liyuanxi – Chinese 'Pear Garden Theatre'
978-1-3501-5739-2
Josh Stenberg

Modern Tragedy
978-1-3501-3977-0
James Moran

Pageant
978-1-3501-4451-4
Joan FitzPatrick Dean

Romantic Comedy
978-1-3501-8337-7
Trevor R. Griffiths

Satire
978-1-3501-4007-3
Joel Schechter

Tragicomedy
978-1-3501-4430-9
Brean Hammond

Korean Pansori as Voice Theatre
History, Theory, Practice

Chan E. Park

methuen | drama
LONDON • NEW YORK • OXFORD • NEW DELHI • SYDNEY

METHUEN DRAMA
Bloomsbury Publishing Plc
50 Bedford Square, London, WC1B 3DP, UK
1385 Broadway, New York, NY 10018, USA
29 Earlsfort Terrace, Dublin 2, Ireland

BLOOMSBURY, METHUEN DRAMA and the Methuen Drama logo
are trademarks of Bloomsbury Publishing Plc

First published in Great Britain 2024

Copyright © Chan E. Park, 2024

Chan E. Park has asserted her right under the Copyright, Designs and
Patents Act, 1988, to be identified as author of this work.

For legal purposes the Acknowledgments on p. xix constitute an extension
of this copyright page.

Series design by Charlotte Daniels

All rights reserved. No part of this publication may be reproduced or transmitted
in any form or by any means, electronic or mechanical, including photocopying,
recording, or any information storage or retrieval system, without prior
permission in writing from the publishers.

Bloomsbury Publishing Plc does not have any control over, or responsibility for,
any third-party websites referred to or in this book. All internet addresses given
in this book were correct at the time of going to press. The author and
publisher regret any inconvenience caused if addresses have changed or sites
have ceased to exist, but can accept no responsibility for any such changes.

A catalogue record for this book is available from the British Library.

A catalog record for this book is available from the Library of Congress.

ISBN: HB: 978-1-3501-7488-7
ePDF: 978-1-3501-7490-0
eBook: 978-1-3501-7489-4

Series: Forms of Drama

Typeset by RefineCatch Limited, Bungay, Suffolk

To find out more about our authors and books visit www.bloomsbury.com
and sign up for our newsletters.

CONTENTS

List of Illustrations ix
List of Tables x
Series Preface xi
Preface xvi
Acknowledgments xix
Notes on Transcription xx
Notes on Translation xxii

Introduction: Orality of Storysinging 1

Part One Technique and Practice of Pansori

1 Voice, Drum, Listening Ear 31

2 *Jangdan*, the Heartbeats of Storytelling 53

Part Two Historical Development

3 Eighteenth–Nineteenth Centuries 81

4 Negotiating Dramatic Modernization 115

Part Three Beyond the Twentieth Century

5 Preservation and Reinvention, Mutually 143

6 Singing Who You Are: An Autoethnography 169

Conclusion 187

Notes 191
Bibliography 209
Index 217

ILLUSTRATIONS

1 A page from *sorichaek* (songbook). A learner will make and annotate their own *sorichaek* throughout their studies   30
2 A scene from "Fox Hunt and the Death of a Queen," October 2012 performance at the East-West Center, University of Hawai'i at Mānoa. The dolls depict (from left to right), Regent Daewongun, Emperor Gojong, Queen Min. On the far right are three dolls of Korean independence activists, including Yu Gwansun (center). Kathy Foley, puppeteer   80
3 A scene from "Fox Hunt and the Death of a Queen," October 2012 performance at the East-West Center, University of Hawai'i at Mānoa. Chan Park in the doll-character of Queen Min sings of her worries and fears. Master Cho Owhan, Preserver of the Jeollanam-do Intangible Cultural Heritage the Jindo-Jodo Fishing Song, plays the *daegeum* flute   80
4 An illustration of pansori recording   142

TABLES

1.1	First three lines of a *danga*	34
2.1	Pansori rhythms and their articulations	57
2.2	Excerpt from *Song of Shim Cheong*, in *jajinmori* rhythm	59
2.3	Excerpt from *Song of Shim Cheong*, in *jungmori* rhythm	61
2.4	Excerpt from *Song of Shim Cheong*, in *jinyang* rhythm	64
2.5	Excerpt from *Song of Heungbo*, in *hwimori* rhythm	67
2.6	Excerpt from *Song of Heungbo*, in *eonmori* rhythm	69
2.7	Excerpt from *Song of Shim Cheong* in *eotchungmori* (also called *danjungmori*) rhythm	73
2.8	Three variations on *jungjungmori* rhythm	75
3.1	Artist contributions (from late Joseon to early twentieth century) to the libretto of *Song of Chunhyang*: A partial list.	100

SERIES PREFACE

The scope of this series is scripted aesthetic activity that works by means of personation.

Scripting is done in a wide variety of ways. It may, most obviously, be the more or less detailed written text familiar in the stage play of the Western tradition, which not only provides lines to be spoken but directions for speaking them. Or it may be a set of instructions, a structure or scenario, on the basis of which performers improvise, drawing, as they do so, on an already learnt repertoire of routines and responses. Or there may be nothing written, just sets of rules, arrangements, and even speeches orally handed down over time. The effectiveness of such unwritten scripting can be seen in the behavior of audiences, who, without reading a script, have learnt how to conduct themselves appropriately at the different activities they attend. For one of the key things that unwritten script specifies and assumes is the relationship between the various groups of participants, including the separation, or not, between doers and watchers.

What is scripted is specifically an aesthetic activity. That specification distinguishes drama from non-aesthetic activity using personation. Following the work of Erving Goffman in the mid-1950s, especially his book *The Presentation of Self in Everyday Life*, the social sciences have made us richly aware of the various ways in which human interactions are performed. Going shopping, for example, is a performance in that we present a version of ourselves in each encounter we make. We may indeed have changed our clothes before setting out. This, though, is a social performance.

The distinction between social performance and aesthetic activity is not clear-cut. The two sorts of practice overlap and mingle with one another. An activity may be more or less aesthetic, but the crucial distinguishing feature is the status of the aesthetic element. Going shopping may contain an aesthetic element—decisions about clothes and shoes to wear—but its purpose is not deliberately to make an aesthetic activity or to mark itself as different from everyday social life. The aesthetic element is not regarded as a general requirement. By contrast a court-room trial may be seen as a social performance, in that it has an important social function, but it is at the same time extensively scripted, with prepared speeches, costumes, and choreography. This scripted aesthetic element assists the social function in that it conveys a sense of more than everyday importance and authority to proceedings which can have life-changing impact. Unlike the activity of going shopping, the aesthetic element here is not optional. Derived from tradition, it is a required component that gives the specific identity to the activity.

It is defined as an activity in that, in a way different from a painting of Rembrandt's mother or a statue of Ramesses II, something is made to happen over time. And, unlike a symphony concert or firework display, that activity works by means of personation. Such personation may be done by imitating and interpreting—"inhabiting"—other human beings, fictional or historical, and it may use the bodies of human performers or puppets. But it may also be done by a performer who produces a version of their own self, such as a stand-up comedian or court official on duty, or by a performer who, through doing the event, acquires a self with special status as with the *hijras* securing their sacredness by doing the ritual practice of *badhai*.

Some people prefer to call many of these sorts of scripted aesthetic events not drama but cultural performance. But there are problems with this. First, such labeling tends to keep in place an old-fashioned idea of Western scholarship that drama, with its origins in ancient Greece, is a specifically European "high" art. Everything outside it is then potentially, and damagingly, consigned to a domain which may be neither "art" nor "high." Instead the European stage play and its like can best be regarded as a subset of the general category, distinct from the rest in that two groups of people come together in order specifically to present and watch a story being acted out by imitating other persons and settings. Thus the performance of a stage play in this tradition consists of two levels of activity using personation: the interaction of audience and performers, and the interaction between characters in a fictional story.

The second problem with the category of cultural performance is that it downplays the significance and persistence of script, in all its varieties. With its roots in the traditional behaviors and beliefs of a society, script gives specific instructions for the form—the materials, the structure, and sequence—of the aesthetic activity, the drama. So too, as we have noted, script defines the relationships between those who are present in different capacities at the event.

It is only by attending to what is scripted, to the form of the drama, that we can best analyze its functions and pleasures. At its most simple, analysis of form enables us to distinguish between different sorts of aesthetic activity. The masks used in *kathakali* look different from those used in *commedia dell'arte*. They are made of different materials, designs, and colors. The roots of those differences lie in their separate cultural traditions and systems of living. For similar reasons, the puppets of *karagoz* and *wayang* differ. But perhaps more importantly the attention to form provides a basis for exploring the operation and effects of a particular work. Those who regularly participate in and watch drama, of whatever sort, learn to recognize and remember the forms of what they see and hear. When one drama has family resemblances to another, in its organization and use of materials, structure and sequences, those who attend it develop expectations as to how it will—or indeed should—operate. It then becomes possible to specify how a particular work subverts, challenges or enhances these expectations.

Expectation doesn't only govern response to individual works, however. It can shape, indeed has shaped, assumptions about which dramas are worth studying. It is well established that Asia has ancient and rich dramatic traditions, from the Indian sub-continent to Japan, as does Europe, and these are studied with enthusiasm. But there is much less wide-spread activity, at least in Western universities, in relation to the traditions of, say, Africa, Latin America, and the Middle East. Second, even within the recognized traditions, there are assumptions that some dramas are more "artistic," or indeed more "serious," "higher" even, than others. Thus it may be assumed that *noh* or classical tragedy will require the sort of close attention to craft which is not necessary for mumming or *badhai*.

Both sets of assumptions here keep in place a system which allocates value. This series aims to counteract a discriminatory value system by ranging as widely as possible across world practices and by giving the same sort of attention to all the forms it features. Thus book-length studies of forms such as *al-halqa*, *hana keaka* and *ta'zieh* will appear in English for perhaps the first time. Those studies, just like those of *kathakali*, tragicomedy and the rest, will adopt the same basic approach. That approach consists of an historical overview of the development of a form combined with, indeed anchored in, detailed analysis of examples and case studies. One of the benefits of properly detailed analysis is that it can reveal the construction which gives a work the appearance of being serious, artistic, and indeed "high."

What does that work of construction is script. This series is grounded in the idea that all forms of drama have script of some kind and that an understanding of drama, of any sort, has to include analysis of that script. In taking this approach books in this series again challenge an assumption which has in recent times governed the study of drama. Deriving from the supposed, but artificial, distinction between cultural performance and drama, many accounts of cultural performance ignore its scriptedness and assume that the proper way of studying it is simply to describe how its practitioners behave and what they make. This is useful enough, but to leave it at that is to produce something that looks like a form of lesser anthropology. The description of behaviors is only the first step in that it establishes what the script is. The next step is to analyze how the script and form work and how they create effect.

But it goes further than this. The close-up analyses of materials, structures and sequences—of scripted forms—show how they emerge from and connect deeply back into the modes of life and belief to which they are necessary. They tell us in short why, in any culture, the drama needs to be done. Thus by adopting the extended model of drama, and by approaching all dramas in the same way, the books in this series aim to tell us why, in all societies, the activities of scripted aesthetic personation—dramas—keep happening, and need to keep happening.

I am grateful, as always, to Mick Wallis for helping me to think through these issues. Any clumsiness or stupidity is entirely my own.

Simon Shepherd

PREFACE

The Republic of Korea, hereafter Korea, has inherited a rich legacy of musical performance. The origins of its performance cultures are, as with many other preindustrial cultures, in the lived experiences of communal labor, leisure, ritual, and storytelling. Since the beginning of the twentieth century, Korean performing arts have evolved through modern and Western Art influences in consonance with global trends. The practices of its indigenous past have either disappeared or entered the national registry of cultural preservation, eccentric to the trajectory of development and modernization. Outside modern popular music trends, the indigenous music termed *gugak* continued among marginalized circles of mostly geo-cultural kinships. In a society still entrenched in the class divisions of the Korean monarchic past, and a monarchy that ended in 1910, in which indigenous musical performances and performers were outcasts, *gugak* was not an average urban Korean choice of career or hobby. Its performative rootedness in the tabooed indigenous ritual tradition came to be synonymous with barbaric ignorance that had ushered in the twentieth-century Korean trauma.

Among the performative traditions of *gugak*, *pansori* (hereafter, "pansori"), National Intangible Cultural Heritage No. 5 and the subject of this book, is singularly exemplary of oral storytelling as a form of theatre. By "voice theatre" I mean the totality of dramatic enactment occurs within a trained solo vocal performance. The history of theatre locates the origins of performance in the tradition of the Homeric singer of epics. These narratives were composed through a combination of formulaic improvisation and received tradition.[1]

However, few storytelling traditions have carried their vocal musical components into the twenty-first century. Pansori, which was first discovered in a town marketplace in 1700s Joseon dynasty Korea (1392–1910), is one notable exception. In my lived experience, I have been fortunate to encounter firsthand the changes in the culture and institutions of *gugak*. Attending school in postwar Korea, I received the standard Western Art music theory and practice, while embracing American pop music on the American Forces Korean Network (AFKN) Radio. In the 1970s, college women were expected to assiduously complete their studies and excel in English to find a suitable marriage partner. In contrast, there was a lively counterculture scene in South Korea which afforded me a substantial amount of American drama and popular music exposure. My brief romance with becoming a singer-songwriter came to a screeching halt when my record debut failed to pass the scrutiny of the government censorship committee. I found solace in studying pansori, and I am currently rounding up my fifth decade as a practitioner and scholar of this storysinging tradition. In teaching such technical elements of pansori as singing and drumming, Master Chung instilled the value of humanity and humility as the basis of telling stories about people. Master Chung's residence in the Eastern part of Seoul was our place of rediscovery, the Forest of Arden.[2]

Crossing between performance and theory, and communicating through pansori with audiences outside Korea, I have learned to be reflexive and inclusive. This is an art form whose practitioners have had to adapt to abrupt and deep-reaching changes in Korean society. Their art was vulgar in the time of monarchs, subversive under colonial rule, and atavistic during the postwar economic success of the "Miracle on the Han River" (*Hangangeui gijeok*). Through my journey with the singing practice and inquiry on the discourse of *gugak*, I have come to adopt a holistic vision of pansori as an open-ended living tradition and demurred from any custodial role of canonical pansori. It has served as my experimental platform for formulating diverse intercultural visions of storytelling, including the theory and performance of bilingual pansori and its audiation.

Without a separate drummer (*gosu*) to accompany me, I have for the past three decades presented my self-accompanied bilingual pansori before audiences around the world. I have carried my drum through many airports on the way to share my talk and performance. Most airports were curiously friendly toward my drum. Following the September 11, 2001, attacks, however, there was one time a customs officer was about to dismantle my drum by pulling out all the decorative brass nails holding its side drumheads to the shell in the middle: he intended to check for any contraband hidden within. I proved its innocence to him by banging out a few rhythmic cycles for all to hear, eliciting laughter and smiles from the surrounding people in an ordinarily tense environment. Here, I express gratitude to my parents for the hardy constitution that has sustained me through these many travels. I hope my commute between performance and research will enrich the reader's understanding of the dramatic dimension of pansori singing.

The building block of the pansori theatre of storytelling is the trained voice of the singer. I do not claim to decipher each singer's mindset, but the term and concept of *seongeum*, "voice," continues to be of ultimate importance that singers continue to strive to acquire. It is the window through which the singer reveals the depth of his humanity, as my teacher repeatedly emphasized: "If you want to be a singer, you should be a human being first." We have in our theatre practice the Stanislavski method designed to enhance the mental aspects of the make-believe. *Seongeum* in performance builds on the kind of focus and verisimilitude comparable in emotional intensity or truthfulness to that of a stage actor. Pansori singing is not make-believe or "acting" per se, but a truthful deliverance of its lyrical reality requires no less concentration, especially since its archaic literacy embedded in traditional orality often jars with the singer's consciousness here and now. In this sense, pansori has also been for me a performative archaeology of the realities left behind in Korea's rapid modernization process.

ACKNOWLEDGMENTS

My gratitude goes to all who rendered me support, encouragement, and inspiration to carry this book project forward: my teacher, Chung Kwonjin (Jeong Gweonjin, 1927–86), who continues to nurture me through his teachings; my research advisor, the late Marshall R. Pihl, for his constant guidance; my late father, Park Kyu-Soh, for teaching me through his example *par excellence* of modern scholarship; my late mother, Kim Ki-Sun, who imparted to me her dearest love for traditional singing and oral history; my loving family for their unwavering faith in me; the scholars, practitioners, and supporters of Korean music and folk arts, and others with whom I have enjoyed critical friendships over decades; my colleagues at the Ohio State University and elsewhere who share a keen interest in the vital and enduring role of the oral traditions of Korea and East Asia in world cultures; Dr. Christopher Sungkyu Lee for his unwavering support for the Korean Performance Research Program at Ohio State; the Bloomsbury Editorial and Publishing team for their wonderful, patient collaboration that allowed me to finish this work in the midst of Covid, and my humble gratitude to the anonymous reviewer(s) for invaluable suggestions. Last but not least, everlasting thanks go to my friend Kyung Ae for allowing me the *Chuu-Gangnam* ("Follow my friend and cross the river south") to that pansori studio on that early summer day in 1974, where it all began.

NOTES ON TRANSCRIPTION

No writing system could capture all the facets of orality, let alone the transcription of foreign words, yet this book will serve as another brave attempt. For the transcription of Korean terms into English, I use the Republic of Korea Ministry of Culture Revised Romanization of Korean (introduced in 2000). There are several exceptions detailed below:

- Where possible, already established and publicized personal names and places are rendered as they are.
- The McCune-Reischauer system is partially adopted where standardized romanization leads to awkward or undesirable pronunciation; for example, 굿 (ritual) is romanized as *kut* (McCune-Reischauer) instead of the unsightly *gut* (Revised), or 박 (a surname) as *Pak* (McCune-Reischauer) or *Park* instead of *Bak* (Revised) or *Bark*.
- Sino-Korean names and Sinitic terms that have long since been nativized into the Korean intellectual and cultural literacy are transcribed and romanized as Korean pronunciation with some exceptions. I also add the *hancha* (Classical Chinese script used in Korea) for further semantic clarity.
- For the examples of pansori lyrics, words are transcribed according to sung diction in order to render elements of oral acoustics that predate any Korean writing systems.
- Romanization of Korean words that begin with "ㄱ" in the newly standardized spelling begins with "g"; however, McCune-Reischauer spelling ("k") is retained

for direct quotations. Similarly, "p'ansori" is used in citations where the original used McCune-Reischauer.
- Although pansori is an originally Korean term, this book will hopefully support its inclusion in the English lexicon as a familiar, therefore non-italicized, term.

NOTES ON TRANSLATION

Transmission of folk musical and dramatic tradition followed the orality's route that entered modernity as its culture of oral composition, transmission, and recognition of individual creativities. In pansori, the Five Narrative Canon comprised of the *Song of Chunhyang*, *Song of Shim Cheong* (alternately, *Shim Chong (or Chung)*), *Song of Heungbo*, *Song of the Water Palace*, and *Song of the Red Cliff*, as well as the seven balladries that did not make it into the canon but are referenced in this text do not have the copyright attached to specific person(s). For several centuries, largely dating back at least to eighteenth-century Joseon, the lyrics have been transmitted in the voices of the singers to remain in the public domain. As teacher lineages are an integral part of pansori transmission, particular singers are popularly credited with having transmitted specific works. For particular songs that were taught to me, I have indicated the teachers in the Notes.

All translations of Korean traditional, creative, and scholarly works are mine, unless otherwise specified.

Introduction: Orality of Storysinging

A person's first encounter with pansori may inspire feelings of intrigue, perplexity, or even aversion due to its acoustic unfamiliarity or a preexisting sociocultural stigma. Some listeners with a direct connection to Korea such as first- or later-generation immigrants would respond emotionally with tears and yearning for Korea. At a high school in an affluent New York City community at which I once performed, a student in the audience questioned whether pansori could legitimately be classified as music as, to them, it sounded like ranting and raving. In contrast, the young audience at a juvenile detention center where I once performed in my state of Ohio, raptly listened to my pansori and asked earnest questions about the plot development and character dynamics in the story of the filial daughter Shim Cheong. They also asked many questions about musicianship and techniques required in training. The contrast between listener expectation and the performative situation may also have piqued their curiosity, in the way Walter Ong notes that as "thought itself relates in an altogether special way to sound."[1]

Pansori is a sound that also has "a special relationship to time,"[2] as its rhythmic accompaniment is essential to the telling and the listening of story. The synergy of voice, drumming, and informed aural reception expands the dramatic dimension of this narrative art. The "telling" in pansori involves multiple levels of complex interactions between singing and speaking, language and vocalization, meaning and style, vocal and percussive, and the aural dimension of "listening" that completes the definition of pansori as a form of narrative drama. The active, creative function of listening is evident in the role of *gwimyeongchang*, "great singer (critic) who sings with an ear." Rhythmic distinctions mark affect, for instance, from slow pensive beats for mourning passages, to dance-like, even syncopated beats to indicate effervescent or playful moments in the narrative.

Modern audiences, however, need guides to appreciate these aesthetics, in the form of program notes or other orienting explanation. As Eklund observes, there is already a "problematic expectation of entertainment and make-believe that has been associated with orally transmitted folklore ... dominant cultures have a strong ethnocentric bias that honors the written text over the oral form."[3] As a traditional storytelling form, pansori faces its share of cultural dismissal of the old traditional acoustics that are categorically considered unentertaining. Still, traditional orality continues to be a high point of critical discourse on human ludic behavior. A major question addressed is whether storytelling is alive, dead, or, as Macdonald's terms, "simply jumped to a new host in the revivalist teller."[4]

The ways of revival are numerous, from sharing stories at storyteller networks and media channels to insulating them as cultural archetypes by preserving from further changes or losses. An ancient Korean oral dramatic interplay of story and singing called *pansori* seems a closer example of the latter. It emerged from the pre-eighteenth-century Korean storytelling, music, and provincial ritual singing, and continues to undergo its identity transformation. The early innovation was by the *gwangdae*, male performers whose ritual functions included percussion and countermelodic backstage chants to the healing songs and dances of their shaman wives or other female relatives. On the testimonies of singers orally transmitted and documented, the names of three *gwangdae*, Ha Handam, Choe Seondal, and Wu Chundae are historicized as the forefathers of pansori. From its etymology of *pan* ("stage," "context," or "publicized occasion") plus *sori* ("sound," "speech," or "song"), we can surmise that pansori emerged as staged storysinging or dramatic storytelling substantiated by singing.

The central aim of this book is to explicate pansori as a form of voice drama composed of singing, drumming, and listening. The theatre is constructed in the imagination through the audience's listening, which evokes the whole stage with characters, scenes, situations, and such. Today, Korean society is actively invested in the promotion of national cultural products for a world audience via the *hallyu* ("Korean wave"). In pansori, there are strong currents to join this art form to contemporary highbrow and popular arts, hoping to ride the *hallyu* with new ways of staging pansori. The singing, listening, and, to a lesser extent, the drumming is thereby reassembled through discursive and material shifts in the contextual surround. But the interplay of these three aspects of voice theatre function as Bakhtin's centripetal force holding the tradition together, from the reinventive popularizing spirit.[5] This book focuses in particular on pansori as a dramatic genre and its realization through the vocal element of performance.

The twenty-first-century singers and audiences of pansori inhabit a lifeworld much different from that of the predecessors who first brought the art to the kingdom's capital, and later, the world. On the origins of the pansori singer, Pihl observes:

> The Korean singer of tales is called a *kwangdae*. His oral narrative is known as *p'ansori*, a long form of vocal music in which he sings a work of narrative literature with appropriate dramatic gesture. *P'ansori*, a folk art and a popular art, evolved at first without the aid of scores or libretti. Some writers have used the expression "one-man opera" to explain the term. The oddity of the expression aside, it does succeed in conveying the four essential characteristics of *p'ansori*: it is a solo oral technique, and it is dramatic, musical, and in verse.[6]

As a lyric dramaturgy inculcated through mimetic training, pansori progressed from a popular premodern marketplace entertainment to entering the registry of the cultural heritages of the modern nation and the world. The singer in performance is the de facto director, actor, and storyteller, simultaneously. In this theatre of the voice, the singing sets scenes, denotes actions, and deciphers the labyrinthine minds of characters. From early on, scholars from multidisciplinary arts and humanities intent on settling the pansori's genre question probed its thematic, musical, and dramatic aspects and concluded, "pansori is pansori."[7] Practitioners who aspired to official recognition tended to emulate the narratives and singing styles of their teachers rather than crafting new stories, songs, or manners of telling. From the angle of national and cultural preservation, pansori seems less a storytelling-in-the-making than an archetypal Korean classical music. The goal is less a cultivation of artistic individualism than artisanal competence resulting from years of copying your teacher. The frequently asked question is whether pansori could also revive as storytelling of the changing times without sacrificing proficiency in the craft.

Our social life has mostly parted ways with the primal orality exclusive in cultures yet untouched by writing, as literacy settled as standard means of communication and knowledge transmission. As Ong notes, literacy has revolutionized social, cultural, and intellectual dynamics: "More than any other single invention, writing has transformed human consciousness."[8] As a matter of fact, Korea's swift adaptation to modernization in the twentieth century was due in part to the acquisition of *hangeul* literacy in the twentieth century. An interesting question is how such revolutionary transformation from oral to literal influences the performative and pedagogical existence of the oral narrative and musical traditions such as pansori in our era of hyperliteracy.

Pansori's vocal repertoire is an archive of pre-twentieth-century orality, and its diegetic flows often tap into the reservoirs of folk and work songs that exude the ambience of the premodern village life of communal labor, leisure, observance of rites, and ceremonies. Those songs all but disappeared in the massive industrialization, urbanization, and depletion of the countryside population. In the story-world of pansori, however, they help reinvoke the old village ambience: *Nongbuga* (Farmer's Song) in the *Song of Chunhyang*, *Manga* (Funeral dirge), *Gilsori* (Road Song), and *Baennorae* (Boat Song) in the *Song of Shim Cheong*, for example. Though delivered in solo voice, it conjures a chorus of multiple voices of that imagined community. Today, the teaching and learning field of pansori and folk singing utilizes literacy and modern technology to transmit these very historic oralities.

The founders of Joseon, Korea's last monarchy (1392–1910), led the mainstream populace to "subsume their native ways, indeed their cultural autonomy, to the foreign ideology of Neo-Confucianism,"[9] with its literary canon as the basis. The textual study of *hanmun*, logographic literacy in *hancha* script credited to the ancient people and land of Sang (商 1600–1046 BCE), settled as foundation for scholarship and political advancement. Its access was limited to the legitimate male heirs of the aristocracy, and the ordinary people and women resorted to oral performativity for expression and transmission of thoughts and artistic creativities. Fashioned as storyteller entertainment, pansori functioned also as transmission of knowledge on popular as well as utilitarian levels. As a result, we have in pansori encyclopedic songs cataloging historical details, natural science, foodways, ceremonies, dress, architecture, geography, and medicinal cures and acupunctures to list but a few. In this way, pansori has served as traditional public education by means of storytelling.

In the mid-fifteenth century, King Sejong the Great, abetted by his team of researchers, delivered to his people the phonetic writing system of *hangeul*.[10] Ki-baik Lee observes that "It was an awareness that his people must have a writing system designed to express the language of their everyday speech, and a concern that all his subjects be able to readily learn and use it."[11] The king's consummate work and noble intent were met with strong objections from the *yangban* ruling class, protective of their monopoly "on access to learning by continuing to use the difficult Chinese writing system. Sejong, however, with the intent of furthering the moral education of the populace as a whole, pushed firmly ahead."[12] As one of the 1894 Gabo Reformation ordinances, *hangeul* was honored as *gungmun*, "national writing," for official documentation, 449 years after its promulgation. Wider use of *hangeul* beyond gender and class division facilitated more ways to enjoy storytelling. The cadenced reading of a novel as self-entertainment favorite is an example of the creative encounter of orality and literacy, a favorite pastime for my late mother. From my childhood after the Korean War of 1950–3, I recall my mother's voice chanting to herself from the weathered pages of her handwritten storybooks. Not every mother was favorably disposed to this retroactivity, and my mother definitely was a minority of one comfortable in continuing old ways, also in dressing, hairstyling, and other manifestations of femininity. Her favorite stories were popular tales from mid-to-late Joseon, mostly anonymously written and hand-copied onto booklets of *hanji* (mulberry paper). As with many women of her generation, when a lull in household duties allowed for a spare moment, my mother entertained and educated herself by retelling these stories in sung recitative. The 1999 film *My Heart* (*Jeong*) by the director Bae Changho, unfolds in the early-twentieth-century juncture of old and new: the protagonist Suni endures a life of difficulty in an unhappy, oppressive marriage. She finds solace and encouragement with her heart unwaveringly in the right place, thanks in part to her therapeutic pastime of story-chanting.

Prior to the introduction to writing, private or public communication was only possible through mnemonic repetition. The speechcraft in primal oral culture had to fit in systemically with oral composition and articulation, and Milman Parry and Albert Lord broke ground with the theory of "formulas," the metric system of oral deliverance of Homeric epic storytelling without verbatim memorization. The pansori rediscovered in modern Korea is a collection of several hundred songs making up the *Obatang*, "Five Narrative Canon," to be memorized verbatim, breath by breath. A new formula or alternate system for mastering the *Obatang* has yet to gain currency with learners today. For readers new to pansori, I share a retelling of my original synopses of the five narratives here.

The Five Narratives

These five selected and embellished narratives represent the five cardinal Confucian virtues: loyalty to superiors, filial piety to parents, wifely chastity to husband, sibling order and respect, and fidelity in friendships according to the gentlemanly code of conduct.

Song of Chunhyang (Chunhyangga)

During the early reign of King Sukchong the Great (1674–1720), a dashing young gentleman named Yi Mongnyong came to Jeolla Province (Jeollado), where his father was appointed as magistrate of Namweon township. One spring day, Mongnyong closed his book and rode out to the scenic Gwanghallu pavilion with the servant Bangja as guide. There he saw on a swing the beautiful Chunhyang, daughter of the retired *gisaeng* Weolmae. That very evening, Mongnyong went to Weolmae's house to woo Chunhyang. The days passed and their love deepened. Mongnyong's father was promoted to a post back in Seoul. As an exemplary Confucian son, Mongnyong had to accompany his parents home to study for the royal licentiate examination and wed a lady of noble birth. Pledging to meet again, Chunhyang and Mongnyong parted.

An official named Byeon Hakto in the north of Seoul heard of the beautiful Chunhyang and petitioned to be the new magistrate of Namweon. One of his executive orders was for her to serve him, and Chunhyang rebuked him saying she was already pledged to a man. Byeon ordered her flogged and imprisoned, to be beheaded as the highlight of his birthday celebration. Meanwhile in Seoul, Mongnyong studied diligently and earned top honors in the royal examination. Assigned the royal inspector of Jeollado, he led his secret troops to where he had left his heart years prior, Namweon, determined to set things to rights. On the eve of Chunhyang's execution, Mongnyong dressed as beggar and turned up at her gate. Weolmae, who had been fervently praying for his return to save her daughter, was devastated at his appearance. Unperturbed, Chunhyang assured him of her undying love for him. At the height of the next day's merriment, there were thunderous shouts, "The Secret Royal Inspector is here!" Havoc ensued as the Royal Inspector's secret police swooped down, hammering and pummeling those running, falling, or crawling for cover. Justice was restored for the innocent and the powerless. Led out of her cell, Chunhyang was made to identify the jade ring she had given Mongnyong at their parting. His identity revealed, the story ended happily.

Song of Shim Cheong (*Shimcheongga*)

In Peach Blossom Village, there lived a blind gentleman named Shim Hakkyu with his resourceful and talented wife Gwak-ssi. He had a comfortable life thanks to her, except they did not have a son to carry on the family name. Their prayers were answered, and Gwak-ssi became pregnant. Unfortunately, she died shortly after giving birth to a girl, leaving the newborn Shim Cheong in the care of her blind husband. Owing to the kind women of the village who nursed her, Shim Cheong grew up to become a beautiful, kind-hearted girl.

In Cheong's fifteenth year, Lady Jang, widow of the late Minister Jang, heard of Cheong's extraordinary virtue and beauty and invited her to the mansion. The sun was setting, and Blindman Shim was cold, hungry, and anxious. He felt his way in the drifting snow, calling for his daughter and fell into an icy stream. A mendicant monk rescued Shim and promised the Lord Buddha of his temple would restore his vision with the donation of three hundred bags of sacrificial rice. Blindman Shim unthinkingly pledged to donate the impossible sum. Hearing of her father's promise, Cheong from that day forth prayed to the guardian spirits to help her procure the rice. One day, a group of merchant sailors entered the village, loudly announcing they would pay any price for a maiden to be sacrificed to the Dragon King of the West Sea as insurance for their safe and prosperous voyage. Cheong sold her dear life for the sum of rice her father had pledged to the temple. She followed the sailors to the sea and drowned herself.

Moved by her self-immolating devotion, Heaven restored Shim Cheong's life in a magical lotus bud to float where she drew her last breath. Meanwhile, the sailors had amassed a fortune and were on their return journey when they spotted the lotus floating where Shim Cheong drew her last breath. They brought it home and presented it to the emperor, who had recently found solace in floriculture after the passing of his queen. One sleepless night, the emperor decided to take a stroll through his flower garden. He was drawn to the fragrance of the lotus bud, and suddenly it opened to reveal Shim Cheong. Convinced she was sent to him by Heaven, the emperor married her.

Though she was happily married, Empress Shim was sad and worried about her father's whereabouts. To help her find her father, the emperor held a hundred-day banquet for all blind men of the country. On the last day, Blindman Shim arrived at the banquet, and in the intensity of the surprise at meeting his daughter he thought had died, Blindman Shim regained his sight. Blessed by Empress Shim's heaven-sent piety, all the blind creatures of the whole world regained their sight.

Song of Heungbo (*Heungboga*)

Once upon a time, there lived two brothers: the younger brother Heungbo was kind and generous, and the older brother Nolbo was obnoxious and greedy. In conformity with Confucian family inheritance protocols, Nolbo inherited the family assets to fulfill his duty as head of household, only to drive out Heungbo and his family in destitution. They wandered in search of shelter, all the while suffering hunger and humiliation. They were about to hang themselves when an eremite from a nearby mountain sanctuary chanced by and took pity on them. Assuring Heungbo to persevere, as fortune belongs to no one in particular, the ascetic found him an auspicious homesite deep in the valley. Heungbo built a mud hut and moved his family there. Spring returned, and with it a pair of swallows that built a nest under his eaves. Two babies hatched. One flew away, while the other fell and broke its legs. Kind Heungbo and his wife nursed it back to health.

The winter, the Great Hall of the Swallow Kingdom in the Southern Hemisphere was bustling with the swallows returning from around the world. Heungbo's swallow limped in to report its arrival. Moved by the story of a human saving one of their own, the Swallow King gave him a magic seed to take back home. Heungbo was delighted at the swallow's return the following spring. In gratitude, he planted the seed that the bird brought. Behind his shed, it sprouted vines which climbed their thatched roof, yielding three beautiful round gourds against the clear autumn sky. It was Chuseok, Korean Thanksgiving, and having nothing else to celebrate the holiday with, the family gathered to saw open the gourds one by one. Miraculously, out poured money, rice, gold, and they became the wealthiest family in the country.

Hearing of his brother's sudden good fortune, Nolbo came to investigate and was incensed with jealousy. Determined to outclass his brother, he caught multiple swallows and one by one broke and bandaged their legs. Nolbo in turn received a seed from a returning swallow, which he eagerly planted. The next fall, he harvested three handsome gourds. What came out of them, I could only leave to your imagination. Nolbo was humiliated and left destitute, but Heungbo took in Nolbo and his family to share his mansion and wealth.

Song of the Water Palace (*Sugungga*)

The Dragon King of the Water Palace was bedridden with an illness, and neither medicine nor doctor could cure him. One day, a mystic descended from the sky to advise the diagnosis and only cure—a hare's liver. None among the king's cabinet except Minister Turtle had the courage to travel to the land in search of the cure. With a portrait of Hare, Turtle came ashore. After numerous life-threatening adventures, Turtle found Hare and successfully lured him to travel to the Water Palace.

Upon arrival, Hare realized he had been tricked. Gathering his wits, he told the Dragon King that regrettably he had left his liver in his mountain dwelling and had to go back for it. In desperation, Dragon King ordered Turtle to take Hare back to land. Turtle would not dare contradict his king and brought Hare back on the false hope that perhaps Hare was speaking the truth. Landing safely, Hare hopped away. A different version offers a Confucian happy ending: Turtle's devotion moved Heaven, and he was awarded a heavenly decoction for his king. Still another version offers raunchy comedy and blighting ridicule: the feces Hare deposited in the fold of Turtle's neck while riding on his shell were the magic pills after all.

Song of the Red Cliff (*Jeokpyeokka*)

The *Song of the Red Cliff* is the pansori version of a third-century Chinese historical event which appeared in Classical Korean oral and written literature. One account is the *Romance of Three Kingdoms*.[13] In contrast to the other *Obatang* texts which emerged from unknown origins through indigenous, multivalent narratives, the *Song of the Red Cliff* adheres to the more linear chronology of Luo Guanzhong's historical novel. For readers familiar with the episodes and characters, I include their names in Chinese characters and romanization in both Korean and Chinese.

In the waning years of the Later Han, the empire was being enervated by factional strife among warlords, bandits, court eunuchs, dowager queens, and members of the scholar gentry. An adoptive son of a eunuch, Cao Cao (曹操) rose to the seat of prime minister and brought one warlord after another to surrender until all of Northern China came under his control.

In the southwest was Liu Bei (劉備), descendant of the founder of Han dynasty, who was keen on restoring the glory of Han. In the Eastern territories was Sun Quan (孫權). In 208, Cao Cao led his 830,000 troops southward to crush the allied forces of Liu and Sun and complete a decisive unification of China. At the Red Cliff (赤壁, Chibi) along the Yangzi River, Cao Cao was utterly defeated.

The first episode of the pansori *Song of Red Cliff* tells of Yu Bi (Chn. Liu Bei, 劉備) who, having lost his trustworthy strategist to a snare set by Jo Jo (Chn. Cao Cao, 曹操), secured the counsel of Jegal Yang (Chn. Zhuge Liang, 諸葛亮) by paying "three humble visits to Jegal's grass hut."[14] Jegal Yang helped Yu Bi win a minor battle, then visited the headquarters of Son Gweon (Chn. Sun Quan, 孫權) to instigate his adviser Ju Yu (Chn. Zhou Yu, 周瑜) to join forces against Jo Jo. The next episode takes place at Jo Jo's camp on the eve of the battle of the Red Cliff. The soldiers were drunk, homesick, and anticipating a bloody battle. Jegal Yang prayed to Heaven to send down a southeasterly wind, an unlikely phenomenon in midwinter. The southeasterly wind did blow, and Jegal Yang destroyed Jo Jo's forces. Gwan U (Chn. Guan Yu, 關羽), the noble warrior, captured Jo Jo as he was escaping on the Hwayongdo (Chn. Huarongdao, 華容道) path but, remembering the favor he received from him previously, spared him.

Transmission of Oral Tradition

Memorization has been an integral part of learning and in turn performing oral tradition. As Goody and Watt note, "The social function of memory—and of forgetting—can thus be seen as the final stage of what may be called the homeostatic organization of the cultural tradition in non-literate society."[15] Oral societies "live very much in a present which keeps itself in equilibrium of homeostasis by sloughing off memories which no longer have present relevance."[16] The emergence of literacy in the developmental history of pansori makes messier and ambiguous its separation of oral and literal. The notion of memory is not so simply divisible between pansori past and pansori present: it has been modified due to the cultural needs of the present. We have today a popular entertainment transmitted from the eras that no longer capture the popular imagination, but are still performed in the capacity of national treasure and valuable cultural property. It had been discarded and forgotten, to be remembered and relearned via literacy and technology.

What pedagogical adjustments might have taken place when literacy entered pansori teaching and learning in terms of transcription of what the teacher orally gives? Every learner aspires to emulate all aspects of his teacher's singing by listening, observing, and repeating, and it has not changed over time. Imaginatively, the permanence of writing at a learner's disposal could distract the process of primary oral learning by deferring the process of mental and acoustic learning. Increased dependency on literacy may have thus played a part in the overall estrangement of pansori as an archetypal verbatim learning.

Writing is also viewed as an artificial technology different from the fully natural oral speech that every human being learns to talk.[17] What is today a painstaking verbatim learning, pansori in the primary oral past imaginatively may have been a more spontaneous learning and composition just as trot, hip-hop, or other popular genres are more readily learned by singers of today. Interestingly, the advent of recording technology makes up for the impaired naturalness with unlimited replay and repetition. Another pertinent question concerns the effects of the shifted pattern of transmission of pansori from the traditional master–disciple *gujeonshimsu*, "pass orally, receive it heartfully," to the modern bookkeeping of lesson fees and time management. By the late 1970s, the majority of learners arrived at their lessons with cassette recorders, on the way to tablets and smartphones. The investigation of technological intervention in pansori training and innovation is timely, given the direction of all fields of pedagogy moving toward distance and virtual learning and of popularization of pansori by means of technological adaptation.

Origin and Kinship

Pansori narratives are derived from folk tales, myths, legends, ritual narratives, and classical novels (*gu-soseol*). The storytellers indexed popular songs, labor tunes, prayer chants, and poetry recitations to punctuate the unfolding drama. Prosodically, pansori draws upon *gasa* style, which was popular among the mid-Joseon Neo-Confucian literati. For these *yangban* poets, *gasa* discursive style and variable length suited their representations of nature. Expressive of a singer's geo-temporal context, *pansori* amalgamated *gasa* prosodic elements with colloquial Jeolla dialects.

In terms of the musical origin of singing, pansori is irrefutably connected with the healing ritual (*kut*) of the Korean Southwest, as the two domains historically have shared blood-kinship and performative profession. Korean shamans (*mudang*) are predominantly female, and their techniques of healing are more about appeasement than conquest of natural or spiritual forces. The invocation progresses to entertain the attendant spiritual and human audience with songs, dances, music, and storytelling. The human living space is also the habitat for the house spirits: the presiding Seongju, the kitchen god Jowang, Dragon in the well, and Cheuksin regulating the outhouse activities, for example. The format of performance is mobile: with the living parlor and/or courtyard as mainstage, the healing performance sometimes moves outdoors into the street, shrine, mountain, riverside, oceanside, on a boat, or to ancestral gravesites.

With bells in one hand and fan in the other, the entranced shaman stages her spiritual drama, with spirit-actors as the invisible cast. The symbolic and realistic props heighten the dramatic ambivalence of liminal reality. Pansori singing appears to have adopted the spatial protocol and *mise-en-*

scène of the ritual performance, i.e., indoor–outdoor storysinging and dancing on a straw mat, making symbolic gestures with a fan. Pansori as a singing voice reveals a strong connection with the singing voice, rhythm, and musical groove of the southwestern *musok* ritual. The improvisational *gueum*, literally "mouth music," meaning "vocable" or "vocalize," performed in both domains, impressionably links spiritual healing chants and pansori.

Historically, the Korean mainstream attitude toward their native spiritual practice has been highly equivocal. The everyday Korean's typical approach is to discreetly consult a *musok* practitioner for life advice while maintaining a distance from its publicly tabooed image. It was not always so, however. From the Neolithic era of clanship, political leadership was concentrated in spiritual leaders who were assumed guardians over the forces of nature, but "the two became distinct as more formidable political power developed ... now content with secular power alone and entrusted religious ceremonies to masters of ritual."[18] With the separation of political and spiritual authority and the circulation of newer belief practices, including Buddhism and Confucianism, the social standing of indigenous ritual practitioners declined further. The ill-fated word-pair, *hwarang* and *hwaraengi*, signals this transition. *Hwarang*, "flower youths," was a system initiated in the sixth-century Shilla kingdom of training sons of elite households as future leaders. For a fuller understanding of mind and body integration, the *hwarang* scouts trained in martial arts, meditation, and musical and poetic performances to feel at one with nature. However, gradually the term *hwaraengi*, a slang term debasing *hwarang*, became synonymous with the *gwangdae* performer:

> Modern Korean scholarship assumes that this degraded *hwarang* tradition merged with other shamanistic aspects of the popular culture during the Koryo period. In the shadow of a Koryo state policy favoring Buddhism, the *hwarang* became displaced and dispersed; and their religious activity

took on the form of popular shamanistic rituals. Their martial skills were turned to tumbling, acrobatics, and rope-walking; and their music became accompaniment for shaman ritual or the stuff of itinerant band performances. Furthermore, after the establishment in the middle tenth century of the Koryo examination system and the subsequent growth of a bureaucratic class with no less a status than the noble officialdom of Shilla, the scattered *hwarang* were demeaned as a group of wandering outcasts who were unregistered and difficult to control, reminiscent of Europe's Gypsies.[19]

The kingdom of Goryeo (918–1392) appropriated *musok* and geomancy to designate Buddhism as the state religion. The result was "a distinctively hybrid form of Buddhist practice"[20] that reformulated native practices into a pseudo-indigenous Buddhism. The Joseon dynasty (1392–1910) at its inception denounced Buddhism for Neo-Confucian ideology but upheld the hereditary slave and outcast system of Goryeo that relegated musicians, actors, and shamans as subalterns.[21] Owing to the strict caste segregation of Joseon, traditional Korean performance arts have a relatively undiluted genealogy.

Under Epic Construction

By late Joseon, pansori singing had gained in popularity and esteem, and some aristocrats were patronizing the art. This new visibility in turn led to textual and artistic gentrification. The existing pansori narratives were trimmed to the *Obatang* (Five Narrative Canon) to correspond to the ideology of *samgang oryun*, "three principles, five human relationships." Superficially, each story promotes one of the five virtues dictating individual acquiescence to social hierarchy: loyalty to superiors, filial piety for parents, wifely chastity, observance of sibling order, and faith between friends. Each narrative's subtextual content, however, is rich with irony. Under the ideological patterning, pansori narratives are compelling revelations of human complexity: "conflict among the dramatic characters betrays the inside story, the social awareness that struggles to be freed of the medieval social bondage."[22] In this regard, pansori's textual hybridity presaged the onset of Korean modernist heteroglossia.

The standard definitions of epic, originated from ancient oral traditions, contain three basic elements: long narrative poem, heroic deeds, and elevated language. For Bakhtin, the epic crystallizes the imagined origins of the national past, literally an origination that is disjoint from the experience of the present.[23] This conceptualization of epic is especially descriptive of Korea as described in pansori. Given the ruptured chronology of Korea's past and present, common perceptions of pansori today conforms more with Scholes and Kellogg's analogy of epic poem as a fossilized, extinct predecessor to living organisms of the present.[24] Preserved as a national treasure, pansori aligns more with these definitions of epic. In practice, its practitioners and audiences grapple with performative realities that are entangled with the cultural politics of preservation. Removed from its original context, pansori singers today focus on maintaining the status quo, i.e., repeating the old songs from their teachers. So transmitted, the tradition gives rise to new conditions and variations. Pansori in this regard is a counterexample, an ancient organism incorrectly declared extinct while it adapts to new conditions. The story begins with the quintessential introduction, "Long ago ...," then animates the long-ago to the present imagination of the audience.

Pansori Singing as Knowledge Depository

As folk tradition, pansori is a product of the views and expressions of the common-to-marginalized populace, serving not only entertainment but also a public knowledge-sharing function, especially since the power that came with literacy was stringently guarded by the male *yangban* elites. There exist in pansori songs that substantiate its epic dramatic construction that may be likened to a kind of public cultural education different from the Confucian heavy hand of its moral didactic contents. These songs recite long lists of material or immaterial things people aspire to possess or be curious about. The songs are hardly essential to plot development, but their exuberant listing of things inserted as part of the storytelling provides rhythmically enhanced breaks from the intensity of the unfolding drama while making you feel better informed. To pansori listeners today, they bring back the forgotten knowledge of old Korea that modernity left behind.

The catalogs of life's details are inexhaustible: cooking, weaving, sewing, building, birth, death, prayer, healing, production, consumption, war, to name but a few. All the canonical pansori narratives contain "cataloging songs," and here are some examples. In the *Song of Heungbo*, the once destitute Heungbo becomes the richest man thanks to his swallow friend. From his magic gourds, out come money, rice, bundles of silk in every color, texture, design, thickness, and manufacturer, followed by a construction crew, tools, and materials to build a palatial mansion for him. In the *Song of Shim Cheong*, the titular heroine sacrifices herself at sea and is miraculously summoned to the Dragon King's underwater palace. At the banquet in her honor, dozens of legendary musicians play their instruments while, one by one, the guests from heaven descend, riding all of those mythological animals. In the *Song of the Red Cliff*, Jo Jo (曹操) loses the battle and runs away, accompanied with the melancholic *Ballad of Birds*, brilliantly interwoven between a voluminous taxonomy of birds and the tragedy of defeat. In the *Song of Chunhyang*, the procession of the new magistrate comes down, passing dozens of still existing locations between Seoul and Namweon. The song is a cultural geography of the love story joining Seoul and Jeolla three centuries ago. In *Song of the Water Palace*, calamity ensues as the Dragon King falls ill. In the frenetic rush to find a remedy, the textbook details of Korean traditional herbology and acupuncture are tabulated in the *Song of Medicines*. I end with a translation of a few of the beginning lines from the song:

> The Dragon King gives his arm, the mystic examines his pulse.
> Heart and small intestines are fire, Liver and gallbladder, wood,
> Lung and large intestines, metal, Kidney and bladder, water,
> Spleen and stomach, earth. When the liver's enlarged,
> wood suppresses earth and damages the spleen and stomach,
> Gallbladder overactivity causes nerve hypersensitivity.
> Lung and large intestinal overactivity weaken the liver and gallbladder.
> According to the Book of Medicine, the spleen is the source of life
> and gall its manifestation. When the heart is calmed, ten thousand illnesses rest,
> When stirred, ten thousand sicknesses rise.
> From a bruised heart, what sickness wouldn't surface?[25]

Narrative Convention and Structure

In conventional theatre, physical staging and movement are important aspects of production. However, in pansori, staging and action are minimized. Instead, an abundant cast emerges in the imagination, generated by singing, drumming, and listening. The staging and props are also minimal: *buchae*, folding fans with spokes made of double slips of bamboo the singer carries. In the possession of the drummer are a wooden barrel-shaped drum wrapped in hide called *buk*, and *bukchae*, drumstick, typically made of birch or citrus wood. The first public pansori performances may have been informal busking-style arrangements in town marketplaces, and this basic staging is still used today for festivals and special outdoor events. The *pan* or stage is set with a *dotchari* (straw or sedge mat) at the center. If available, a *byeongpung*, folding screen with calligraphic writing or painting, serves as a backdrop. The singer stands stage center, facing the audience while the drummer sits on the floor to the left, facing the singer and scans the audience for their responses. On the fringe of the *dotchari* are two *bangseok* or square-shaped flat cushions for the drummer and drum. Singer and drummer are typically dressed in traditional *hanbok*. The traditional hairdo seems more compulsory for women than men: patriarchal conventions percolated into *gwangdae* norms during Joseon.

A pansori song begins with the singer's rousing utterance of the first word of the song. The drummer instantly answers with a matching beat and *chuimsae*, vocal cheer such as *Uh-huh!*, *Olssigu ha jotta!* (*Hiya*, cool!), *Gurae*—! (Indeed!), or *Gurochi*! (That's it!). Some connoisseurs of pansori claim this first singer–drummer exchange is a critical litmus for gauging competency and energy level, by which the audience discerns the quality of the performance about to take place. Throughout the performance, members of the audience are most welcome to pitch in their *chuimsae*. Pansori audiences of the 1970s–1990s were more subdued than today, negotiating conventions of theatrical fourth walls, public etiquette, and Korean *chemyon* ("face" or self-presentation). But a pansori performance no longer stays tranquil since the Koreans attending traditional music events today are more vocal. Lacking the inhibitions of older generations, and not unlike the fan performances characteristic of Korean pop music concerts, younger audiences today give out hearty *chuimsae* in the form of whistles and shouts. For the singer and drummer, most welcome are those *chuimsae gosu* (experts) friends and associates who are familiar to the narrative, rhythmic, and melodic punctuation and thereby provide generous *chuimsae*. But take what you can get, for any encouragement from the floor would be better than silence.

The singer wields *buchae* like an extension of the arm to portray imaginary objects, scene changes, or emphases. The cracking sound of the *buchae* unfolding and folding commands attention, like a Zen master's bamboo club sounding the threshold of emptiness. Draw an arc upward in measured tempo and thwack it open: you have opened the sky; flutter, it is the wind blowing; wave, the tide is rising; fold it slowly and you are gently back on land; spread it out and lay it before you, it is a banquet table, book, altar, or palace courtyard; dry away your sweat, it is simply a fan.

Pansori may be described as a minimalist theatre as the drama unfolds not in the physical stage acting but in the listener's auditory power of imagination. A nineteenth-century poet named Shin Wi (d. 1847), having attended a performance of the *Song of Chunhyang* by the famed Go Sugwan, left an intriguing firsthand observation under the title, *Gwangeuk jeolgu shibisu* (Twelve Seven-Character Quatrains on Viewing a Play, 1826):[26]

> Chunhyang, finished with her makeup, casts an amorous glance,
> Dressed up and holding a fan, how odd she looks!
> How the fair Royal Inspector Yi
> Still dominates the show![27]

These lines lead readers to imagine a pair of actors playing two flirtatious lovers in person. But it is an unlikely scenario since women did not enter pansori until the later part of the nineteenth century. The next possibility may involve a pretty boy actor cross-dressed to play the character of Chunhyang. But this, too, is less likely, given the poem was written to applaud the legendary expressiveness of the *gwangdae* Go Sugwan's singing. I conclude that the poet illuminates not a realistic impersonation by the actor, but the imagined flirtatiousness of the lovers Go's singing graphically conjures up without corrupting the minimalist theatre of the voice conventionality.

Poetics of Storysinging from Past to Present

For Plato, music is a double-edged sword in that it disposes the listener toward not only virtue but also vice. There is grace and gracelessness. Gracelessness lacks rhythm and harmony like bad words and character, while grace is the emulation of a moderate and good character through education of music and poetry. Rhythm and harmony permeate the inner part of the soul more than anything else.[28] Equating music with emotion, Aristotle likened musical modes to emotional states, and prescribed musical education as a means of cultivating ethical character.[29] To Confucius, music was primarily a prescriptive means of maintaining social order auguring peace and prosperity, and his theory explains how the sound of music implicates the mind that moves:

> Music rises in the mind
> Touched by things the mind moves
> So risen sound merges with sound
> Stirring and impelling due patterns the sound of music.[30]

Music in the Confucian school was, like a game of chess, an acoustic confirmation of the correct political positionalities. Their social existences manifest in the modulations of the voice sprung from the mind. The five prescriptive notes diagnose the society's state of affairs. For example, if the king is arrogant, the note prescribed to the ruler (宮) turns rough: if the administration is reeling, the note representing the minister (商) is teetering; if people are aggrieved, the note representing the people (角) is perturbed; when state affairs are troubled, the corresponding note (徵) is sorrowful; when state resources decimate, the corresponding note (羽) sounds impending devastation. The tone, pitch, interval, colors of costume, props, orchestral map, notation, and even the material and make of instruments were molecules of this ideological quantum. The mind of the Sage unperturbed by emotion "stays the course of the Way with ceremony, harmonizes sound with music, unifies action with governance, circumvents vice with punishment."[31] The Korean court music (*jeongak*) comprising of the indigenous *hyangak*, ritual music of Tang dynasty (*dangak*) and their fusion, continues to safeguard the Confucian musical poetics in performance.

Rooted in the poetic disposition of indigenous folk music (*minsogak*), pansori is vernacular, spontaneous, and emotional. The human in the pansori voice converts the unreachable ideals of *samgang oryun* to human experience. Through the vocal performance of pansori, even the most unreal self-sacrifices the protagonists make sounds engagingly real. Perhaps this was the reason those aristocrats became avid pansori listeners and patrons in the nineteenth century.

Unlike the court music for official ceremonies and celebrations, folk music was a more transparent portrayal of everyday life. Songs and dances were specific to life rituals, labor, and leisure. Canonical pansori narratives express both folk sensibilities and Neo-Confucian morality: under the prescriptive veneer, there was folk knowledge beyond the exaggerated emotionalism often associated with mass culture. From onomatopoeic language, vernacular humor, diegetic elements, and other textual components, there are rebellions and narrow escapes from authority, anti-heroes, improper female conduct, and many other departures from Neo-Confucian literary didacticism.

Korea's sociopolitical transitions in the twentieth century were also moments of crisis and innovation in performance traditions. While mainstream popular music developed in conjunction with modernism and electricity, traditional labor, leisure, and storytelling were considered outmoded. Pansori had almost entirely lost currency as a popular entertainment form, and instead entered into a conservatory mode as a national treasure. If the nineteenth-century canonization of pansori was a propagation of the dynastic ideological foundation, the twentieth century witnessed its ossification as a cultural icon. With the implementation of cultural preservation systems in the 1960s, styles officially designated as "archetypes" (*weonhyeong*) were taught by officially recognized masters to their students and in higher education and graduate degree programs. Today, the field is producing far more college-graduated singers than can be accommodated within the national and regional human cultural property framework.

The postmodern performative poetics of pansori is progressively toward boundary-breaking and transnationalism propelled by the strengths of the continuing transmission. Pansori is a refreshing subject of intercultural or fusion experimentation geared for regaining the hearts and minds of contemporary popular music and theatregoers. The innovative among singers collaborate with theatre, film, independent music composers and singers as well as Western classical and other ethnic instruments. They strive to situate their performative identities in the popular cultural sphere, probing intercultural possibilities in collaboration with other dramatic or musical genres presumably more palatable to the audiences today. The media as a whole exercises much more relaxed playfulness than before when introducing pansori, indicative of a larger shift in manner of representation: pansori is embraced less as a "national treasure" than a popular cultural phenomenon.

Between Speaking and Singing

An aphorism in traditional music goes, "The word is short, sori is long (*eodan-seongjang*)." In pansori, there occurs not only a structural alternation of speaking and singing but also tonal variation within the hybrid language of the lyric. Spoken introductions are brief and followed by longer melismatic detour through the lyrics. Singing enhances poetic elevation of language with rhythmic repetition and harmony. Aristotle's definition of mimetic art of poetry either accompanied with the "music of the flute and of the lyre" or "by means of language alone,"[32] resounds in pansori where language and rhythm harmonize between stylized speaking (*aniri*) and singing (*sori*). The setting and assembly of characters occurs in spoken *aniri*. Pansori narration enters song mode when the singer's spirit, *heung* or *shinmyeong*, "moves" or "animates," then returns to advancing the diegetic flow. Metaphorically, the singer traverses the narrative by alternately walking then dancing.

On the energetics of poetry, O'Shea and Holub observe, "poetry is energy, it is an energy storing and an energy releasing device."[33] These dynamics are elongated and amplified through *sori*. The relationship between speaking and singing also involves the dramatic tense shifting between past and present. In general, the spoken narrative of *aniri* is typically in past tense in moving the plot of the story forward, while the *sori*, sung narrative, claims the here-and-now for the character's thought and action as well as the storyteller witnessing them. In this regard, singing is comparable to stage acting, where the actor's consciousness converges with the character's consciousness.

Orality, Literacy, Technology

Transcription, notation, and other technologies are now mainstream in the performance and learning of traditional music (*gugak*). In his study of pansori schools of stylistics, Bae Yeon-hyung notes that hand-scribed *hangeul* scripts called *sorichaek* serve as a manuscript of the singer's narrative with the designation of *jangdan* for each song.[34] Its pedagogical function goes much further to make room for the suprasegmental and microtonal elements of the vocal legacies of teacher. Because of the individual nature of its making, *sorichaek* is an essential learner text for the very personal business of *sori* acquisition. The teacher recites the day's lesson, the learner writes it down in their *sorichaek*, the teacher demonstrates how it is sung, the learner transcribes the performance as added annotation to practice later. Even with today's advanced digital literacies, the pencil-and-paper *sorichaek* is a widely used pedagogical tool.

Since the first Korean music recording by Columbia Records including a few excerpts of *Chunhyang* and *Shim Cheong*, Osaka 1906, recording technology has found crucial functions in the oral transmission of pansori. In pansori education, recording has substituted a large portion of the traditional face-to-face training and practice: it is less essential to physically remain within hearing range of your teacher's voice for as long as it takes to acquire the narratives. Students can go away after making sure the recordings made during lessons are good to go. Smartphones and other devices are widely used to record teacher demonstrations. Recording technologies also make it possible to continue learning from singers who have passed on.

In the continuing tradition of Korean court music, there have been in use various notational systems including *jeongganbo*, boxcar or square bar notation of pitch and interval, the twelve-pitch *yulchabo*, and the instrumental onomatopoeic *yukpo*. Outside the limited use of sound notation in instrumental music, folk music pedagogy and performance was left to the realm of mnemonic improvisational variation. Since the twentieth century, staff notation from Western Art music has served as standard musical literacy in Korea. Transcription of one of the five canonical pansori narratives into staff notation is now a standard requirement toward the fulfillment of a graduate degree in pansori, although in practice staff notation is rarely used in learning to sing pansori. Many practitioners realize that Westernized annotation systems lead to fragmented and deconstructed performances. In acquiring the teacher's *sori*, descriptive illustration or a shorthand transcription of the teacher's demonstration helps the student to visualize and reproduce its acoustics, and in turn, develop their own *sori*. Despite the prevalence of Western Art musical staff notation, in academic settings in particular, it is the *sorichaek* that endures as a pedagogical standard in the domain of performativity.

Outline of the Book

This book is comprised of three parts and six chapters. Part One explains the technical elements of pansori's voice theatre. Chapter 1 explores the coordination of pansori's vocal and rhythmic aspects using a wide range of examples from the corpus of pansori and folksong. Warm-up singing is of particular focus as an entry to the lyrical enactment of narrative. The chapter goes further to examine the connections between pansori and other folk-singing styles, lyrics, and techniques. The discourse of *seongeum* refers to "voice music" or "music of the voice" that every singer aspires to for the purpose of aligning with *imyeon* (interior dimension). Through their vocal technique, pansori singers create a signature or identifying *deoneum* (individual artistic contribution), which marks the work of famed singers in the construction of the pansori canon. *Deoneum* signatures also mark major and subsidiary modalities and regional stylistics. Chapter 2 introduces the structures of the *jangdan*, rhythmic cycles essential to pansori drumming and singing.

Part Two examines the concept of voice theatre through Korea's historical trajectory with a focus on the eighteenth through the nineteenth centuries. This period in pansori was characterized by formal discovery and aristocratic patronage and gentrification. The canonical form developed in this time has continued mostly unaltered due to preservation efforts. Chapter 3 examines the developmental phase of canonization and resultant shifts in dramatic imaginaries. A small cohort of *sadaebu* scholar-intellectuals had appropriated the syncretic folk music of pansori to render a palatable version for royal and aristocratic audiences. While gentrification would have excised diegetic elements that were deemed too vulgar for highbrow audiences, it is possible that street performers and *gwangdae* artist guilds continued to include these omitted parts in their repertoires for some time. Into the twentieth century, Chapter 4 examines the dialectic of preservation and innovation that parallels Korea's changing place in the world.

Part Three uses ethnography to examine the cultural contexts of pansori's past and future, given the rise of digital literacies and the ascendancy of Korean popular music in global culture. Both preservation and reinvention are mutually inclusive: maintenance of the pedagogical and artistic competence in the realm of familiarity is requisite for reinvention in a popular context. Chapter 5 gives a bird's-eye view of the pansori musical scene of the modern and contemporary times through a description of main currents in the subculture. Outside of the mainstream, there are countercurrents of innovation that converge with other musical traditions. Finally, Chapter 6 conducts an ethnography of pansori learning and transnational adaptation specifically introducing my own works. Reflecting on lived experience in the field, I examine the future directions of pansori among other indigenous traditions in Korea and in the world.

PART ONE

Technique and Practice of Pansori

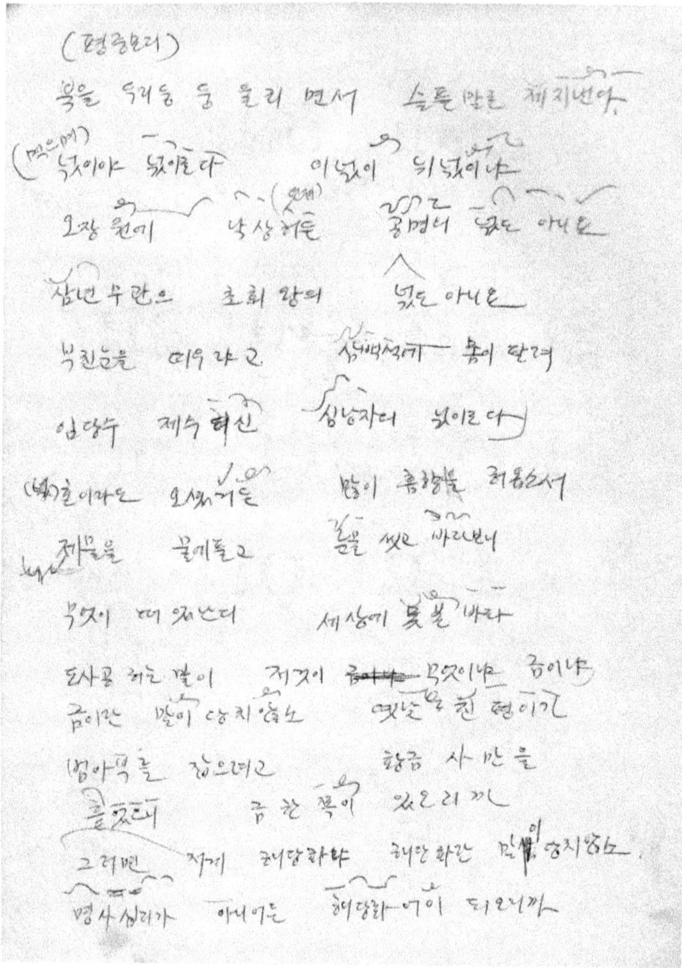

FIGURE 1 *A page from* sorichaek *(songbook). A learner will make and annotate their own* sorichaek *throughout their studies.* Credit: Chan E. Park.

1

Voice, Drum, Listening Ear

In today's Korean performing arts, one can readily find adaptations of traditional storytelling, exemplifying Henry Jenkins' concept of transmedial narration. However, pansori origins are not always apparent. For instance, the Universal Ballet's 1986 original repertoire *Shim Chung* presents a non-lyrical choreographed version of the *Song of Shim Cheong*. Another well-known adaptation is Im Kwon-taek's feature film *Chunhyang* (2000). In retelling this classic romance between a beautiful *gisaeng* and her gentleman-scholar, Im employs a double-frame diegesis in order to retain signature elements of pansori. Though the film diverges in many points from traditional pansori, Im's artistic direction closely follows the Obatang source material. The transmedial diegesis of *Chunhyang* is juxtaposed with another stage or *pan* framing a singer, drummer, and audience. Im's *Chunhyang* combines voice theatre and feature film, where live performance and filmic adaptation result in a fused storytelling. Each action sequence of the film is clearly a visualization of the pansori.

This chapter presents an analysis of pansori storysinging, the triangular performative coordination of singing, drumming, and listening, with textual examples. The trained pansori voice evokes a long-established tradition, but an individual singer's voice should also convey individual style and persuasion. Likewise, drumming combines prescriptive patterns along with spontaneous and innovative elements. The drumbeat confirms and accentuates the singer's performative interpretation, and the audience's auditory power of interpretation actualizes this theatre of storysinging. Warm-up singing is of particular focus as an entry to lyrical enactment of narrative. The chapter goes further to examine the connections between pansori and other folk-singing styles, lyrics, and techniques. The discourse of *seongeum* refers to "voice music" or "music of the voice" that every serious singer aspires to for the purpose of aligning with *imyeon* (interior dimension). Through their vocal technique, pansori singers create a signature or identifying *deoneum* (individual artistic contribution), which marks the work of famed singers in the construction of the pansori canon. *Deoneum* signatures also mark major and subsidiary modalities and regional stylistics.

Warm-Up

Unlike today's conventional theatre where performers customarily do vocal, physical, or psychological preparation backstage before the actual show, pansori warm-up consists of a short song (*danga*) before the audience prior to the main repertoire. In the case of abbreviated performance times (as in a variety show), warm-up singing is often skipped or featured as the main. The warm-up pansori also allows the drummer to attune their performance and the members of the audience to likewise hone their listening and warm up their *chuimsae*. These preparatory song lyrics typically derive from classical Sino-Korean expressions decorating the provincial colloquial Korean, a poetic reality removed from contemporary discourse. Translated below is one such warm-up song from classical Korean oral literature, *Gangsangpungweol* (Wind and Moon on the River):

> Leisurely boat on the river, off to gather wind and moon?
> A trade boat over the blue waves of Janggang(長江)?

Beomnyeo (范蠡)'s[1] fishing boat in the foggy moonbeams over the Five Lakes?
Neither. Enter the Hansongjeong forest, cut a pine long and straight,
Fashion a small canoe, float it with wine and snacks galore!
Let us to the scenic Gyeongpodae of Gangneung.
This agony of waiting for the one at the deadly crossings to the land of Chok (蜀).[2]
Outside the gate the waning moon hangs from the tip of the highest paulownia branch.
Mount that moon on turtleback, let us hurry home.[3]
Time passes, it is Dano the Fifth Moon, the best season when lazy daylight lingers at the window.[4]
From the thicket, the oft singing of wood thrush, *Ee-oh-lay!* A hen takes flight.
Clear wind and bright moon,[5] this wide world, kites fly and fish jump.[6]
White gulls, stay, I'm not after you. His Majesty deserted me, so I followed you.
I build a wooden shed by the river, wine and dine on season greens and water, pillow my head on my arm to stretch. How about it for the life of a real man? Keep your head up, Buddy.[7]

Danga is typically sung in *jungmori*, a medium 12-beat cycle of four triple-beat phrases invoking the agrarian calendrical metaphor: spring planting, summer growth, autumn harvest, and winter repose. The first three lines are given in Table 1.1.

The speaker, a poet-official, has lost His Majesty's favor and is banished from court. Biding time in exile, he soothes his bitterness through a newfound appreciation for nature, struggling not to let political adversity hamper his masculine pride. For the pansori singer, this energetic warm-up song could promise a successful performance. Several dozen such *danga* lyrics remain in circulation today. They share well-

Table 1.1 First three lines of a danga

1				2			3			4		
1	2	3	4	5	6	7	8	9	10	11	12
강 Gang	상 sang	이 eu	누 du-	응 -ung	동 doong	떤 tteon	난 nan	배 bae			
		풍워 pungweo	열 -ol	실 seel	러 lo	가느 ganeu	은 -un	배앤 bae-aen	가 ga		
시임 siim	니 ni-i	장 ja-ang	강 ga-ang	벽 byeok	파 pa	상으 sangeu		왕 wang	래 lae	허 ho	든 Deun
거 Geo	룻 ruut	배 Bae		오 oh	호 ho	사 sa	앙 ang	연워 yeonweo	올 ol	소 so	그 Geu
어 Eo	-	-	엄 om	자 ja	르응 reu-ung	낙 nak	시 si	밴 baen	가 ga		

Note: The columns appear to be of different width. However, all squares are of the same intervals. The vacant squares are where the voice rests or syncopates. The hyphenation marks show that syllables between boxes connect in one breath instead of breaking into two staccato articulations. For example, the 4–5th beat in the second phrase in Line One, *du-ung* should be one drawn-out articulation.

known citations from the classical poetic tradition and historical anecdotes that reflect the singers' rapport with the changing listener profile. I include here the titles and key messages of three of the songs I have become familiar with:

Jinguk myeongsan 鎭國名山, "Auspicious mountains," praises the mountains safeguarding the capital city of Seoul and the nation, so Hail His Majesty's grace! The song ends with an injunction: "When you reach your middle age, let someone else have your worldly ambitions while you find a nature spot big enough to fit a tiny shack on, invite your soul-friends to enjoy music and poetry."

Jukchang manghye 竹杖芒鞋, "Bamboo staff, straw sandals," captures the altered consciousness of a hermit entering an imagined pristine gorge to view the legendary anchorites. He is star-struck by the Seven Sages of the Bamboo Grove, Strategist Jegal Yang (諸葛亮, 181–234), Poet Baek Nakcheon (白樂天, 772–846), and the steadfast eremites So Bu (巢父) and Heo Yu (許由) of the legendary era of the emperors Yo and Sun (堯舜). "Why did Heo Yu roll up sleeves and wash his ears when So Bu herded his cow away?" reflects the asceticism idealized in traditional Korean poetry and singing. Convinced of Heo Yu's leadership, Emperor Yo (Yao) urged him to step up as king in his stead. At the Yeongsu (潁水) River, Heo Yu was washing his ears to be cleansed of the unwholesomeness of the emperor's proposition. Berating the apparent hypocrisy of gaining fame for renunciation, So Bu herded his cow away upstream, refusing to let it drink the unsavory water that washed Heo Yu's ears which heard the emperor's nauseating invitation. The two friends were never seen again.

Sacheolga 사철가, "Four season song," also known as *Isan-jeosan*, "This hill, that hill," reflects on the inevitabilities of aging and death through a seasonal metaphor. In place of higher Confucian principles, it

adopts the tone of an ordinary law-abiding citizen
dreaming of an ethically wholesome society:

Hills here, hills there, flowers abloom, it is spring for sure.
Spring's here indeed, yet I feel gloomy.
Yesterday I was young, today I'm pathetically grey.
My youth forsook me with no promise of return,
Spring comes only to leave, so why welcome it?
Spring, be gone if you will!
Know the old saying, "Lush leaves and sweet grass of summer surpass spring flowers"?
Autumn returns with shivery dews and north wind,
Yet golden chrysanthemums and red maples stand unfazed.
Winter returns on fallen leaves with freezing wind, snow blizzard covers the world in silver,
Moon white, snow white, world white, they're companions to my hair's white.
Heartless time fleets by, my youth, once old, cannot return.
Listen, my friends, to what I say.
Assuming all of us make it to one hundred years
Taking away sick days, sleep hours, worries and anxieties,
We have barely forty years.
When death comes a sudden, we're just a handful of dirt in the north mountain burial.
A groaning board at your memorial is still inferior to a cup of coarse wine drunk while living.
Time! Stay! Don't let the beautiful youths grow old.
Stay! Time is heedless so what could anyone do?
Let us hang time from every drooping cinnamon branch,
Let us round up and away to the world of dead those who steal from government, mistreat parents, create sibling discord,
Let the rest of us enjoy one another with "Have another drink" and "No more for YOU."[8]

Pansori and Its Connections to Folk, Popular, and Ritual Singing

In end-of-life matters, premodern Koreans practiced *cheondo-kut*, where *mudang* (shamans) led the rite of passage guiding the soul to its resting place. The provincial varieties include: *jinogwi-kut* of Seoul and Gyeonggi; *ogu-kut* of the Eastern Coastal region; *segyeong bonpuri* of Jeju Island; and *ssitkim-kut* of the Jeolla regions. Following industrialization and wide-reaching conversion to Christianity, these shamanic practices have declined in prevalence. Yet, their performative connection endures in their folkloric connection with pansori. Marshall Pihl identifies the beginnings of pansori in the secularization of shaman culture in later Joseon: "To satisfy changing popular tastes and a growing demand for secular entertainment, shamanistic performances became popularized and the narrative shaman song itself grew increasingly vulgar as it tended to incorporate comic expressions."[9] Geography also contributed to the secularization of shaman song and the emergence of pansori.

Korea has a varied topography with scenic mountain ranges, gorges, and winding rivers, surrounded by seashores and islands serving as natural borders of local cultures. Thus, each province developed homologies between geography and language use, music style, and sacred and secular performativity. Affixed with *-tori*, they include *gyeongtori* of Gyeonggi Province (including Seoul), *seodo-tori* of the Northwest (including Pyeongyang), *menari-tori* of Eastern coastal and Southeastern Gyeongsang provinces, *jeju-tori* of Jeju Island, and *yukchabaegi-tori* of the south of Han River, including the Jeolla provinces where pansori as we have it was discovered. Drawing the sympathy of guardian spirits through song, dance, storytelling, symbolic gestures, costumes, and props, shamans divine and placate misfortunes of fellow humans and transmit their spiritual arts and crafts to succeeding generations. There are two main categories of Korean shaman practice: "possessed shaman" (*gangshin-mu*) largely north of the Han River, and "inherited shaman" (*seseupmu*) to the south of Han River and *yukchabaegi-tori*. In the case of possession, it should be the possessing spirit endowing the shamanic power to whom it chooses. Although newly minted ones often come from a shaman ancestry or connection, the possession occurs unpredictably and unprepared insofar as the arts and crafts of the profession goes. The new awakening of the chosen seems more spiritual than performative, and during my field ethnography I encountered some of those learning to sing, dance, and play the *janggo* drum needed for their new profession.

On the other hand, endowment of inherited shamans operates as an inheritance system of human society. The mudang profession together with the arts and crafts of the ritual performativity and transmission are protected within the kinship circle, from mother-in-law to daughter-in-law, for example. So transmitted from generation to generation, there accumulated an abundant corpus of performative artistries, not unlike that of pansori or other genres. I conclude that the mournful *yukchabaegi tori* of the Korean southwest had nurtured the spiritual affect of the regional ritual music and fostered the tonal foundation of pansori.

National Intangible Cultural Heritage No. 72, the *ssitkimkut*, "cleansing ritual," of the Islands of Jindo is a riveting harmony of spirituality and art in improvisational 4-triple *salpuri* beat (literally "purgation"). The musical accompaniment for *ssitkumkut* is an ensemble of flute, fiddle, zither, drums, and gong termed *sinawi*. Of note is the improvisational *salpuri* in *gu-eum*, a vocalization that imitates instrumental sounds. Though utility separates ritual practice from entertainment, the link between them is clear in overall tonality, rhythm, and acoustic imaging. In fact, pansori is often misidentified with the mourning rituals of *kut*. Pansori singers often cross between sacred and secular context singing *gu-eum*, especially where *salpuri*, *sinawi*, and *ssitkimkut* are played both as the real funerary event and as a staged cultural event. Here is a beginning invocation of *ssitkimkut*:

*Naha-ah-naanyeo . . . . . . yeo, na-na-i-eu-eu-eu-eu, nani-
i-i-i . . . . na—yeo na--yeo
Nahana eu-eu-eu-eu, nani eu-eu-eu
Nan nan nansiro nan-nan na-na-nan na-neu eu-eu-eu,
na-nansi-nansi nansiro nanna-a
Daruji jirujiru jiru-nan-neo, na-neol neo-neu-ni-neo . . .*
Never knew I am but a dead soul, today I know I am.
When did I die and become a spirit?[10]

In the realm of popular music, the southern folksong genre also termed *yukchabaegi* closely resembles the contemplative tone of the slow six triple-beat *jinyang* in pansori singing. The lyrics open to a wide range of thought-provoking realizations about life, love, joy, and hardship. The genre spans resources from popular entertainment, labor chant, and spiritual invocation. It also borrows from the language of *sijo*, three-line poetic chant, and motifs from the storytelling of pansori. While pansori is tailored as dramatic storytelling and protected as a national treasure, *yukchabaegi* is a less-policed genre that contains heterogenous lyrical truths in a verse or medley.

At the time I was starting to learn pansori, many teachers used to discourage learners from singing *yukchabaegi* during training, lest the entrainment of their pansori voice be sabotaged by the more liberally emotive *yukchabaegi* style. Master Chung Kwonjin would explain that an ideal voice moves hearts and minds with dignity and not emotional excess. Pursuit of dignity by reining in emotion may have been a guideline left from the nineteenth-century gentrification of pansori that found new application for the newfound status of pansori as a national treasure. *Yukchabaegi* nonetheless remains a welcome respite for pansori singers from the technical and affective restraints of their craft. I translate below a few verses:

(slow 6-triple comparable to *jinyang* in pansori)

Refrain: *Sa-a-ni----ro---guna—he------------*
My heart is the blue mountain,

Your heart is the green river.
The river flows,
Would the mountain move?
Unable to forget,
The green river whirls and swirls around the blue mountain.[11]

(faster 6-triple comparable to *semachi* in pansori)

My love fair as flower, firm as fruit
many as branches, deep as roots.
I miss him, I can't see him, why?

A kite is caught!
Stuck in the juniper tree a kite is.
Gentlemen of the Samcheongdong district,[12] would you free it?

(medium 4-triple comparable to *Jungmori* in pansori)

I plant chrysanthemums outside my window,
Place my fresh brew below.
Wine's ready, mums bloom, friends come, moon rises.
Child, strum on geomungo, play all night we will.

Dream, dream, all's but a dream.
You and I are in a dream, everything is a dream.
I wake up in another dream, waking, too, is a dream.
Born in dream, live in dream, die in dream, gone in dream.
Waking is futile, dreaming is useless.

(faster 4-triple comparable to *jungjungmori* in pansori)

O bright moon Yi Taebaek (李白) befriended.
Its luminous incandescence enslaves this tough-guy heart.
Enjoy, relish, for you can't when old.
No flower stays florid after Day Ten,
That moon, once full, declines.

Before the youthful days are done,
Before this night is done,
You two enjoy each other to your hearts' content.

(Dynamic 6-duple beats, contrasted with 4-duple *hwimori* in pansori)

The Samgak Mountain of Seoul, let me ask you.
You've been here a long while,
How many talented and beautiful people have you
 brought and sent?
This town is still packed with eligible dandies,
Isn't it sensational? I love it![13]

Seongeum, Physiology of Pansori Aesthetics

A product of both nature and culture, *seongeum* is vocal sublimation of storytelling. Voice is cultivated through a lifetime of discipline to become an instrument of storytelling. The production and maintenance of the pansori *seongeum* can pose a physiological mystery for those acclimated to Western operatic traditions. The relative hoarseness of pansori contrasts with the ideal of "tonal beauty, pure line, and clarity of enunciation"[14] of the *bel canto*. Tonal depth in Western operatic singing is enhanced by the additional spaciousness in the pharynx secured by "a high velum, a low tongue, and a lowered larynx."[15] In the case of pansori singing, the pressure building by not lowering the larynx effects a pharyngeal tension and the characteristic hard-pressed and husky pansori timbre.

The preference for a natural *suriseong* of a strained voice reflects the pansori aesthetic of perseverance over ease. Other preferred voices include the strong metallic *cheolseong* and crystal springy *cheonguseong*. The undesirable voices include the sticky and shapeless *tteok-mok*, overly decorative *norangmok*, dried-up *mareunmok*, stiffened *gudeun-mok*, or dampened *nugeunmok*.[16] These terminologies are largely allegorical illustrations of people's natural voices. The forebears of pansori left room for improvement via a metaphysical understanding of the mind–voice symbiosis, *Jeongshim-jeongeum*, "Correct mind, correct tone." If the voice conveys the harmonizing warmth (*hwaseong*) of the singer's personality, nature has done its share.

Seongeum is also cultural acquisition of technical skills referred to as *sigimsae*, vocal grooves reflecting a singer's geo-cultural marker, and technical mastery over their natural tone. Some define its root word as *sak-ta* (digested),[17] thus interpreting the term as "a degree of ripeness." The late zither master Kim Yundeok proposed *siki-da* (to compel an action or result from someone),[18] emphasizing the players' self-direction in performance. Without sheet music, the teaching and composition of pansori depended on physical imaging and evaluation of acoustic moves. Examples of these pedagogical metaphors include *saengmok*, a "voice undisciplined or out of practice and gone raw"; *seseong*, thin or falsetto voice; *hangseong*, nape-ringing voice; *biseong*, nasal voice; *paseong*, cracky voice; *balbalseong*, "voice like a hyperactive puppy"; *gwigokseong*, "weeping of ghost," and *agwiseong*, "devilish voice from hell"; *unmuljin sori*, "wrinkled"; *mul deuryeojin sori*, "stained."[19] Master Chung Kwonjin's inimitable specialties included *tongseong*, "tubular voice," strong unblocked voice, and *peobunneun seongeum*, "torrential gushing voice," demonstrating his preference for unassuming, unadorned, powerful, and straightforward voice.

Imyeon, Interior Dimension

The concept of *imyeon* (interior dimension) refers to psychological layering. In pansori song, physical acoustics are thought to correspond to the narrative truth that animates the performance, just as a soul takes form in physical reality. Thus, *imyeon* is the inner aspect of *seongeum* which attempts an acoustic representation of cognition.[20] The psycho-auditory concept of *imyeon* as externalization of the invisible recalls the somatic aesthetic of Nō formulated by Zeami Motokiyo (1363–1443) for achieving "internalization" in rejection of "External." From comparative perspective, Zeami's notion of performance in relation to text is applicable to the current discussion of pansori singing in relation to text. He locates the metaphoric principle of "flowering" in the "deepest recesses of our art" preceded with acquisition of the knowledge of the skills, the seed.[21] Such endeavor carries the artistic truth deeper into the inner dimension, as "an actor who adds strength to his natural abilities through constant practice and rehearsal, understands quickly, and puts himself totally into the object of his role is one who can truly be said to have achieved internalization."[22]

Performing artists strive to sound, look, think, or feel real on stage. In Western theatre, the Stanislavski method was used to create believable characters by "becoming" characters. Calibrating their worldview and storytelling craft, my teacher and his predecessors sought to make real the feelings and thoughts of the characters. In transmission of the philosophy of the "Correct heart, correct sound," he advanced an ethos of advancing the reality one wished to create in drama. His vision of symmetry of art and humanity was his "method" to reach the inner chords of narrative truth: you sing who you are.

For its association with Korea's past(s) and generous use of what are considered minor modes making up the bulk of pansori singing, its voice is at times equated with *han* (恨), an elision which erases the other affective dimensions of comedy, satire, and vaudeville alongside more sober elements. In the larger discourse of Korean traditional aesthetics, the term has been alleged to mean a deep-seated sorrow or grievance unique to Korea. Often, the vocal narrative expression of pansori is reduced to the singular notion of *han* from national or ethnic tragedy. The narrative of *han* tends to politicize not only the past historical challenges but also recent traumas. In pansori narrative, however, *han* may also simply be a colloquial utterance equivalent to "alas" or "woeful." In the Song of Chunhyang, for example, the retired *gisaeng* Weolmae, mother of Chunhyang, utters *Neulgeungeosi han-iroda*! ("Grown old is my *han*.") while gazing at the moon. She sounds more like simply talking to herself about the passage of time rather than stirring up the national pain. On the face of it, the narrative of *han* appears to oversimplify pansori's vocality to a mere tonal expression of *han*. Could the logic of *han* be more effectual than causal, that this problematic notion of a fundamental sorrow unique to Korea was in fact an entrepreneurial discovery on account of the acoustic impression of pansori? As cohabitants of this world, all ethnicities share hardships and griefs universally if not always equally, and each ethnicity has different ways and means of expressing them. The discourse of the "interior dimension" of pansori singing is another channel of internalizing its vocal semantics as a more nuanced meaning-making beyond what its tonal impression of *han* alleges.

Deoneum, Individual Artistic Contribution

What tonal or stylistic directives did singers invoke in new compositions? Unlike many other vocal music genres, pansori singing enacts drama without melodic accompaniment. The *seongeum* constructs the basic tonal foundation (*sigimsae*) of ascent (*chuseong*), descent (*toeseong*), rolling vibrato (*jeonseong*), tremble vibrato (*yoseong*), and glottal stop (*kkeongneunmok*), among others. Over time, singers aggregated original narrative or musical compositions (*deoneum*) into shared repertoires, with rhythm as a centripetal framework. Pre-twentieth-century singers left these signatures, named or anonymous, in the canonical Five Narratives. Until the mid-twentieth century, there was a convention of naming *deoneum* authors at the beginning of spoken narratives. For example, the singer would begin, "This song was the *deoneum* (*badi* or *che* alternately) of the illustrious master so-and-so, so how could I attempt to imitate even a little of their greatness?! But allow me to muster everything I have to try at least!" By using the tone of formulaic self-effacement, the singer simultaneously highlights his artistic pedigree and secures a *pan* for performing someone else's invention as his own, comparable to the conventions of written citation in our scholarship world. The drummer would seize it as a cue to give out a hearty bang and cry of encouragement, "*Olssigu!*" I once heard a recording, place and time unknown, of Master Chung Kwonjin's recognition of the legendary nineteenth-century Shin Manyeop during his performance of *Sugungga Song of the Water Palace*.

Sugungga, an allegory of survival against power, deception, and exploitation, is a narrative of poetic justice. In the story, the Dragon King of the Sea has fallen ill, and the only cure is the Hare's liver. Tricked into coming to the Water Palace, Hare in turn fools Dragon King into believing that he had left his liver in his mountain abode and will bring it back if released. Captain Devil Stinger hears gurgling coming from Hare's innards and shouts, "He's got the liver in him!" In the recording I heard half a century ago, Master Chung Kwonjin at this narrative juncture was switching to citing performatively Shin Manyeop and his brilliant *deoneum*. In a closer reading of Jeong Noshik's compilation, I observed Master Chung Kwonjin inherited semantic content and historical references in Shin's *deoneum* and adapted these in turn with vernacular expressions and sensibilities of his school, style, and time. At the end of his compilation of Shin's *Tokki barrack* (Hare protests), Jeong Noshik adds, "Pak Mansun emulated, Jeon Doseong (1864–1944) transmitted," opening to how the salient individual inventions were reproduced and transmitted among singers.[23]

Aniri   Stunned Hare collapses, then bolts up angrily. The color of his face instantly changing, he shakes head and rolls his eyes.

Sori Dumb-Ass Turtle and Devil Stinger, His Majesty's order is stern, how could I deceive him? Listen to the old saying: Tyrant Geol of the Ha land slayed the honest Yong Bang and wrecked the nation soon after. Have you never heard of the foul-minded Sang Ju that ordered opening of Bigan's belly and found no seventh hole, causing the start of the national ruin? You want to open me up to see for yourself. If the liver is in me, great, if not, what will happen to your country? All of you will perish, your king will return to the netherworld called *hwang* (黃)-*cheon* (泉). You two will croak first. Cut me open, you'll find nothing but a pile of shit!

Ujo and *Gyemyeoncho*, the Complementary Modalities

In the matters of stylistics, the frequently interchangeable suffix terms, -*cho* and -*che*, broadly apply to geographic, stylistic, or tonal modalities. A set of terms used in the court music domain migrated to the folk music genres, including pansori: the *ujo* scale, approximating the pentatonic *sol-la-do-re-me*, corresponds to courtly, grandiose, or awe-inspiring ambience; *gyemyeoncho*, mainly built on the scale of *me-la-si-do*, conducive to the expression of sorrowful, nostalgic, or passive, settled as a dominant mode in folk music, dance, and singing, including pansori. A moderate *ujo* or *pyeongcho*, "peaceful mode," is suitable for the warm-up song category before the main act.

Ujo and *gyemyeoncho* are the main axles, *yang* and *yin*, of pansori singing. They mark stylistic differences among the existing schools of singing: the Eastern style (*dongpyeonche*) is more replete with *ujo*, and the Western style (*seopyeonche*) with *gyemyeoncho*. These differences are thought to align with geo-cultural features: singers residing on the majestic Jiri Mountain slopes east of the Seomjin River cultivated styles bursting with the masculine energy of *ujo* in resemblance of its geography; the singers located west of the river that meanders through the vast stretch of plains to the West Sea developed the sorrowfully melismatic and feminine expressions of *gyemyeoncho*. Generally assumed to be extant in name only is *junggoche*, "middle-old style," associated with the relaxed tempo and supposed even temperament of Chungcheong people.[24] The masters Yi Dongbaek (1866–1947) and Park Dongjin (1916–2003), both from Chungcheongdo, are known as principal forerunners of *junggoche* style.[25] In his teaching and performance, Master Chung Kwonjin would fondly introduce *hogeolche-Junggocho*, a style of quixotic bravado or playful uninhibitedness.

These style distinctions served as key criteria for designating schools of pansori as cultural heritages. In the process however, regional distinctions were elided by the collaboration among singers of different schools. The father of the River and Mountain Style (*Gangsanche*) originally from Sunchang of North Jeolla, Pak Yujeon (1835–1906) started as a Western-style singer. Following his debut in Seoul, Pak realized the *gyemyeon*-dominant Jeolla style was too melodramatic for the urban Seoulites, and through his encounters along the pansori scene, developed his own syncretic *Gangsanche*.[26]

Among the various style distinctions, some of the most striking features of pansori involve the style and forms denoting gender, which follow from the tonal complementarity of *ujo* and *gyemyeoncho*. In pansori, ujo is typically associated with traits of ideal masculinity such as nobility, valiance, and leadership, while gyemyeoncho is associated with drawn-out melancholic sentence endings with femininity. The dynamic of the two lovers in the Song of Chunhyang is a great example. As the all-male pansori was shifting to a unisex practice toward the end of the nineteenth century, an ethnographer/theorizer of pansori named Shin Jaehyo pioneered the creation of separate Song of Chunhyang narratives for male, female, and juvenile singers. Shin's male and juvenile adaptations have been transmitted by ways of their copies, but his female version has not. From his analysis of Shin's different versions, Gang Hanyong concludes that Shin intended the male version for adult readers, the female version for an imagined commoner audience, and the juvenile version for youth.[27] There is no known record or anecdote of any dramaturgical attempt to implement these experimental narratives into music.

When women entered the all-male singing territory unmarked by gender-specific tonal division, adjustment in its pedagogical exchange may not have been too major, except in pitch. Such precedence can be found in the lyrical chanting preserved in the category of *jeongak* (court or elite music) known as *gagok*, *gasa*, or *sijo*, where male and female versions are largely differentiated in the pitch ranges. The female part is raised by a fifth interval as part of a flexible vocal range. In contrast to court music chanting, pansori singing minimizes the use of falsetto, so the adjustment between male teachers and female learners, or vice versa, should have been limited to a tuning to the pitch ranges of one another. Some male singers have a very high register, as the mastersinger Cho Sanghyun whose singing in the film *Chunhyang* remains a high point of pansori singing: the poetic description of what the young scholar Mongnyong's eyes capture in the shimmering spring air, the historic Gwanghallu Pavilion surrounded by the amazing Jiri Mountain peaks and gorges, unfolding in Master Cho's amazing pitch and timbre. Insofar as pitch goes, my own experience of learning from Master Chung Kwonjin may be described as less strained and more manageable: notwithstanding losing my voice countless numbers of times in the process, the fact that my range was lower and deeper than an average female and my teacher's range was not over the top, but its being comfortably conversational was a saving grace.

Some women singers discovered a boost of feminine expressiveness in the tonal difference between *ujo* and *gyemyeoncho*, and most of the mastersingers I have met, especially male, were disproving this phenomenon in their belief that too much *gyemyeon* makes the *sori* weak, flighty, or overly melancholic. They are connoisseurs of the simple *gotche* (old style) pronounced with muscular and unadorned stylistics in *ujo* flavor. For them, centuries of exclusively male aesthetics accumulated as standard values and ways may not easily be replaceable. Imaginatively, the women's efforts to satisfy the stern expectations of mainstream critics' preference for copying their ideal masculine vocal expression also had to antithetically accommodate the socially prescribed traits of feminine charm and mannerism. In this context, female singers may have found a kind of natural affinity in the melancholic vocal expression of *gyemyeoncho*.

Female pansori singing may not have progressed according to a preexisting technical or structural protocol. Psychoculturally, in the absence of such protocol, the practice has involved the chemistry of what one learns and what one is. In the same breath, a male singer learning from a female teacher must also be experiencing similar challenges. I came to emulate my teacher's voice as I became more acutely aware of the depth of his interpretive vocal genius regardless of gender. This does not mean I have never questioned my vocal gender identity, and I am a fan of several female masters. The importance of the question of assigning or reassigning voice gender decreases against the storyteller's function of pansori indiscriminately impersonating all creatures and genders. The aesthetics of pansori *seongeum* hinges on your vocal power of interpretation such as *imyeon*, the revelation of the interior dimension of not only the narrative reality but also who you are as a soul.

Subsidiary Voices

Menari-che is the bouncy Gyeongsang provincial style reminiscent of a wandering shepherd's cheerful call. Master Chung Kwonjin's version of the *Song of Shim Cheong* features it in two travel scenes: the lead singer's funeral dirge for Shim Cheong's mother toward the beginning of the story, and the road song duet by Cheong's blind father and his adulterous new wife bartering pathos and humor on their way to the capitol banquet for the blind.

Hogeolche, "gallant-man style," playfully commanding a tone full of jocular energy, is credited to the nobleman-turned-*gwangdae*, Gweon Samdeuk (1771–1841). The timbre is generated by a "tubular" voice straight from the abdomen known as *tongseong*. In his *Song of Gwangdae* (*Gwangdaega*), Shin Jaehyo (1812–84) compares the voice of Gweon to the loud gushing of a gigantic waterfall over a steep cliff.[28] Blindman Shim's pride and joy in raising baby Shim Cheong against all the odds is a good example of this voice. Cheong's mother dies, and he raises the baby by soliciting the nursing mothers of the village to help feed her. His daily routine includes the baby's nursing rounds, back home to put her to sleep and out again to beg for daily food and supplies, and he could not be prouder and pluckier.

Gyeongdeureum (Gyeonggi or Seoul mode) is credited to the nineteenth-century singer Yeom Gyedal from Gyeonggi Province.[29] This style reflects class distinctions in pansori. Over the past six centuries, the Seoul dialect has been the standard language of the political and cultural center, and pansori *gyeongdeureum-cho* caricatures the Seoul elite male voice. One notable example is Yi Mongnyong in the *Song of Chunhyang*. Yi is the aristocratic Seoulite who falls in love with Chunhyang of Namweon of Jeollado. He reluctantly leaves Chunhyang but returns just in time to rescue her from a vengeful magistrate. Their falling in love, parting, and reunion are sung as a duet, with Chunhyang's *gyemyeon* and Mongnyong's *ujo-gyeongdeureum* taking turns. Their passionate affair comes to a screeching halt as Mongnyong returns to Seoul to fulfill his filial duty, i.e., study and pass the royal examination, land in the network of the political insiders, and be properly married to a lady of noble birth. In the "Parting Song" (*Ibyeolga*), their entwined voices uniformly express profound resentment at the class differences that determine their fate. Mongnyong, the aristocratic scholarly male from Seoul, maintains a superior rational grasp of the situation while Chunhyang, the local *gisaeng*, performs a self-disparaging act of emotional outburst and clinging. Her nagging voice expresses her resentment at how he will marry a proper lady from a ministerial family, pass the royal examination, climb to a high rank, and cast out all thoughts of her. But her sarcasm gives way to pleading:

Chunhyang (in *jin-gyemyeon*, "heavy *gyemyeon*")

Look here Sir, give me the date of your return at least.
Will you return when the Sangsang Peak on Diamond
   Mountain turns flat?
Will you return when the oceans east, west, south, north
   turn to land?
Will you return when a horn grows out of horse's head?
Will you return when a crow's head turns white?
"Clouds chase dragon, wind follows tiger," they say.
Where you go today, your mate for eternity follows.

Here is an opportune moment for the singer to recapitulate to the masculine *gyeongdeureum* for Mongnyong's valiant attempt to dispel the turmoil in their hearts:

Mongnyong (in *ujo-gyeongdeureum*)

Chunhyang, do not cry.
Enemy I have none except my own *yangban* propriety.
The wives of the invaded land of O, lovesick for their
   husbands,
Grew old in their lonely rooms "asking one another's
   welfare on the chilling riverside."
In the autumn moonlight on Gwansan mountain, the
   chaste women soothed their loneliness by harvesting
   lotus roots while recalling their husbands.
For what we share between us, we will surely have our day
   of reunion.
Your steely steadfast heart shall withstand the smelting
   furnace,
With your faith unbending as bamboo, wait for my
   return."[30]

In this chapter, I have introduced and explicated the range of technical elements in pansori singing that coordinate to create dramatic effects. These technical elements can be traced through historical and geo-cultural contexts in the schools of various pansori masters. The dimension of pansori singing is an intricate system of a musical storytelling stage even with a built-in warm-up. As an art of storysinging, these elements are a vocabulary that maintain grammatic coherence. Further, the vocal techniques serve as the foundation of the continuing dialectic of preservation and innovation that has informed public discourse, national regard, and even experts' understanding of pansori. The next chapter examines pansori drumming and its coordination of vocal dramatic enactments.

2

Jangdan, the Heartbeats of Storytelling

Korean drumming is many in kind and much in artistic prowess. Referred to as *jangdan* ("long and short"), ancient Koreans saw rhythm as an interplay between "long and short" intervals. As the heartbeat of labor, leisure, worship, and storytelling, Korean rhythms have a wealth of regional and contextual variation, while adhering to natural elements, including the seasonal cycle and the principle of balancing complementarity of *yin* and *yang*. Developed around Korean indigenous spiritual practices, its nature-friendly symbolism finds an ancestral genesis in neolithic prehistoric eras, the foundation myth of the genealogy of Dangun to begin with. Dangun, the founder of Ancient Joseon (2333–108 BCE), was the son of Hwanung, illegitimate son of the heavenly ruler Hwanin:

> The Old Record notes that in olden times Hwanin's illegitimate son, Hwanung, wished to descend from heaven and live in the world of man. Knowing his son's desire, father surveyed the three highest mountains and found Mount Taebaek the most suitable place for his son to settle and help man. Therefore he gave [Hwanung] three heavenly seals and dispatched him to rule over the people . . . Leading the Earl of Wind, the Master of Rain, and the Master of Clouds, he took charge of some three hundred and sixty

areas of responsibility, including agriculture, allotted lifespans, illness, punishment, and good and evil, and he brought culture to his people.[1]

The wind, rain, and cloud are the nature elements that sustain life between heaven and earth, and their symbolism continues down to the traditional Korean percussive performance referred to today as *pungmul* and its contemporary reinvention known as *samulnori*. The four basic ensemble instruments are explained as four nature symbolisms: a small metal gong called *kkwaenggari* is lightning thunder, a large metal gong called *jing* is wind, the hourglass-shaped *janggo* drum is the pitter-patter of rain, and the barrel-shaped drum called *buk* signifies clouds. The *pungmul* and *samulnori buk* are slightly larger in size, lighter in weight, but have louder acoustics than a pansori drum. The organic association it has with agricultural sustainability such as planting, transplanting, harvesting, and thanksgiving can furthermore be attested by the fact that *pungmul* has also been referred to as *nongak* (Farmers' band music).

In pansori, rhythm cannot be an independent solo expression as in the percussion ensembles but is an accompaniment to the singing voice. It is a prudently measured interplay between structure and anti-structure, with the drumming blending learned structures and unscripted fillers. The cyclical rhythmic patterning is referred to as *jangdan* ("long and short") and is as self-explanatory a term as the art of rhythm is variation of interval and speed. Another term for rhythm is *bak*, most likely the root word of *bak-ta* ("stitch," "stud," "ram," "drive"). The individual names of the beat patterns typically end with the suffix, *-mori*, "drive," or "herd," an interesting imagery of drumming in relationship with singing.

In pansori, the critical role of the drummer as the singer's co-performer is evident in the ironic saying, *Il-gosu, yi-myeongchang*, "Number One is drummer, Number Two is singer." Drummers should know enough of the songs and textual flow to provide adequate accompaniment. The singer's performance depends on the drumming. For pansori singing, the execution of *buchimsae*, patterns of integration of beats and words, is of critical importance. *Buchimsae* includes on-beat and straightforward *daejangdan* and varieties of off-beat or asymmetrical patterns such as *eot-buchim*, *milbuchim*, *ingaegeori*, *wanjageori*, and *goedaejuk*.[2]

While *gosu* were there to complement the singer's style and technique, they faced a culture of discrimination within artistic and larger hierarchies. Yu Giryong compares their uneven treatment: "The singer rode a palanquin while the drummer walked behind carrying his drum. The singer would be received in the guest parlor with drinks and hors d'oeuvres and generous honoraria, while the drummer stayed in the servant quarters and received coarse fare and lousy pay."[3] Some drummers, including Song Gwangnok and Yi Nalchi, had enough of the second-class treatment and became singers in their own right.

Other drummers had a more equitable experience with their co-performers and patrons. The drummer Han Seongjun (1875–1935), known for his enchanting looks and skills, was sought after by all the prominent singers competing for his drum accompaniment.[4] Drumming is an active repartee to singing—sympathizing, encouraging, rebutting, countering, coaxing, consoling, conjuring, provoking, grappling, and sparring. These complements of pansori merge into a single flow.[5] On more than one occasion, Master Chung Kwonjin would declare how fortunate a singer he was to have the "amazing" Ilsan[6] as his drummer: "When Ilsan dies, I will stop singing."

There are a variety of types and sizes of Korean drums. The construction of each matches particular functions, such as singing, dancing, procession, ritual, instrumental or percussion ensemble. Pansori singing is paired with *sori-buk*, a barrel-shaped drum resembling a marching snare drum in size and shape but much heavier. While a snare drum is played on one drum skin with two sticks, the *buk* has three surfaces comprising two drum skins and the drum shell in between, using one stick and a hand: *Deong!* (right drum head struck with drumstick), *Ttak!* (wooden drum shell wrapped in hide hit with stick), and *Gung!* (left drum head tapped with left palm).

Due to its acoustic versatility, some listeners might wonder where "the drum set" is hidden. The theatrical economy of *buk* accompaniment relates to position and technique: the drum is floor-seated together with the drummer with the drum shell facing up and functioning as the third drumhead. The drummer sits cross-legged with the right foot slightly forward to brace the drum so that it does not roll away. The right hand holds the drumstick, and the left hand rests on the left drumhead. Left-handed drummers use the opposite arrangement. While *soribuk* is not the largest, its heavy wooden shell produces a deep reverberation that heightens the drama in pansori. Below, I introduce the basic phonologies of pansori drumming, with the matching symbols in parentheses for notational use. The annotations are my own style and not a universal transcription method:

(gD)	"gDeong"	soft left palm then hard right with stick almost simultaneously
(D)	"Deong"	hard right beat with drumstick
(d)	"deong"	right soft beat with drumstick
(T)	"Ttak"	hard beat on top with drumstick
(t)	"ttak"	light beat on top with drumstick
(tgr)	"ttageurak"	light bouncing atop the drum barrel
(G)	"Gung"	tapping on left with left palm
(g)	"gu"	light tap on left with left palm
(.)		inaudible tap with left fingers
(gg)	"gugung"	light bouncing with left palm

Table 2.1 shows the rhythmic syntax of pansori, each holding one cycle of the basic *jangdan* in pansori singing. To better represent the continuous flow of pansori rhythm, each rectangle equally represents one triple-beat interval. For example, one *jungmori* cycle stretches to 12 beats, while one *jinyang* cycle holds 18 beats. The speed varies from pattern to pattern, singer to singer, and drummer to drummer, so they cannot be compared metronomically.

Table 2.1 Pansori rhythms and their articulations

	3	6	9	12	15	18
Jungmori	Deong-gung-tta	Gung-tta-tta	Gung-gung-tta	Gu--ng	**	**
Jungjungmori (faster jungmori)	Deo--ng	Deo--ng	Deo-ng-tta	Gu--ng	**	**
Jinyang	gDeo---	---	---	--ng	Tta-a-ak	Tta-a-ak
Semachi (faster jinyang)	gDeo---	---	---	--ng	Tta-a-ak	Tta-a-ak
Jajinmori	Deo--ng	Deo--ng	Deo-ng-tta	Gung-ta	**	**
Eot-mori (eonmori)	Deong-gung-ta	Gu-ng ta Gu-ng	gung-ta-gung ta	** **	**	**
Hwimori	Deong	gung	gung	gung	**	**
Danjungmori (1st half of jungmori, also called eotchungmori)	Deong-gung-tta	Gung-tta-gung	**	**		**

Note: ** No beat as it is a shorter rhythm cycle.

Categories of Rhythm

The section below provides lyrical samples in romanization and in *hangeul*, onomatopoetic sounds and matching symbols, and English translations, showing how rhythm syntactically corresponds to the progression of storytelling.

Jajinmori, Frequent Beat

The beginning of the *Song of Shim Cheong* in the *Gangsanche Poseongsori* version introduces Gwak-ssi, the talented and devoted wife of Blindman Shim, in *jajinmori*, "frequent beat." One of its major functions is listing or cataloging an abundance of items or actions. This song (Table 2.2) strings together the endless list of her talents and skills in weaving, cooking, sewing, washing, and more. With the money she earns from labor, she takes great care of her husband.

The song could also count as *jungjungmori*, faster *jungmori*. Its kinetic vibrancy approaches *jajinmori*. Both are constructed with four triples to a cycle, however, the more syncopated *jajinmori* beat generates the feeling of swinging or swaying while the triples of *jungjungmori* stays within a waltz-like structure.

Jungmori, Medium Twelve-Beat

Owing to Gwak-ssi's tender loving care, Shim lacks nothing except a male heir to carry on their family name. Seeing how serious he is about the matter, Gwak-ssi launches costly prayers and pilgrimages. The next song (see Table 2.3) employs the medium-speed four-triple beat of *jungmori*, in iterating a compelling story development: Gwak-ssi devotes her thoughts and prayers to conceiving a son, and travels to all sacred sites to beseech Lord Buddha. She then begets a fantastic *taemong* (birth dream).

Table 2.2 Excerpt from Song of Shim Cheong, *in jajinmori rhythm*

1			2			3			4		
Ssa	-k	pa	nu	ji	-l	gw	-an	dae	do	bo	-k
쌱	-	바	느	지	ㄹ	과	ㄴ	대	도	보	ㄴ
Do	-	ng	do	-	Ng	do	-ng	ttak	gung	tta	-ak
gD	g	D	g	t	T	g	g	T	·	·	·

Sewing official caps, belts, gowns for pay,

hae	-ng	eui	cha	-ng	Eui	jing	Nyo-ngi	myo		tta	-ak
해	-ㅇ	의	챠	-ㅇ	의	직	룡이	묘			
Do	-	ng	do	-	ng	do	-ng	ttak	gung	tta	-ak
gD	g	d	g	g	t	g	g	T	·	·	·

Scholar's jackets with black trims, long gowns, lapels,

(continued)

Table 2.2 (continued)

		sop	su	qwae	ja	ju	-ng	chi	mak		kwa
		섭	수	쾌	자	주	-o	지	막		과
Do	-	ng	do	-	ng	do	-ng	ttak	gung	tta	-ak
gD	g	d	g	t	t	g	g	T	.	.	.

Narrow-sleeved long vests, wide-sleeved coats with open armpit,

na	-m	nyo	eui	bo	geu	jan	nubi	jil		
나	-ㅁ	녀	의	복	의	잔	누비	질		
Do	-	ng	do	-	ng	do	-ng	ttak	gung	tta	-ak
gD	g	d	g	t	t	g	g	T	.	.	.

Densely quilted male and female street clothes.

Table 2.3 Excerpt from Song of Shim Cheong, in jungmori rhythm

1		2			3			4		
Gwak	ssi	bui-	-n		geu	nal	bu	teo		
곽	씨	부인	-ㄴ		그	날	부	터		
gD	g	d	g	t	t	G		T	·	·

Lady Gwak   From that day forth

1		2			3			4		
pum	pa-	-a-	-	-	mo	in	jaem-	-ul		
품	파	아	ㄹ	-	모	인	재	물		
gD	g	d	g	t	T	G		T	·	·

Worked hard for pay   saved and saved

(continued)

Table 2.3 (continued)

1			2			3			4		
		oen	gat	go-ng	eul	da-	a-deu	ril	che		
		원	갓	공	을	다 아	드	릴	제		
gD	g	d	g	t	t	g	g	T	.	.	.
	Spent unsparingly for her prayers

Jinyang-jo, Slow Six-Beat

Jinyang is a slow six-triple beat rhythm generating the blues-like calm, serenity, or sorrow often associated with pansori poetics. To new listeners, its pace gives the impression of pansori as unbearably slow and tedious. Its etymology is likely *jin-nyang*, meaning "endless," "strung-out," or "protracted," like adding two more triples to the already slow-motion feel of *jungmori*. Jeong Noshik credits two founders of *jinyang*. The early nineteenth-century singer Kim Seongok was sick in bed when his singer brother-in-law Song Heunglok entered the room crooning his greeting in *jungmori*, "How are you holding up lately?" Kim crooned back that he was sad and lonely in what has since developed as the never before heard *jinyang*.[7] The uncalculated discovery of *jinyang* with two additional triples to *jungmori* brought out a whole new expression of protracted sorrow, and it was, according to Jeong Byeongheon, an upgrade of pansori from simply playful forgetfulness to artistic creativity based on retrospection.[8]

In answer to Gwak-ssi's prayers and devotions, Lord Buddha granted them a child. To their profound disappointment, it was a girl. Gwak-ssi is bedridden after the birth. Realizing her end is near, she imparts her last words to her blind husband in woeful *jinyang* (see Table 2.4).

The boxcar notation for *jinyang* shows that beats and the words are farther apart and fewer in between than in *jungmori*. The lexical sparsity of *jinyang* demands greater technical skill. The singer needs a higher-level art of *seongeum* to fill intervals with a voice embodying truthful emotional expression.

Semachi, Faster *Jinyang*

New rhythmic patterns are generated through changes in tempo. In a faster mode, the frequent omission of beats creates new and intriguing acoustic imaging. *Semachi* is frequent in folk music as a triple-beat, waltz-like rhythm. In pansori, this pattern is a faster *jinyang*. While *jinyang* allows for protracted

Table 2.4 Excerpt from Song of Shim Cheong, in jinyang rhythm

1		2		3		4		5		6	
Ga	gu	-	-	eu	-	-	-				
가	구	-	-	으	-	-	-				
gD			·		·			T		t	

Her dear husband's --------

1		2		3		4		5		6	
son	ki	reu	-	ja	-	-p	ko-	-			
손	기	를	-	자	-	ㅂ	고	-			
gD			·		·		·				
hand						Holding			T		tgr

1		2			3		4			5			6		
yu	eo	-	-		n	heo	go-	-	-	-	-	-	-	-	-
유	어	-	-		ㄴ	허	고	-	-	-	-	-	-	-	-
gD		·				·	·			T			t		

saying her final words

1		2		3		4		5		6	
juk	teu	e	-	u	ni	-	i	ra					
죽	드	으	-	으	니	-	이	라					
gD		·		·		·		·	gg	G	gg	G

dies.

vocalization, dramatic context or temporal constraints often call for accelerated tempi of *semachi jangdan*.

Hwimori, Sweeping or Vortexing

Hwimori, "sweeping or vortexing," is a rushed four-duple cycle. As the name indicates, *hwimori* emphasizes speed and energy-building. It bides no time for carousing or playfulness, but portrays flight or surprise attacks. Examples of *hwimori* usage include the unannounced appearance of the inspector-general incognito in the *Song of Chunhyang* or the magical outpouring of wealth in the *Song of Heungbo*, a true gentleman who virtuously endured his older brother's maltreatment. This song (see Table 2.5) is his hour of heavenly reward, in the form of money and rice gushing out to make him very rich and full.

Eonmori, Asymmetrical Drive

Eonmori, "asymmetrical drive," is a ten-beat cycle generating an ambience of unbalance or other-worldliness essential to Jeolla *muga* (shaman song), also known as *sinim changdan* (monk's rhythm). There can be multiple configurations, including 2+3 and 2+3, 3+2 and 3+2, or 3+2 and 2+3. The beat is a unique variation utilizing the odd numbers in place of the comfort of even numbers, thereby creating an esoteric, mysterious atmosphere. In the *Song of Heungbo*, the first bearer of Heungbo's heavenly blessing was a mendicant Buddhist monk. Succumbing to the starvation and humiliation of this world, Heungbo and his whole family are about to hang themselves from a rafter when the monk appears before Heungbo's shack to beg for the alms. Table 2.6 is the song of the monk coming down the mountain in *eonmori*.

Eotchungmori, Asymmetrical *Jungmori*

Eotchungmori, asymmetrical *jungmori*, is also called *danjungmori*, severed *jungmori*. The arc of a regular *jungmori*

Table 2.5 Excerpt from Song of Heungbo, *in* hwimori *rhythm*

1		2		3		4	
Heung	buga	joa	rago	Heung	buga	joa	rago
흥	부가	좋아	라고	흥	부가	좋아	라고
gD		g		g		g	
Heungbo's ecstatic				Heungbo's on cloud nine			

1		2		3		4	
gwe	du	tcha	geul	ttoro	butko	namun	doro
궤	두	짝	을	떨어	붓고	나믄	도로
gD		g		g		g	
No sooner he empties the two chests							

(continued)

Table 2.5 (continued)

1	2		3	4	
su	bu-	u-	-k	tok	tok	teo-	-lgo
수	부	-	옥	톡	톡	티어	ㄹ고
gD		g		g		g	

Than they pile up in heaps   *tap tap*, he shakes them empty

1	2		3	4	
dora	seota	dora	bomyun	doro	hana	gaduk	hogo
돌아	섰다	돌아	보면	도로	하나	가득	하고
gD		g		g		g	

Turns around, turns back around, they're piled up like mountains again

Table 2.6 Excerpt from Song of Heungbo, *in* eonmori *rhythm*

1	2	3	4	5
Ju	ng	na	ryo	-
주	o	나	려	-
D	g	d	g	d

1	2	3	4	5
o	-n	da	-	
오	ㄴ	다	-	
G	L	D	g	

Monk is coming downhill

1	2	3	4	5
jung	ha	na	na	ryo
중	하	나	나	려
D	g	d	g	d

1	2	3	4	5
o	-n	da	-	
오	ㄴ	다	-	
G	L	D	g	

A monk is coming down

(continued)

Table 2.6 (continued)

1	2	3	4	5
jeo	jung	e	geo	dong
저	중	이	거	동
D	g	d	g	d

Look at his attire

1	2	3	4	5
ho	-	-	di	-
허	-	-어	디	
G	g	d	g	d

1	2	3	4	5
u	-l	bo	so	
의	ㄹ	보	소	
G		D	g	

1	2	3	4	5
ho	-	-n	ju	-ng
허	-	-언	쥬	ㅇ
G		D	g	

Abjectly tattered and ragged a monk

1	2	3	4	5	1	2	3	4	5
da	-a	tto	ro	jin	so	ng	la	-a	
다	아	뗠	어	진	소	옹	라	-	
D	g	d	g	d	G		D	g	

His hood is down-at-the-heel

crests from the sixth through ninth beats. With asymmetrical *jungmori*, the cycle is cut and restarts after the sixth beat. This abrupt end creates a sense of finality and is typically employed in epilogues. This asymmetrical rhythm signifies a curt, decisive end to a story.[9] Table 2.7 gives a few beginning cycles from the epilogue of the *Song of Shim Cheong*.

In pansori, the drumbeat is critical to the singer-storyteller's pace in variant performative schemes. The solo-singer format can be rearranged into several forms in terms of division of artistic labor: "consecutive singing" (*yeonchang*) is where a group of singers divide the narrative among themselves to take turns sequentially, and "dramatic divided-role singing" (*bunchang*). Also referred to as "dialogic singing" (*daehwachang*) or "three-dimensional singing" (*ipchechang*), *bunchang* is the prototype of operatic *changgeuk* where singing is divided into dramatic role-play.[10] Divisions by performance duration include "excerpt singing" (*ttomaksori*) and "entire narrative singing" (*wanchang*). *Wanchang* can take several hours or more, and the drummer's artistry and vigor is critical for retaining attention and energy. A performance of longer *wanchang* narrative typically employs more than one drummer to share the labor of sitting cross-legged, drumming for hours.

The drummer may not be the centerpiece of pansori performance, but pansori performance is unimaginable without the drumming. It optimizes cognitive and physical entrainment by energizing and synthesizing drumming, singing, and listening. The flow invokes the "autotelic" experience theorized by Mihaly Csikszentmihalyi in his study of optimal experience and attention based on intrinsic motivation.[11] Pansori drumming is in large degree improvisational on set cyclical parameters. The drum accompaniment in pansori is an art of omission, i.e., skipping or suspending beats in balancing sound with silence. Table 2.8 provides three *jungjungmori jangdan* for readers to try their own variation.

Accompaniment drumming in numerous Korean traditional singing, dancing, and instrumental genres is dialogic in its supportive role. It is empathetic exchange of performative

Table 2.7 Excerpt from Song of Shim Cheong *in* eotchungmori (*also called* danjungmori) *rhythm*

1		2			3		4	
Gut-tae	yeo	Shi-m	sae-ng	wo-n	eun	**	**	**
그때	여	심	생	원	은	**	**	**
gD	g	D	g	d	d	**	**	**
At that time,		Sir Shim			**	**	**	**

1		2			3		4	
eo	gyo-rul	Ip	sil	si	kyo	**	**	**
어	교를	입	실	시	켜	**	**	**
gD	g	D	g	d	d	**	**	**
Escorted into palace on royal sedan								

(*continued*)

Table 2.7 (continued)

1			2			3		4		
pu-wo	-n-gu	Nul	Bong-heo	si	go	**	**	**	**	**
부위	ㄴ군	을	봉허	시	고	**	**	**	**	**
gD	G	D	g	d	d	**	**	**	**	**

Dubbed with the Lordship of Royal Father-in-Law

Table 2.8 Three variations on jungjungmori *rhythm*

1		2			3			4		
Dong	ttak	gung	ttak	Ttak	gung	gung	Ttak	gu	ung	gung
동	딱	궁	딱	딱	궁	궁	딱	구	으	궁

1		2			3			4		
Do	ong	do	-	Ong	tta	-k	Ttak	gung		
더	엉	더	-	옹	따	악	딱	궁		

1		2			3			4		
Do	-ng	ttak	gungjara	jat	Tcha	gung	gung	Ttak	gung	
더	엉	딱	궁자라	잣	쩌	궁	궁	딱	궁	

reality with *jangdan* as the shared language. I have the vivid image from five decades ago of the two famous partners in pansori: *sori* master Chung Kwonjin and drum master Kim Myunghwan banging out yet another magic *pan* of play and flow. I also witnessed a less than fortunate situation another master endured during her otherwise stellar performance: the *gayageum* Master Seong Geumnyeon (성금년) once lamented with metaphoric description how her *sanjo* performance got ruined "thanks" to her *janggo* accompanist: "I would barely set it back up, only to have him capsize it again!" The accompanist apparently had not been familiarized with the intricacy of her *gayageum sanjo* rhythm, and this is baffling since her version was already establishing as the most popular in teaching, training, and performance.

Early in the 1980s, I bought my first pansori drum. One day, a trustworthy drum maker from Jeollado brought a new batch for sale. Master Chung tested all of them and selected one for me that was a bit smaller in size yet hardy. For half a century, the drum has traveled with me extensively while affording me to practice singing while drumming. Since moving to this part of the world with rarely a chance to find a drummer in residence, I transitioned to seated and self-accompanied pansori. Instead of a fan, I hold a drumstick during performance. In the absence of the wonderful dialogic energy of the singer–drummer interplay, I hope the monologic interplay between me and my voice sufficiently amplifies the elements of storytelling instead. And self-accompaniment singing is hardly unique: many artists sing and play the piano or guitar flawlessly.

The variant lengths and patterns of pansori drumming are more complicated than simply repetitive duple, triple, or quadruple beats that you can easily retrieve when offbeat. If you are lost in the middle of counting the twelve beats of *jungmori*, or six-beats of *jinyang* for example, recovering the synchronicity is easier said than done, especially if there are syncopations or long drawn-out notes. For me, the most challenging when self-accompanying is *jajinmori* with heavily syncopated and elongated notes, thoroughly enjoyable to sing or drum, but quite challenging to do simultaneously. It takes extra practice and mental concentration to get it right. Master Chung cautioned us to "stay with the basic beat" (*weonbakdaero*), especially at the beginning of training. Someday, enlightened and skilled in the art of pansori drumming, you could put your innovative spirit to boldly adding or subtracting beats to create novel structures and designs amenable to adaptation and improvisation. These technical aspects of drumming serve as complement to the voice in theatrical staging of the narrative.

PART TWO

Historical Development

FIGURE 2 *A scene from "Fox Hunt and Death of a Queen," October 2012 performance at the East-West Center, University of Hawai'i at Mānoa. The dolls depict from left to right, Regent Daewongun, Emperor Gojong, Queen Min. On the far right are three puppets of Korean independence activists, including Yu Gwansun (center). Kathy Foley, puppeteer. Photo: Chan E. Park.*

FIGURE 3 *A scene from "Fox Hunt and Death of a Queen," October 2012 performance at the East-West Center, University of Hawai'i at Mānoa. Chan Park in the doll-character of Queen Min sings of her worries and fears. Master Cho Owhan, Preserver of the Jeollanam-do Intangible Cultural Heritage the Jindo-Jodo Fishing Song, plays the daegeum flute. Photo: Daniel Miller.*

3

Eighteenth–Nineteenth Centuries

Joseon Korea (1392–1910) was an absolute monarchy structured around Neo-Confucian class and gender hierarchy. Under the royal household, aristocrat clans wielded superiority over commoners. The bottom strata included slaves and outcasts such as butchers, shamans, and male and female entertainers (*gwangdae* and *gisaeng*). The musical arts had their own hierarchy: ancient sacrificial music supposedly created by the sages of the idealized past was the proper music for the nobility called *aak*, "graceful music," or *jeongak*, "correct music"; the music practiced among the common and lower class was *sogak*, "crude" or "lewd" music. Even Jeong Yagyong (1763–1836), a leading scholar of the *Sirhak* (Practical Learning) philosophy with affiliations to Catholicism, while challenging Neo-Confucian indoctrination, was discriminating with the regional indigenous performances:

> Prohibit the likes of actors, puppeteers, performers of shamanic music, masked dancers, acrobats, anyone selling wicked words and skills. The extravagant waste by petty officials and officers in the southern regions sets bad precedents. Every spring and summer they lose their minds to the actors' nonsensical acts, all day and all through the night. The officers in charge of educating people do not

prevent this but drag them into the official courtyards, even letting their female dependents come out to watch this. This obscenity is most irregular.[1]

In a society where human worth was measured along class division, music was not merely entertainment but a reconstitution of class. Yet, change was inevitable although lamented by many strict neo-Confucians such as Official Heo Eui of the Royal Music Institute (1657):

The music that is played for the court has undergone a change since Prince Kwanghae (1609–1623) took the throne. It has begun to sound like the awful music used by shamans, raucous, promiscuous, and is played far too fast. Lately it has gotten even worse.[2]

Prior to the discovery of pansori, popular music had already been a matter of concern for the mainstream aristocracy, who associated faster tempos with folk "impropriety."

Though class and gender hierarchies pervaded society, boundaries were not impermeable to individual desire. The genre paintings of Shin Yunbok (d. 1817) depict *yangban* gentlemen partying with *gisaeng* girls, stealing amorous glances at women bathing at the streamside, or transfixed by shaman performances. *Samil yuga*, "three-day leisurely procession," is a painting credited to Kim Hongdo (1745–1806), showing a ritualized interaction between different classes. Top scorers of the *gwageo*, royal examination for the upper-class males, would have a celebratory parade home to visit relatives, master teachers, or peers along the way. The convention involved a liminal collaboration of aristocrats and commoners. Kim's painting shows the winner on horseback, proudly sporting the tri-colored flower hat and official blue cloak. Clowns, troubadours, dancers, and musicians enliven the spectacle for those watching with envy and admiration.

For winners without sufficient means, poetic imagination could substitute for an actual *yuga* event. Song Manjae (1788–

1851), a *yangban* pansori enthusiast, was the proud father of a *gwageo* winner. Lacking the means for an actual *yuga*, the elder Song instead composed the narrative poem *Gwanuhui*, "Observing the Performers in the Act" (1826). The introduction and fifty quatrains in *hancha* evoke a *yuga* panorama: musical prelude, audience, twelve repertoires of pansori in circulation, performer–spectator interaction, and *gwangdae* performing tightrope (*jul-gwangdae*) and other acrobatics. In this tableau, the *gwangdae* are ritual masters and entertainers appealing to the *yangban* intelligentsia.[3]

In mid- to late Joseon, narrative imagination crossed existing class boundaries. This was due in part to the eventual spread of *hangeul* and a rise in literacy, coupled with the rise of a market economy and the development of leisure culture. The two periods of warfare and invasion, i.e., Japanese (1592–8) and Manchus (1636–7), also signaled a major shift in public discourse. The Practical Learning School challenging neo-Confucian mores as well led to the onset of a new collective Korean consciousness. Performing arts of folk origins and wider appeals in both their making and appreciation could not have been immune to these social changes and cross-class interactions of the time. The gentrification and canonization of pansori that occurred may have been a counterbalancing recontextualization of Confucian ideology in the popular spheres of storytelling. In diegesis, dramaturgical analysis of the canonical pansori offers more complex interpretations of humanity absurdly imposed with a human class system. For example, the story of Heungbo on the surface upholds brotherly loyalty according to the sibling order, but the human practice of prioritizing the older at the expense of the younger pales as heaven intervenes with more durable causality of punishing evil and rewarding good.

Joseon Korea, beginning with its founder, strengthened the ties with Ming through greater inculcation of neo-Confucianism as an official ideology, while moving away from Buddhism, which was associated with the predecessor Goryeo dynasty. Outwardly, the mendicant monk who secures Blindman's pledge of 300 bags of sacrificial rice is a scam artist: Shim Cheong sacrificed her life for the rice, but her father's recovery of sight did not materialize. It was their magical reunion at the end that opened the healing hand of Buddha to enable the efficacy of her filial piety by restoring her father's sight. The *Song of the Water Palace* is a sardonic depiction of the beastly existence of the human jungle. Under the propagandic banner of loyalty, greed and nincompoopery represent the politics of power, and survival is the key for the food-chain animals. The plot of the *Song of the Red Cliff* unfolds within the historical imagination of China within a specific time frame. The limits and delimits of adaptation may have been in close observation of the time's view of the relationship between China and Korea. The song also represents Korean cross-cultural literary and musical interpretation of one of the highlights of the East Asian historical storytelling.

From the beginning of the history of pansori, the *Song of Chunhyang* dominated the wider ranges of readership and creativity, and its origin story included a ghost-story version: a plain-looking girl died of a broken heart, followed by a series of overnight deaths of every succeeding magistrate. A ritual of purging (*salpuri*) was accompanied by the Chunhyang story of fulfilled love duly dedicated to placate her grieving ghost, and peace was restored soon after. At the time of pansori's discovery in the early eighteenth century, the story of Chunhyang as we know it was circulating in several dozen hand-copy, woodblock, and printed versions as well. The protagonist Chunhyang is no ordinary *gisaeng* but a hardened warrior of love protecting her wifely chastity with her own life. In the strict class distinction of the time, her posing as a virtuous lady by rejecting the advances of her political superior was a serious transgression, punishable by death. But the character of Chunhyang breaks the norm to emerge victoriously, adding creative traction to Korean popular storytelling as a whole.

The *Song of Chunhyang*, a three-century transmission, shows mature narrative development devoid of premodern mythological trappings. The character of Chunhyang as found in my singing practice is unlike the idealized image of pure and chaste Chunhyang along the question of her social identity, i.e., whether she is *gisaeng* after all. The answer is found in a song: learning that Chunhyang refuses to attend the *gisaeng* roll call against his direct order, the new magistrate dispatches the head *gisaeng* to Chunhyang's house. Welcoming her opportunity to insult and injure the saucy Chunhyang acting as if she were a highborn lady, the head *gisaeng* derides "her Lady Chastity." Chunhyang responds: "Sister, you know I have been in this trade [*gisaeng* profession] since eight, and I'm sixteen. And what have I done to you?" This softens the antagonistic head *gisaeng* to become comradely. It can be surmised that such a realistic treatment of characters and actions in the midst of a premodern propensity for ideal feminine virtue is what makes Chunhyang a timeless storytelling.

The earliest text of pansori narrative in written form is *Gasa chunhyangga ibaekku* (The Two Hundred Lines of the *Song of Chunhyang*), each line consisting of a couplet of 7-character phrases, totaling 2,800 *hancha* and included in *Manhwajip* (1754), a literary collection by Yu Chinhan (1711–91).[4] When he visited his relatives in Jangheung in Jeolla Province in 1753, Yu toured the local cultural scene and happened upon a pansori performance of *Song of Chunhyang*. Returning home the following spring, he reconstructed the song in *hansi* (poetry in literary Chinese) from his recall of lyrics, melodies, characters, and locations. In recognition of the poem's critical importance as the earliest source material, Kim Donguk also raises the question of how faithfully he transferred what he saw and heard to his *hansi* version.[5] The first couplet goes: "The front of Gwanghallu pavilion, the Crow-and-Mackpie Bridge, I'm Gyeonu (Herdsman) and you're Jingnyeo (Weaver)."[6] From the start, Poet Yu appears to be collecting the pieces of his eyewitness memory for later reconstruction, in shorthand style for creative reading or enactment. According to Yu Geum, his son, his father was slandered by his *yangban* peers for bringing such a prurient folk story into their esteemed midst.[7]

For pansori as a genre, the nineteenth century was a nexus of innovation, yielding abundant singers, texts, and styles. In *Joseon changgeuk sa* (1940), Jeong Noshik documents the anecdotal ethnography of singers and their artistic contributions from the premodern era. Jeong's ethnography along with the oral testimonies of senior practitioners provides a rich understanding of early pansori text and style formation. This era is also known as the time of the Five Professional Generations: "On the whole, one generation of *kwangdae* generally served as teachers to the next."[8]

Excluded Seven Ballads (*Taryeong*)

In the early nineteenth century, at least twelve narratives existed in pansori format. By the late nineteenth century, the repertoires were reduced to the canonical five *sori* that thematically aligned with the five Confucian cardinal virtues. The other seven were left out as simply *taryeong*, "ballad" or "folk song," as pansori was commonly referred to at the time, to experience gradual erasure of their vocal *sori* contents. More recently there have been sporadic attempts at recovery or recreation of these seven *taryeong*, as either solo pansori or multi-singer operatic *changgeuk*. The National Changgeuk Company in 2012 launched the *Pansori Ilgop Madang*, the Seven Pansori Repertoires, an effort to expand the mainstream *changgeuk* repertoire beyond the canonical five. Their rediscovery will allow for a fuller understanding of the nineteenth-century culture of Korean storytelling. I include the titles and storylines of the excluded seven.

Garujigi Taryeong, Ballad of the Femme Fatale

There exist two interpretations of the word *Garujigi*: it is the body of a dead man wrapped in a straw bale for transport. The original, obscene connotation was that of female genitalia structured horizontally, so believed to enhance sexual pleasure. In the story, both interpretations fit into one causality where the female protagonist's fatal attraction is the beginning of the male protagonist's demise. The heightened level of vulgarity was likely one of the reasons for its exclusion from the canon. However, Shin Jaehyo, credited with the canonization of the Five Narratives included this particular story in his *Saseoljip* collection.[9]

Garujigi Taryeong is also known as *Byeon Gangshoe Taryeong* after the name of the protagonist's male partner. The most libidinous man in the south, Byeon Gangshoe marries the infamously hypersexual Ongnyeo. However, their daily business of living is compromised by an excess of fiery lust. One day, Ongnyeo urges her husband to go and gather firewood. Reluctant to exert himself except in sex, Byeon opts for the shortcut of chopping down the closest tree, which happens to be the totem pole safeguarding the village. Consequently, all the guardian spirits gather to deliver punishment commensurate to his desecration, death.

The many lusting suitors for the widowed Ongnyeo offer to help prepare Byeon's remains for the funeral in exchange for her hand in marriage. One after another, they fall dead or are fastened to the ground. Only the spirits have the power to undo the curse, and the occasion calls for an absolution. The story concludes with Byeon's funeral, and a touring company of performers appear to fulfill the task. *Garujigi* is a comedy of errors combining spiritual sacrosanctity and *joie de vivre* entertainment.

Onggojip taryeong, *Ballad of the Curmudgeon*[10]

Mr. Ong of the Ongdang Village was a bigoted, stubborn soul. He greatly disdained Buddhism and was particularly cruel to Buddhist monks seeking alms. Finally, an enlightened guru decided to intervene. He crafted another Mr. Ong with bits of straw, and the straw Mr. Ong went to claim the home life of the real Mr. Ong. Straw Ong chased out Real Ong and cohabited with his wife. Left to wander aimlessly, Mr. Ong found his awakening to become a better person. The guru forgave him, and he returned home a new man.

Bae-bijang taryeong, Ballad of Chief Deputy Bae

The *yangban* Kim Gyeong is assigned as new governor of the island of Jeju and recruits Mr. Bae of the West River District as his deputy in cultural affairs. On his departure, Bae's wife makes him promise to avoid the lures of the local Jeju *gisaeng*. Joseon men had tacit license to pursue extramarital liaisons while female chastity was strictly regulated. Bae, however, heeds his wife to the point of declining invitations from his peers, who gather at venues with drinks and *gisaeng*. Governor Kim, likely experiencing profound boredom in his Jeju post so remote from the capitol, formulates a ruse to "loosen" Deputy Bae's chaste conduct, employing the *femme fatale gisaeng* named Aerang and the quick-witted servant Bangja as his operatives.

Smitten by Aerang, Deputy Bae begs Bangja to lead the way to a liaison. At that moment *in flagrante*, they hear a thunderous call from outside. It is Bangja impersonating Aerang's brutish husband. Aerang hides the frantic Bae in her rice chest, and the chest is thrown into the sea. By the grace of spiritual intervention, the chest miraculously opens so the deputy swims back to shore. The story ends with Chief Deputy Bae flailing as if swimming for his life across the governor's courtyard, while the onlookers to this comedy of errors delights in the gallows humor of Bae's misfortunes. Though *Baebijangjeon* features a zealous promotion of Neo-Confucian virtue, namely the segregated lives of men and women (夫婦有別), it was nevertheless excluded from the *Obatang* canon. While speculation is left to the readers, one possible explanation is its unflattering portrayal of a government official who encourages misconduct from his most virtuous subordinate.

Gangneung Maehwa taryeong, *Ballad of the Plum Blossom of Gangneung*

Scholar Gol, secretary of the Commissioner of Gangneung, is in love with the top *gisaeng* Maehwa ("Plum Blossom") when he receives his father's order to return to Seoul to take the *gwageo* examination. The lovestruck Gol has failed the *gwageo* after penning verses of longing for Maehwa in lieu of examination answers, and must return to his former Gangneung post. His boss intervenes: arranging a fake burial mound of Maehwa at the roadside, he tells Gol that Maehwa is dead. Devastated, Gol passes his days clutching her portrait to his bosom and wailing at her gravesite. At dusk one day, at the Commissioner's order, Maehwa appears before Gol feigning as a ghost. The next day, the ghost of Maehwa seduces Gol into accompanying her to the famous Gyeongpodae pavilion for their dance to the otherworldly journey before he gradually realizes he has been tricked.

Compared to the governor's ruse in the story of Chief Deputy Bae, the Commissioner's antics in *Gangneung Maehwa taryeong* are more ethically directive to commit to one's duties. Love, like life, is a fleeting dream. The clear shamanic and Daoist magical subtexts of this *taryeong* would have been difficult to accommodate in the canon.

Jangki taryeong, *Ballad of the Pheasant*

A dazzling pheasant and his sagacious hen have a splendid life together until one day they discover a bean in their path. His wife cautions him against picking up what should be most definitely a trap, as she does not want to be widowed again. The hen does her best to save her swashbuckling husband from the snare, but he refuses to heed the fretting of the "inferior" gender and gets killed. Many eligible pheasants come courting. She rejects all but a widower pheasant to live together happily ever after. The story on the surface is a simple parabolic progression that opens to a serious critique on the fictitious nature of patriarchal authoritarian mandates.

Musugi taryeong, aka *Walcha taryeong*, *Ballad of the Philanderer Musugi*

The married son of a wealthy man of Seoul, Kim Musuk is a ladies' man. One day, Musuk takes one look at Euiyang, a *gisaeng* scouted from Pyeongyang to work at the king's court. He falls for her beauty at once. He buys her out of the *gisaeng* registry, and they cohabit. Musuk's new love interest does not stop him from seeking new affairs, however. Euiyang solicits help from Musuk's wife and a few others for her plot to cause Musuk extreme financial hardship whereby he reforms himself. This story is modernistic in that the protagonist's rehabilitation is realistic. Financial hardship is a bitter potion, but a circumstance that was plausible for premodern and contemporary audiences.

The seventh excluded narrative is *Gashinseon taryeong*, *Ballad of the Fake Immortal*, or *Sugyeong nangja jeon*, *Tale of Miss Sugyeong*. The former is about a man fooled into entering the Diamond Mountain to procure the heavenly peach and nectar. The latter is a lengthier tale of romance continuing through hardships, death, and resurrection.

Obatang, the Gentlemen's Pansori

Mid-nineteenth century Korea was the site of political challenges and influences from an outside world larger than its traditional neighbors, culminating in the Japan–China conflict and Japan's annexation of Korea in 1910. This chapter explores how with the historical backdrop of the nineteenth century, literacy and musical performativity were merged, gentrified, and canonized as the Korean storysinging tradition called "pansori." The artistic productivity of the time was intertwined with the collaboration of literary scholarship and aristocratic patronages celebrating the talents and achievements of the singers. Introducing the key figures in the establishment of pansori canon, two names most readily associated with the historical and narrative development of pansori of this era are: Prince Heungseon Daeweongun (1820–98) who served as the regent when his son King Gojong (1852–1919) rose to the throne at the age of twelve, and the literary talent Shin Jaehyo (1812–84).

As a reigning Confucian patriarch, the Regent Heungseon Daeweongun wielded unrestricted influence in the history of Joseon inching toward its twilight. In foreign affairs, a chain of events involving Western colonial powers turned Daeweongun "bitterly defensive against the West."[11] Domestically, he aimed to consolidate the power of the monarchy over the aristocracy by transcending factional and regional politics and even class in the appointment of personnel.[12] In general, he set in motion the direction of the government toward "a resolute program of reform."[13]

Outside of his political activities and struggles, Daeweongun's deep connection to pansori is hardly mentioned in orthodox Korean history. Daeweongun in fact happens to be one of the most recalled names in the anecdotal history of pansori by virtue of his critical influence and patronage. The stories of his friendship and patronage for talented singers are famously retold through unofficial history channels such as film or drama series. A sixth cousin of the heirless King Cheolchong (r. 1849–64) and highest in the order of succession, Prince Heungseon lost his parents at a young age and had a difficult childhood, with no one to guide him into the elite circles of power. At the same time, he had to survive political slanders and threats of physical harm from the rival powers of the Andong Kim Clan. The prince camouflaged his sanity in scandalous behavior, often in the company of "low lives." As a way of protecting his progeny from political harm's way, he inappropriately mingled with socially outcast *gwangdae*. He once narrowly escaped an assassination attempt by disappearing in the company of a traveling Namsadang performance troupe.[14] From this episode, we could surmise that the prince's association with actors and musicians started years before he came to power, and had to be substantially deeper than a usual patron–singer encounter. Daeweongun's penchant for pansori-listening was favorably rooted in his memory of Singer Song Heunglok (1801–63). Years before he gained power, the down-and-out prince was once staying in Jeonju. On the Fifth Day of the Fifth Month (Dano) celebration, the prince went to the park to attend the *sori* performance by Song and requested to hear him sing again. That evening, Singer Song, then referred to as the King of Singing, swapped life stories with the downtrodden prince, and Song offered the prince his entire honorarium from singing that day. Daeweongun remembered the singer's kindness, and when he came to power, he searched for him across the nation but could not find him.

The *Daesaseup* of Jeonju was initiated in the seventeenth century as a winter martial arts tournament in horse riding and archery. By the early nineteenth century, it also featured ambitious pansori singers' performances as main attractions. It was stopped after the fall of Joseon and resumed in 1975 as an annual three-day summer traditional music festival. It continues as the prime venue for discovering new *myeongchang* or "star singers." It is said that Daeweongun ordered the governor of Jeolla to institutionalize an annual pansori contest in memory of the singer Song Heunglok, the modern inception of the *Daesaseup* national annual contest that continues at the park now called the Deokchin Gongweon. When Daeweongun was living, the first-place winners of the pansori contest were customarily dispatched to perform at the prince's Unhyeon Palace in Seoul for his final approval. Daeweongun's continued patronage for pansori, in addition to his genuine appreciation for pansori singing, may also have been an expression of his undying nostalgia for the unlikely friendship developed between their uneven classes and in the ruthless world in which they lived.

The man of the hour in the creation of the Five Narratives (*Obatang*), Shin Jaehyo was son of a wealthy *jungin*, an "in-between" class of people inheriting only half of *yangban* parentage and thus assigned below *yangban* and above commoner. Originally from Yangju, Gyeonggi Province, Shin lived in Gochang of South Jeolla. He combined his literary savvy, political ambition, and cross-cultural outlook to merge the separated cultures of high, low, written, and oral to Korean storytelling. The complexity of Shin's Sinitic literary adaptation of the vernacular performativity of pansori illuminates an intriguing possibility of an oral–literal merger, especially if his collaboration with singers of his time was testing his lyrical reworkings via the singers' musical composition (*buchimsae*). In comparison with the handwritten and print versions transmitted in the singing world, Shin's versions are more for an elite readership, with limited borrowings of lyrics between the singer texts and Shin's. Compiler of Shin Jaehyo's pansori *saseol* (narratives), Gang Hanyeong categorizes them as dramatic literature written in refined poetic language different from pansori as performance.[15]

In 1865, Daeweongun initiated a reconstruction of the Gyeongbok Palace that had been destroyed during the Hideyoshi Invasion three centuries prior. The independently wealthy Shin Jaehyo donated generously to the project, and was rewarded with an honorary military commandership title bestowed from Daeweongun. For Shin, his work with pansori canonization was a means of establishing his public persona despite his non-*yangban* status.[16] Having a personal recognition by Daeweongun, the most powerful man in Joseon, was a major social capital and incentive for his pansori gentrification and canonization project. He used his own financial resources for gathering singers, staging performances, explicating pansori aesthetics, and editing the texts and songs.[17]

The curation of pansori libretti involved literary-linguistic aspects of narrative content as well as musical embellishment.

Shin's literary vision combined with the singers' artistic savvy in this collaboration, testing how his textual revisions and new compositions could be executed technically. In his *Song of the Gwangdae* (*Gwangdaega*), Shin lists four essential requisites of pansori in their order of importance: appearance (*inmul*), narrative composition (*saseol*), vocal attainment (*deugeum*), and accompanying gesture (*neoreumsae*). Pihl interprets the "appearance" as a "commanding and effective stage presence ... more a matter of native talent than of training."[18] But Shin's own definition is literal in that the appearance is "inborn so cannot be changed."[19] For Shin, the performer's appearance does not disappear into the character, thus a *gwangdae* or actor must have an appealing look just like actors in Hollywood today.

As far as public visibility was concerned, pansori singing was made as a male-only practice, where the female presence appeared only within the narrative reality created by the male imagination. As mentioned earlier, by producing several versions of the story of Chunhyang according to gender and age differences, Shin Jaehyo took pansori one step closer to the new horizon at last of the female storyteller voice. He went even further to debut a female singer on the national stage, another decisive step toward gender-blind pansori-singing practice we have today. The story continues: Shin's endeavors with the pansori canonization project were rewarded when in 1868 he was made director of the inauguration production celebrating the renovation of more than 330 buildings of Gyeongbok Palace. Shin ambitiously debuted several new songs of blessing for the auspicious occasion, to be performed before Daeweongun by his beloved female protégé, Jin Chaeseon (1842–?). Jin's was the first known public performance by a female pansori singer, and it gave Shin greater political visibility as well as irreparable heartbreak.

Born as *gisaeng* and registered at the district office of Gochang, Jin Chaeseon had entered Shin's training center. After her sensational debut at the Gyeongbok Palace inauguration, she was indefinitely detained at Daeweongun's

Unhyeongung Palace as his functionary *gisaeng* until he lost power and was ousted six years later. Jin's fate is unknown: there are speculations that she either ran away to China or was murdered on the orders of the queen, Daeweongun's daughter-in-law and political adversary. The nature of the bond between Shin and Jin has inspired generations of storytellers, including Lee Jong-pil's 2015 film, *Dorihwaga (Sound of a Flower)*, also the title of Shin's love ballad for Jin currently in the care of a Shin family descendant. The poem is written in the pansori warm-up song (*danga*) format, but is much longer: totalling 136 lines, each comprised of four phrases, each made up of roughly four syllables, the lyric is about four times the average length of *danga* leaning towards twelve-beat *jungmori*. The poet reveals his heart by employing the various nature elements with Jin's lovely face shimmering through them. In place of Sinitic verbiages, the poet resorts entirely to *hangeul* construction, bringing focus to what he is feeling more intimately. It is difficult to fathom a man's heart capable of feeling that much longing giving her to his superiors. Whether it was his political move or demonstration of loyalty to his superiors, I leave it to the readers. Below are the first few lines translated:

> Four-n'-twenty spring winds and another flowering
> Let us, let us to view the peach blossoms
> Peach's ravishing crimson, plum's snowy white
> But what flower among flower is this?
> She smiles and speaks, as if hearing my thoughts
> Flute and drum chase the bees from the fragrance
> Monarch butterfly swaggers in.[20]

A literary scholar, poet, critic, and associate of Daeweongun, Shin exerted authenticity in his curation of the genre. His separate versions of Chunhyang for female singers and minor-age singers were dramatic adjustments of pansori singing to gender and age-appropriate expression, tempo, pitch, and narrative perspective. It was the singers' privilege to be in

Shin's inner circle and realize his editorial vision with the best of their abilities, flawlessly musicalizing the often ostentatious parades of Sinitic literacy cluttering up the poetic content. A *yangban* patron named Jeong Hyeonseok (b. 1811) once wrote a letter recommending a singer for admission to Shin's pansori school. In his instructions for the singer, Jeong prescribes articulating the embellished libretto with clarity, along with other stipulations for making a "great singer" free of "certain 'abuses' committed by kwangdae in the performance of p'ansori."[21]

> Furthermore, select from among singers those whose presence is attractive and whose voices are strong and sonorous. Train them in some thousands of characters and, after having awakened them clearly to tones and sounds, teach them with libretti so that they can recite them as their own words. Next, teach them using the singing modes: the basic mode, which must be grand, deep, and harmonious; the commanding mode, which must be clear, brave, and powerful; and the wailing mode, which must be of sad and piteous lament. The reverberations of the voice should make the rafters ring and the clouds stand still. When the singer takes his place and tries to sing, his articulation must be so clear and the narrative so consistent that he can assume that none of his listeners fails to understand. In addition, he must carry himself erect and proper; and, whether he sits, stands, raises his fan, or gestures with his hand, all of these must be done with moderation.[22]

Notwithstanding the literary worth of Shin's gentrification project, the "pansori novels" cropping up after his time were likely substantially reverted to the living oral expressions of singers, evidenced in family-guild transcripts. The narratives became confluences of classical text and vernacular, with the Confucian virtues as figurehead and the sentiments and feelings of ordinary people filling gaps with human drama in diegesis. The surface themes may have served "an excuse for aristocrats to enjoy the vulgarity of p'ansori," while the vernacular "held popular audiences and moved them at heart."[23]

Working through Jeong Noshik's oral history collection, Pihl establishes five professional generations of singers from the late eighteenth through the early twentieth centuries forming their master–disciple relationships.[24] The first generation is made up of Ha Handam and Choe Seondal with no known credit to specific songs, but they occupy a historical importance of the now obsolete pre-performance convention of *soripuri*, oral recognition of singers and their contributions came before the singer himself. According to Jeong Noshik, Singer Jeon Doseong as a child heard all the famous singers, including Pak Mansun, and Yi Nalchi cite Ha and Choe as the two progenitors of pansori during *soripuri*.[25] The second generation is the "Go-Song-Yeom-Mo," the celebrated era of Go Sugwan, Song Heunglok, Yeom Gyedal, and Mo Heunggap mentioned in Shin Wi's poem. The fact that all except the Jeollado native Song Heunglok were from either Chungcheong or Gyeonggi Province indicates pansori singing had circulated "into the central regions of the country in the early decades of the nineteenth century."[26] Historically, perhaps due to its "Land's End" geography farthest from the capitol, Jeollado, including the islands of Jindo, housed the largest number of banished officials from Seoul. Local artists claim the literary, artistic, and performative culture on the islands reached a height of sophistication due to exposure to the cultural expectations of the *yangban* Seoulites serving expulsion sentences on the island. The settling of Jeolla dialects and culture as the dominant foundation of pansori may have been more processual and haphazard than innate, considering the serendipitous momentum in its cultural performances in the land of political exiles.

Defining the third generation of singers as a teaching generation, Pihl observes they "flourished in the middle third of the [nineteenth] century. These teachers established classical interpretations and populated the remainder of the century with their disciples."[27] They also populated new episodes, songs, and stories to expand the repertoires to as many as twelve. They laid the foundation for the gentrification of pansori by setting the precedence of the musico-literary collaboration with men of letters. For example, Singer Bang Manchun trained at a temple in Hwanghae Province while collaborating with a local poet-master and others on *Song of the Red Cliff*.[28]

During the days of advancing modernity in the late nineteenth century, the fourth generation actively participated in Shin Jaehyo's canon-building enterprise. At the threshold of the twentieth century, they were expected both to perform and teach the tradition while innovating through it. The entrance of women unsettled the preexistent taboo against the notion of a female pansori singer, and the modernization of travel and mobility exposed singers to different performative styles and textual interpretations. The fifth generation, who came of age in the early twentieth century, was "to carry the p'ansori tradition into the twentieth century and recite to Chŏng Noshik the oral history of their art."[29]

Jeong Noshik in the *History of Korean Singing Drama* lists 89 singers, including eight females, each credited to a song, spanning from the late eighteenth to the early twentieth centuries. The singers were almost entirely linked in master–disciple relationships, with each generation of *gwangdae* generally serving as teachers to the next generation.[30] The "Eight Eminent Singers" of the first half of the nineteenth century were Gweon Samdeuk, Yeom Gyedal, Song Heunglok, Kim Jecheol, Mo Heunggap, Go Sugwan, Shin Manyeop, and Bang Manchun; those of the second half were Song Uryong, Pak Mansun, Kim Sejong, Jeong Chunpung, Pak Yujeon, Yi Nalchi, Jeong Changeop, and Jeon Haejong. The numeric significance of eight is assumed to reflect literary aspirations for eminence comparable to the "Eight Great Prose Masters of Tang and Song."[31] Considering the literary elevation of pansori working as a possible inroad to social ascendance, gentrification of the narrative content may have been a hot topic of interest and enterprise.

Between the Narrative (*Saseol*) and Its Musical Composition (*Deoneum*)

In his lavishly embellished description, Shin Jaehyo goes so far as to personify the "narrative" (*saseol*) to an ideal beauty waiting for a capable literary mind to grasp:

What is saseol?
It's the stunning flower embroidery with perfectly crafted gold and jade words,
It's the dazzlingly adorned beauty revealing herself from behind the folding screen,
It's the bright full moon coming out from behind clouds,
Bringing a smile of satisfaction to a listening face is difficult . . .[32]

In comparing his work of narrative embellishment to elusive feminine beauty, Shin appears to differentiate his literary craft from the performative role of *gwangdae*. It is now the job of singers to materialize his belles-lettres in their trained voices. In the collaboration of literary and musical, the concept and ownership of individual artistic contribution (*deoneum*) needs clarification: insofar as *deoneum* is musical composition of *saseol*, their relationship appears to be comparable to that of composer and lyricist, or singer and narrative embellisher in the case of pansori. And it is in the singer's singing where lyricist's artistry is demonstrated. To show how different singers contributed their respective *deoneum* in the construction of one narrative, I have created a table of singers and their repertoires constituting some of the major repertoires of the *Song of Chunhyang*. The Korea Britannica Corporation, a subsidiary of Encyclopedia Britannica, Inc., in 1982 produced the *Deep-Rooted Tree Pansori Collection*, containing the recordings of the five canonical narratives by several eminent singers and companion brochures, including scholarly introductions by Yi Bohyeong and annotated *saseol* narratives.

In his introduction of the *Song of Chunhyang*, Yi includes the main elements of repertoire constituting the narrative, showing how the individual deoneum came together to create the *roman-fleuve* of Chunhyang's love story (1982).[33] The repertoires are organized by the plot chronology. Table 3.1 visualizes the musico-literary connection and the accumulation of individual creativity and collaboration over time, into the continuous development and transmission of pansori repertoires that exist today.

On the threshold of the twentieth century, I would like the readers to be acquainted with the biographical and professional notes of a few major singers of the nineteenth century and their contributions. The earliest ethnographic record by Jeong Noshik combined with the orally transmitted and gathered anecdotes from the twentieth-century circles of the late masters serve as the sources. Their anecdotes, interesting in and of themselves, provide windows from which we can view the social–performative relationship of the time and place manifested in the historical performative development of

Table 3.1 Artist contributions (from late Joseon to early twentieth century) to the libretto of **Song of Chunhyang**: *A partial list*

Name	Dates	Song
Jang Jabaek	n.d.	At the scenic Gwanghallu in Namweon, Mongnyong sees Chunhyang.
Kim Sejong	1825–98	Back home, Mongnyong flips through *The Thousand Characters* while thinking only of Chunhyang.
Yi Seoksun	n.d.	That evening, Mongnyong visits Chunhyang's home. While waiting for her, he looks around Chunhyang's tastefully decorated room.

Song Gwanglok	n.d.	Slow "Love Song" in *jinyang* beat.
Go Sugwan	n.d.	Faster "Love Song" in *Jungjungmori*.
Yu Gongnyeol	1859–1934	Mongnyong on his way to see Chunhyang; he agonizes over having to tell her he needs to end it since he must return to Seoul.
Mo Heunggap	1822–90	"Parting Song I"
Pak Yujeon	1835–1906	"Parting Song II"
Jeong Jeongnyeol	1876–1938	The procession of the new magistrate is coming down to Namweon.
Yeom Gyedal	n.d.	Chunhyang is beaten for her refusal to serve the new magistrate; the dandies of Namweon harshly criticize the new magistrate for his cruelty.
Song Heunglok	1801–63	Chunhyang, beaten and tortured, laments in her jail cell.
Yi Nalchi	1820–92	Chunhyang yearns for Mongnyong in her cell.
Pak Mansun	n.d.	Chunhyang in her dream encounters the ghosts of the two legendary chaste wives.
Im Bangul	1904–61	"Uncombed and Messy," Chunhyang yearns for Mongnyong in her cell.
Song Mangap	1866–1939	Farmers' Ballad (*Nongbuga*), contains farmers' criticism of the new magistrate, and the Inspector General Incognito Mongnyong on his way to Namweon hears it.
Song Heunglok	1801–63	Ghosts, howling and weeping, daily visit Chunhyang in her cell.

pansori. I hope the catch phrase titles introducing them help identify the nature of their social identities or artistic achievements. The lyrical *deoneum*, albeit *sans* the vocal execution, hopefully serves as linguistic illumination of the vocal theatre of pansori singing at its best.

"Aristocratic *Gwangdae*"

Bigabi is a name given to *gwangdae* of *yangban* origins. The term is technically an oxymoron, since *yangban* and *gwangdae* could not be the same person given the strict class division of the time. Assuming nature is stronger than culture, there are those born to sing or play music who relinquish class privilege or parental wishes to follow their hearts to become singers or composers. In the history of pansori, those few equipped with critical literacy plus the embodied knowledge of singing were regarded as assets as attested in the saying, "There is Jeong Chunpung in the north and Shin Jaehyo in the south."[34] Chunpung ("Spring Wind"), a name unbefitting of a *yangban*, was Jeong's self-chosen name for his new *gwangdae* identity. Born in a *yangban* clan of Chungcheong Province, he passed the first examination for office and received the title of *jinsa*. The year of his birth is not known, but he was close to Daeweongun, who admired Jeong's scholarly prowess and narrative innovation. The prince also enjoyed Jeong's dignified *ujo* style of singing, expressive of the pedigree of nobility. Credited to Jeong is *Sosang palgyeong*, a warm-up-style eulogy of the eight scenic beauties along the rivers So and Sang in today's Hunan, China. The locale's eight-beauty theme was imported into the poetic canon during the Goryeo kingdom.[35] Jeong adroitly adds his own poetic dexterity to the syntax of pansori. From Stanza Four:

> Blue waves, clean sand, moss-covered banks,
> Unable to resist the urge to return,
> A goose flying hither with a reed flower in its beak

One after another, dot-dot-dot, dive in a queue
Is this not the "geese falling on sand bank" echoing back?[36]

The first two seven-character quatrain lines borrowed from *Gwian* ("Return of Geese") by the poet Jeon Gi (錢起) of the Tang dynasty bluntly affirm the Sinitic erudition for an audience profile shifting toward elitism. The easy listening that follows in vernacular Korean is poetic and musical justice for all. The final line is a literary–vernacular merger, the typical syntax of pansori narrative. In singing, Jeong intended a seamless pollination of his key asset, i.e., literacy. His erudition, coupled with poetic merit, helped set the standard direction of textual gentrification. Jeong's *Sosang palgyeong* found wide adaptability across the canon and beyond. For example, the entire passage is interpolated in *Jebi nojeonggi* ("Swallow's Flight Itinerary") in the *Song of Heungbo*. It was also arranged for the *gayageum byeongchang*, where the singer sings while also playing the *gayageum* zither. Jeong's rendering of his *Sosang palgyeong* was transmitted to Song Mangap (1866–1939), and a recording by his son Song Gideok remains in the pansori archive.[37]

Jeong Chunpung's senior by several decades, Gweon Samdeuk (1772–1841) was born in Jeonju of Jeollado to a prestigious Andong Gweon clan. In his twelfth year, he chanced upon a performance of pansori on his way home from the village schoolhouse and pleaded with the singer to teach him. To avoid possible capital punishment for corrupting a son of *yangban*, the *gwangdae* pleaded with the boy to forget the idea. The boy insisted and the singer finally agreed to teach him. Several years passed before his family found out and ordered him to stop singing, but he did not. The clan leaders handed down the verdict: death by beating and granting his last wish to sing one more time. It was the Song of Ten Lashes (*Shipchangga*), Chunhyang's aria at the scene of her torture for refusing the lustful advancement of her superior. Rolled up in a straw bale, the boy sang his finale. His sorrowful voice moved everyone to tears, and the clan leaders commuted his punishment to excommunication and banishment. Stripped of his station and privilege, he worked as a temple servant while perfecting his *sori*.[38]

Gweon Samdeuk is credited with *hogeolche*, "heroic mode," playing on the trope of masculine straightforwardness in Nolbo's Swallow Calling Song in a rousing *Jungjungmori* beat in the *Song of Heungbo*. Determined to outdo Heungbo's wealth, one spring day Nolbo is out to catch and break as many swallow legs as possible so he can become many times wealthier. The song of Nolbo out to catch swallows was transmitted to Jeon Doseong (1864–1944), Song Mangap (1866–1939), Kim Changnyong (1871–1935), and the female virtuoso Pak Nokchu (1905–79). Pak Nokchu's version transmitted to Han Nongseon (1934–2002) is translated here:[39]

Jebiga (Song of Swallows)

Spring passes, summer comes, it's Buddha's birthday, butterflies flit and flutter,
Oriole on willow branch calls its own name, *kwekkol kwekkol*!
the net Bokhui-ssi wove[40] slung over his shoulder, out to lure swallows, to Bangjang hill.
Right Peak here, Left Peak there, across, opposite, left, right, peaks all around,
"Come, Birdies!" He kicks a thicket calling "Huyeo--Huhhuh, Swallow!"
On Bangjang mountain, he strikes a bush, "Huyeo! Swallow, Hey! Where're you going?"
A black kite circling the sky,[41] "Is that a swallow?"
Crows and magpies heading south, "Are they swallows?"
An oriole glowing golden in the spring sun, "Is that a swallow?"
A dove hovering over a cliffside, "Is that a swallow?"
"Swallow there! Do not enter that house, it was built on a bad-luck day!

When "Fire reaches the girder,[42] you won't even know.
Come to my house, come in!"

"King of *Sori*"

The "King of *Sori*" (*Gawang*) of the nineteenth century, Song Heunglok (1780–1860) founded an influential school of pansori. Within the inner circle of his family, his *dongpyeonche*-style singing was also practiced by his younger brother Gwanglok, brother-in-law Kim Seongok, and grandson Song Uryong. His great-grandson Song Mangap (1866–1939) taught this ancestral heirloom to major singers, including Jang Pangae, Kim Jeongmun, and Pak Nokchu, while leading the modernization of pansori through his work in *changgeuk*. Song Heunglok's lifelong affair with the *gisaeng* Maengnyeol reflects the intimate romantic and artistic chemistry between *gwangdae* and *gisaeng*: they were *similis simili gaudet* as social outcasts and colleagues in the musical arts. Song admired Maengnyeol's beauty, intelligence, and critical ear for pansori singing. The story goes that his efforts to impress her led to his becoming the king of *sori* of his time. In their stormy relationship, a bitter fight broke out one day and she packed her bag and left. His pride would not let him go after her, but he sang in sorrowful *jinyang* mode: *Maengnyeol, Maengnyeol, you witch! Go if you will, I don't care!* Maengnyeol, eavesdropping behind the door, returned to his embrace.[43]

The Korean language is built in an abundance of onomatopoetic phraseologies, and rich sensory expressions abound in pansori. Translated below is part of Song Heunglok's famous *deoneum* in the *Song of Shim Cheong*, where Blindman Shim, abandoned by his wanton new wife on his way to the royal banquet, cools off in a stream to soothe his broken heart. Similar water imagery and onomatopoeic devices occur in *Song of the Water Palace* (*Sugungga*), as Turtle discovers a scenic land-world and stream so different from the realm of the Dragon King. His song of discovery is redolent with nature's colorful sights and sounds in an upbeat *jungjungmori*:

Stream winds around blue mountains, here *kweol-kweol*,
   there *jururururu* ...
Rivulets join and shoot the water upward, downward,
   fanning droplets,
Strike rock wall across, *kkwaang! Kkwaang!* Frothing
   foaming, *bukcheok-bukcheok!*
Sound of water, *Weollireong! Kkweol-Kkweol!* gurgling,
   churning, convulsing, where to?[44]

"True River-Mountain Style"

At the height of his political power in the 1860s, Prince Daeweongun invited the winners of the annual Jeonju *daesaseup* competition to his palace as resident artists. At twenty-five, Pak Yujeon (1835–1906) of Sunchang of Jeolla was the prince's favorite houseguest. During his lengthy residency in the prince's palace in metropolitan Seoul, his singing underwent substantial textual and stylistic gentrification under the generous care of the prince delighted by Pak's clear springy voice and singing style. He bestowed on him an honorary military officer's title (*seondal*) and a pair of black crystal glasses to cover his missing eye during performances. According to Jeong Noshik, the *Seopyeonche* style of singing began with Pak Yujeon, and his style came to be known as *Gangsanche* after the name of his home village.[45] A slightly different story circulated in my teacher's circle goes: learning Pak was from a village called Gangsan ("River and Mountain"), Daeweongun one day praised his singing with "You're the true 'River and Mountain.'" Hence the *Gangsanche* style came to represent the 'truly' nature-invoking Pak Yujeon style.

If the singing career of Pak Yujeon had ended simply as Daeweongun's "royal *gwangdae*," the world would not know his role in the birth of *Gangsanche-Boseongsori*, today's dominant style of singing. Toward the end of Daeweongun's regency, the palace politics was fueling a bitter feud between him and his daughter-in-law the queen, and the surrounding nations were using the opportunity to drive their agendas into Korea's domestic affairs. When Daeweongun's regency ended in 1873, Pak escaped Seoul and returned south. In Naju, a man of *gwangdae* origin named Jeong Jaegeun invited Pak to relocate to his hometown of Boseong. In Boseong, Pak transmitted his *sori* to Jeong Jaegeun, who in turn taught his nephew Jeong Eungmin (1896–1964). Young Eungmin would accompany his uncle to Seoul and at one point was involved in the multi-singer dramatic *changgeuk*, but lost interest in the urban theatre scene and returned home to farm and train his *sori* whenever he could. Aspiring singers flocked to Boseong to be his disciples, including Seong Uhyang (1935–2014), Seong Changsun (1934–2017), Cho Sanghyun (1939–), and his son and my teacher Chung Kwonjin (1927–86). All of them were at one point or another recognized as living human treasures or preservers of pansori.

A "Saddest" Song of Parting (*Ibyeolga*)

The *Song of Chunhyang* that entered the *Gangsanche Boseongsori* repertoire is widely recognized as the legacy of the eminent singer Kim Sejong, contemporary of Pak Yujeon and Jeong Chunpung and Shin Jaehyo's indispensable collaborator. His *Lovers' Parting Song* (*Ibyeolga*) is regarded as a highlight of pansori singing.[46] In terms of the stylistic connection with the song, Master Chung Kwonjin also mentioned Pak Yujeon, opening the possible reality of *deoneum* as a more complex exchange of multiple authorships of lyrical and musical composition. Constructed with three voices, including the narrator and two lovers, *Ibyeolga* builds up their exchange of emotions and feelings of imminent separation. Their exchange employs tonal and modal contrast to dramatically manifest their different regionalities, personalities, and handlings of the situation. In between sympathetic interjections in the narrator's voice, two distinct voices take turns: Mongnyong has just revealed to Chunhyang the news of his imminent departure. When her initial shock subsides, she begins her farewell in grim *jungmori*: it is layered with Chunhyang's vernacular *seopyeonche* in sorrowful *gyemyeon* mode, expressive of her Jeolla origin and feminine gender role. As discussed in Chapter 1, Mongnyong responds in the *gyeongdeureumche* manifesting his Seoul *yangban* identity in measured *ujo* mode, demonstrative of gentlemanly self-control and scholarly pedantry. These serious emotions contrast with the hilarity of Mongnyong's next stanzas, which exploit the gravity of the stream of tears to deliver an impromptu chastity lesson for Chunhyang. He is leaving her with the last-minute instruction of the wifely *myeongbun* (moral duty) to wait for him despite the uncertain reality of his return.

The lengthy exchange of their pledge of love is cut short by the servant Bangja, who rushes the young master up onto the donkey and sends them off. In the *deoneum* of Mo Heunggap (1800–64), the singer featured in the oldest extant painting of pansori performance,[47] Chunhyang indecorously erupts into a histrionic outburst:

> See that drooping pine branch, I'll untie my long travel scarf,
> Tie one end to the tree limb, tie the other end around my neck,
> *Plop!* I fall and dangle from it,
> I'll end my life before your eyes, it'll be the end.
> You can't leave me here still alive.[48]

Chunhyang's suicidal theatrics in Mo's version is absent in the *gangsanche boseongsori* version. The unrestrained outburst from a female of low birth toward an aristocratic male may have fallen out of consideration for ideal textual gentrification. This is the version we learned:

> Bangja grabs the donkey by the bridle and *Whup-ah!* It turns and bolts like a flying tiger,
> Uphill, downhill, round a bend, along the green river,

Chunhyang helplessly watches his receding figure,
Smaller than the moon, than a star, than a butterfly,
Then as if the full moon plunges into the cumulous clouds,
In the blink of an eye, he sinks behind the Bakseokchi hill.
Chunhyang flops down wailing, "He's gone!"
He was talking of leaving, he's really gone!" She bawls unreservedly.[49]

Between the Mo Heunggap and *Boseongsori* versions, the main difference is in the portrayal of Chunhyang's reactions, i.e., between a Chunhyang invoking a gruesome image of herself hanging from a tree limb and another more restrained version. In the *Boseongsori* version, Bangja's timely intervention followed by the physical disappearance of Mongnyong into the distance replaces much of Chunhyang's melodramatic outburst.

Gisaeng Roll Call

In the story of Chunhyang, an array of supporting roles help develop the plot and sustain the focus on the protagonists' situations and actions. For example, there are the clever male and female servants, Bangja and Hyangdan, the lustful Magistrate Byeon who harasses and tortures Chunhyang. Chunhyang's mother and retired *gisaeng* Weolmae represents the outcast element of Chunhyang's birth. The local cohort of *gisaeng* regard Chunhyang as a peer, while she distances herself from them as her love grows for *yangban* Mongryong. The *Song of Chunhyang* includes a generous depiction of the private and public existence of *gisaeng*, as depicted in the Gisaeng Roll Call (*Gisaeng jeomgo*). The song is full of clever metaphors and sharp wit grounded in insider knowledge of the life of *gisaeng*.

The first female pansori singer Jin Chaeseon, introduced earlier in connection with Shin Jaehyo and Prince Daeweongun, is credited with *Gisaeng jeomgo* in the *Song of Chunhyang*.[50]

Given the brevity of history of female singers of pansori, the production of female *deoneum* is still a novelty. The fact that it was a female singer familiar to the ways of *gisaeng* captured the cultural imagination of *gisaeng* in the *Song of Chunhyang* is significant. The amalgam of classical literacy and *gisaeng* mannerism in the lyrics suggests the likelihood of an eccentric yet vibrant textual collaboration occurred between Jin Chaeseon and Shin Jaehyo.

Since Mongnyong's departure, the story of Chunhyang has entered a dark and depressing phase. Lusting after Chunhyang, the lubricious new magistrate comes to town, and a fresh phase of Chunhyang's suffering begins. The festivity of inauguration of the new magistrate includes the roll call of the *gisaeng* listed in the township registry, comparable to a beauty pageant staged today, and the new magistrate can hardly wait to meet the famous Chunhyang. The caricatural pageantry of the *gisaeng*, each vying for the new magistrate's fancy in the swinging *semachi* beat, provides a much needed comic relief from the sorrowful tune of *Ibyeolga*. The assistant manager opens the *gisaeng* registry and rhythmically calls the roll:

> You, Gondolier, rowing to Nampo deep in the night, is the "Orchid Liner" equipped with cassia oar and silk sail?[51]
> "Orchid Liner" the head *gisaeng* enters, she's gorgeous! The tail of her outer skirt stylishly bunched up in her hand raised up to her delicate bosom, she walks in quietly and answers, "Here I aaaammm!"
> Poet So Dongpa floated a boat on Jeokpyeok River and raised a drink to his guest when over the East Mountain the "Moon-Rise"!
> "Moon-Rise" enters, gathering her red skirt for a mesmerizing catwalk! "Here I am, Sir!" She takes her position back left.
> The magistrate complains the introductions are too slow, and he is bored. The officer shifts gear to faster *jungjungmori* to introduce two by two in seven-character quatrain.

Is the Eighth Moon Lotus here? Is the Red Lotus of
  Autumn here? "Here we are!"
Spring Breeze whispering on tree branch! Up and down
  Flying Swallow! "Here we are!"
Where is the tavern? Herdboy points to where Apricot
  Blossoms are! "Here we are!"
Is Half Moon here yearning for love? Is Zither Heart from
  bamboo grove here? "Here we are!"
Chrysanthemum in autumn color, evergreen Bamboo Leaf,
Spring Flower smitten by the wind! "Here we are!"

For a final laugh, the song presents Nakchuni, "Smitten Spring Flower," in a fashion resembling bullying in our society:

Smitten Spring Flower enters, quite done up, the best she could for the occasion. She has pulled back all her hair from her forehead to behind her ears. Determined to win the audition, she has paid the whopping one-*nyang* seven-*don*[52] for facial powder to make a white batter, applied across her face. Tall as a totem pole, she holds up the tail of her skirt right under her chin, thump-thumps in enormous strides, "Here I am!"

Graphic Linguistics of *Sori*

When you sing "When the Sangsang Peak on the Diamond Mountain turns flat, will you then return?", and we all know that the peak is so high it pierces the sky through the clouds. You must sharply raise the tone of "Sangsang peak" in a high-pitched falsetto. At the word *pyeongji*, "flat ground," drop your tone flat and low.[53]

In his analysis of pansori singing, Kim Sejong developed a keen interest in the linguistic elements of vocal music such as pronunciation, intonation, repetition, tonal height, and articulatory length. Kim additionally stressed the importance of facial expression and gesture "since singing is a form of drama, one must not forget the importance of dramatic gesture."[54] As a result of gentrification, pansori came to be where vernacular Korean and Sino-Korean literacy mesh as one syntax, necessitating interlingual adjustment in performance. In his interpretation of the methodological concept of "the word is short, sori is long (oedan-seongjang)", Kim stressed the feeling of ease for both listener and singer. For example, "articulation of names or Sino-literary words and phrases should be short, while descriptive adjectives or verbs and conjugational participles such as -e (에) or -euro (으로) should be elongated."[55]

Under the pervasive influence of Western literary expressions, Korean speech and language arts experienced many irreversible changes since the beginning of the twentieth century. In pansori narrative, many indigenous linguistic elements still remaining challenge our work of interpretation and translation. In the Korean language, the subject and object are often not mentioned or clearly marked as separate entities but diffused in the spirit of communal togetherness of the minds being implicated. The fact that Koreans in communication still use "we" or "our" more than "I" or "my," may serve as a possible explanation for "our mother," "our child," or "our wife," a source of comic relief for those studying Korean as a second or foreign language. The frequently used expression, "One mind transfer to another mind" (*ishim-jeonshim*) reflects the high-context classification of Korean communication. It follows that in pansori narrative, the lyrics are at times indeterminate. Where the logical sequencing of the words appears insufficient, affective and cognitive interpretation completes the meaning. For example,

> Chunhyang helplessly watches [his receding figure],
> [Smaller than] the moon, a star, a butterfly.[56]

Chunhyang stands on a hill watching Mongnyong galloping off, but whose observation of whom is the second line?

Grasping as much as possible the narrative reality necessitates penetration of the subject–object, observer–observed, and singer–listener barrier of the mind. Then we see the inverse proportion between his receding figure and her increasing flood current. In hopes of better situating the minds in accord, I doctored the first line with "his receding figure" and added "smaller than" in the second line.

This chapter has been a critical investigation of the developmental phases of pansori during the eighteenth and through the nineteenth centuries. The pansori narrative singing as we recognize today was largely in place. The singers in concert with literary talents worked to reinvent pansori via gentrification of lyrics and thematic enhancement. Particular attention was paid to the concept and creation of *deoneum* as an individual artistic contribution of literary and musical creativity. The chapter showcased examples of major singers, styles, repertoires, and songs, with the *Song of Chunhyang* as the main frame of reference.

4

Negotiating Dramatic Modernization

In the twentieth century, further removed from its premodern roots, the oral storytelling called pansori faced the existential challenge of performative relevance. This chapter investigates the dramatic and theatrical modernization of pansori that started at the turn of the twentieth century, focusing in particular on the development of the multi-singer operatic pansori referred to as *changgeuk*. *Changgeuk*'s beginning was entwined with the first Korean modern drama production of *Eunsegye* (Silver World), but other forms of "new drama" challenged and influenced the later development of *changgeuk*.

The Gabo Reformation in 1894 was a major proclamation of Korean modernity. It was also the final year of the *gwageo* examination, ongoing since 958. Its abolition meant the *hancha*-based study of the Confucian classics was no longer a prerequisite to a successful political career. Instead, the *hangeul* script promulgated by King Sejong five centuries prior was now the standard of communication and discourse. Michael Pettid asserts that the early modern standardization of *hangeul* appealed to "the desire to bond the language of everyday life with literature."[1] The unity of everyday speech and its written transcription (*eonmun ilchi*) led to a wider channel of written storytelling broadly referred to as a "novel." At the time, English became a new secondary literacy: the first newspaper,

Dongnip shinmun, *Independence Paper*, was launched on April 7, 1896, with three pages in *hangeul* and one in English.

The nascent spirit of Korean modernity emerged during a national crisis, the colonization of the country by neighboring Japan. A major source of subjective horror Julia Kristeva calls "abjection,"[2] colonization mutates behavioral and psychological reality by breaking down the balanced cognition between self and other. Reading abjection through a decolonial lens, Kelly Oliver observes, "colonization perverts affects and turns the negative affects of the colonizers against the colonized through the workings of a cruel superego."[3] A cultural psyche stunted by loss of nation was all the more susceptible to outside influences for better or for worse. In such national trepidation there were new concepts of drama and theatre of mostly European origin coming through from colonial Japan. A new artistic vision of the everyday social environment, realism in theatre mandated a shift toward a naturalistic portrayal in physical staging as well as psychological dimensions, the Stanislavskian "method acting" for example. The awareness of the mental reality of dramatic play corresponded to the physical *mise-en-scène* of the "stage."

"Stage," New Matrix

The concept of theatre as a permanent indoor stage and auditorium was first introduced to Korea in *Seoyugyeonmun* (*Travel Observations of the West*, 1895), which was written by Yu Gilchun, an adherent of the Enlightenment school of learning. In 1881, Yu went to Japan as part of the Gentlemen's Excursion Team, then to the US in 1885 as part of the Korea–US Commercial Treaty. He stayed to attend a Boston-area school for 15 months as the first recorded Korean student in the United States. He visited many countries in Europe on his way home. Upon his return to Korea, Yu was placed under house arrest for seven years for his progressive worldviews, during which time he wrote the book. The volume includes his firsthand observation of the Western dramatic plays and productions, including the physical layout of the theatre interior, realist set design, scene changes, orchestral pit, make-up, and costuming. For Koreans who had never ventured outside the loosely delineated *pan* set outdoors or in a living space, "Yu Gilchun's eyewitness observation was Korea's first lesson in dramatic edification."[4]

After establishing its consulate, Japan began relocating citizens to Seoul. The Japanese expatriates built their theatre buildings for cultural entertainment and as a "strategy of cultural domination of Korea."[5] For Koreans who had never attended dramatic entertainment in a permanent indoor theatre, performance activities in the Japanese or Chinese theatres were a source of creative imagination and curiosity. In addition, Christian missionaries from Western countries also advanced missionary work by staging dramatic storytelling about the life and work of Christ in church productions open to the general public. These influences helped catalyze Korea's own modernization in theatre arts.

Thirteen years prior to Korea's harrowing annexation by Japan, King Gojong elevated Korea from Joseon to Daehan Jeguk, the "Great Korean Empire." This was a gesture of defiance against China's claim to sole imperial status. In 1897, Emperor Gojong performed his enthronement ceremony in the newly raised Weongudan, a dome-shaped royal prayer hall. With his elevated status, the emperor resumed Korea's indigenous state ceremonial dedication to the heavenly guardian spirits. The Korean Empire was short-lived, and the imperial prayer hall was dismantled and replaced with a hotel for the Japanese Government-General of Korea which is now the five-star Josun Hotel. While it lasted, much of the Korean Empire's administrative activity was devoted to the commemoration of the forty-year anniversary of Emperor Gojong's enthronement. The occasion was a chance to present the new empire to the world: the streets of Seoul were being cleaned and improved, the streetcars ran on time, Western time and measurement systems were implemented, and multiple city-planning and architectural projects were underway. The hard work did not go unnoticed even by harsh critics such as Isabella Bird Bishop, a British traveler and author of *Korea and Her Neighbors*. In 1894, she had criticized Seoul as the dirtiest city in the world, and two years later opined that the city was "changing into the cleanest and most civilized of the East."[6]

In 1902, on the property of the Deoksu Palace, the first modern auditorium called Huidae, literally "Drama Stage," was built for the emperor's fortieth enthronement ceremony and continued use for official and unofficial events thereafter. An office named Hyeomnyulsa was inaugurated to oversee the management of the building and the activities "aimed at entertaining both the domestic and foreign guests as well as the public, funded by the emperor himself."[7] The building exterior was known to have adopted the architectural style of the Roman Coliseum, but the filmy photograph remaining in circulation resembles an image of an enlarged Mongolian yurt. The received wisdom is that the building could hold 2,000 people, possibly according to a different measure of auditorium capacity. The interior had a green room and an auditorium with three seating sections facing the stage. The stage and the auditorium were separated by a curtain, and the back of the stage was covered with white drapes. With the pansori singer Kim Changhwan as artistic leader, over 170 top-rated singers, dancers, and musicians went to work preparing for the celebration set for autumn 1902. Due to the outbreak of a cholera epidemic, the event was postponed to spring 1903, and then postponed again to autumn 1903 after the crown prince contracted smallpox. By autumn 1903, with a poor harvest and worsening relations between Russia and Japan for hegemony over Korea, the ceremony concluded as a truncated formality without celebratory fanfare.

Birth of *Changgeuk*

In the wake of seemingly never-ending cancellations, the initial vision of dramatic modernization lost traction, and the players of Huidae resumed traditional popular entertainment, inviting criticisms from both the bureaucratic and the public sectors. Averse to the likes of *gwangdae* and *gisaeng* engaging in "lewd" acts on royal land, the supervisor of Hyeomnyulsa himself submitted a remonstration demanding its closing, and granted in 1906. Those who anticipated a magical dramatic makeover were disappointed by the "continuation of the same old Chunhyang."[8] The building was repurposed as the Officers Club, until in 1908 it was occupied by a new tenant, Yi Injik, a novelist/journalist and confidante of Yi Wanyong who infamously led Korea to annexation by Japan. The building resurfaced as the historic Weongaksa Theatre with 500-capacity, starting with 40 singers and 24 performing *gisaeng*. The repertoires included pansori and traditional musical entertainments, experimental *bunchang* (divided-role pansori singing) of both canonical and new stories. Weongaksa closed shortly before the annexation and burned down a few years later.[9]

Pansori on the surface lacks spectacle such as set, costume, and other special effects, which is one of Aristotle's six elements of drama (plot, character, thought, diction, song, and spectacle). The visual effect in pansori occurs interiorly within the mental realms of singer, drummer, and listener. But spectacle as external sensation was the aspiration for the modern drama movement. At the end of the nineteenth century, there were two popular entertainment venues for pansori singers within the Four Great Gates of Seoul. Gwangmudae Hyeomnyulsa near the East Gate featured a variety of Korean performances with male and female pansori singers. Downtown, near Seoul's Chinatown district, Changgeukkwan catered to the Chinese residents with touring companies from their homeland. Pansori singers Yi Dongbaek (1866–1947) and Gang Yonghwan (1865–1938?) were among the occasional outsiders attending Chinese operas performed at Changgeukkwan. Gang had envisioned multi-performer pansori highlighting individual specialties, and the Chinese operas with role-typical voices and acts inspired him to similar possibilities for the staging of pansori as a modern performing art.[10] Gang was instrumental in the creation of *changgeuk*, ensemble operatic pansori with some dramatic enactment, a negotiation of genre between the narrative, the dramatic, and the lyric. Another innovation coinciding with *changgeuk* was the advent of female professional pansori singers during the early modern period. According to the testimony of Han Seongjun, who in 1908 joined a tour of southern provinces as drummer, there was only one female *gwangdae* playing the roles of both Chunhyang and Shim Cheong.[11] It was presumably the role-playing aspect of *changgeuk* that required the increased participation of female singers.

By introducing the set, prop, costume, lighting, curtain, and individuated role-playing, singers could project onto the visual realm the *sori*, the aural tropes of premodern Korean narrativity. As a dramatic form, pansori is less make-believe than vocal signification of the dramatic truth, and the fusion of narrative and dramatic, i.e., telling and enacting, inevitably continues to be a daunting trial and error. From another angle, a solo pansori singer is their own director in performance, improvising narrative or musical adjustments as needed. In *changgeuk*, the singers coordinate with the rest of the cast, director, crew, and orchestra.

An important dramatic innovation in *changgeuk* is the *dochang* (occasional narrator). The *Akhak gwebeom* (樂學軌範 "Standard music text") compiled in 1493 under the royal edict introduces the *dochang* in court music as the director-singer responsible for leading the orchestral performance. In *changgeuk*, the *dochang* is a traditional singer-storyteller persona connecting the two functions, i.e., telling and enacting, as one play. The dramatic identity and function of *dochang* is as malleable as the directorial vision, for example with *dochang* entering the play as one of the characters or only between scenes.

Although the ambitions for modern Korean stage drama and an independent modern Korean empire fell short of fruition, the early trial and error gave rise to *changgeuk* and its continuing dramatic and theatrical challenges. Further, the emperor's enthusiastic patronage seemed to promise ongoing state support for pansori and *changgeuk* today. In the March 1941 edition of *Chunchu* magazine, Singer Yi Dongbaek and Drummer Han Seongjun nostalgically reminisce about the halcyon Weongaksa days:

Yi   "Yeah, we were untouchable then, His Majesty Emperor Gojong treated us so well, and singing and dancing was so much fun. We were even allowed on the royal parlor in the presence of His Majesty Sunjong."[12]

Yi and Han recount a critical moment when a somersaulting acrobat stumbled and fell on King Sunjong, who became king when the Japanese colonial authorities forced his father, Gojong, to abdicate. The performers had anticipated punishment as was the prerogative of royals. Instead, King Sunjong just laughed. An enthusiastic patron, King Sunjong was so enamoured by his favorite singers that he would sometimes listen to their performances over the telephone receiver, as in-person attendance by a royal was considered undignified. The performers marveled at their royal audience's appreciation of pansori.[13]

Stepping into the Silver World

If the new drama movement espoused linguistic realism over poetically elevated speech, movement, or singing, the "new novel," *shin-soseol*, was an equally adventurous pursuit of the unity of speech and writing. Based on a *shin-soseol* titled *Eunsegye* (Silver World) written by Yi Injik (1862–1919), the *shin-yeongeuk* (new drama/theatre) production under the same title premiered at the Weongaksa Theatre in 1908. Although the staged content of the production is lost to speculation, it is known to have included the story of *Choe Byeongdo Taryeong*, a pansori adaptation by Singer Gang Yonghwan about a real person wronged by a corrupt governor.

At this time, several other true stories were also providing material for experimental *changgeuk*, suggesting a deep mistrust of the bureaucracy and the role of pansori and *changgeuk* as an outlet for grievance sharing.[14] According to the testimony of Singer Yi Dongbaek, the progressive radical statesman Kim Okkyun (1851–94) had drafted the *taryeong* for public awareness, and Singer Kim Changhwan directed and starred in it.[15] The official credit went to Yi Injik and his eponymous *shin-soseol* published several months prior.[16] Yi possibly adopted the story of *Choe Byeongdo Taryeong* as the first part to his multigenerational epic saga *Eunsegye* by repackaging its narrative content with his modern savvy, then used the published volume as the working script for the 1908 premiere. The hyphenated headline, *soseol-yeongeuk*, "novel-drama," on the production announcement signals a protean nexus of genre formation:[17]

Soseol-yeongeuk: President Yi Injik of the *Daehan Newspaper* in improving our national drama opened his shin-yeongeuk company at Hyeomnyulsa in the Yajuhyeon village day before yesterday, to educate the singers with his novel *Eunsegye* for the opening of his shin-yeongeuk two months later. To help defray the cost of singer training, the place opens its commercial venue from July 26 for two months, 7 pm to 12 am, featuring a variety of indigenous performances.

In a millennia-old culture newly encumbered with colonial arbitration, modern literature was extemporaneous and hybrid. Those in search of "true" modern Western literature were dismissive of early modern Korean writers' efforts as "simply mixtures of modern Western literature, modern Japanese literature, and pre-modern Joseon literature."[18] Im Hwa (1908–53) praised *Eunsegye* "as exceptional work equipped with Western content and form."[19] His notion of "Western" as the standard for Korean literary modernity was a typical response among fellow critics. However, it is worth noting that the dual Korean and Western perspectives in *Eunsegye* were part of a deconstruction of Korean lifeworlds in the colonial era.

The language use, narrative structure, and thematic contents of Yi Injik's novel *Eunsegye*[20] combine familiar literary practices of premodern Korea and the yet-to-be familiarized visions for the future. With all of its idiosyncrasies and flaws, the work bridges the orality of Korean storytelling and modern literacy: the novel was appreciated as a new pansori narrative of the changing era. Reflecting the author's impassioned views, *Eunsegye* is a political novel that employs the didactic tropes of classical Korean storytelling to engage contemporary issues of modern Korea.

Synopsis of *Eunsegye*

Choe Byeongdo, a farmer living in a mountain village of Gangneung in Gangweon Province, is inspired by the enlightening ideas of the historical activist statesman Kim Okkyun (1851–94), dedicated to saving the nation. Choe saves every penny to help fund Kim's work, accumulating substantial wealth in the process. The corrupt Governor Jeong arrests him on false charges of seizing his assets. Following months of incarceration and torture, Choe is released only to die on his way home. In shock and grief, his wife succumbs to a psychic illness shortly after giving birth to their second child. Choe's friend Kim Jeongsu steps up to care for Choe's household, assets, ailing widow, and children Oksun and Ongnam. Several years pass, and Kim leaves Choe's financial matters to his son and takes Oksun and Ongnam to Washington, DC, for a modern education. Five years pass. In his prolonged absence, Kim's son has made a series of unwise decisions and dissipated all Choe's assets. The despairing Kim takes to drinking and dies. Oksun and Ongnam are stranded in Washington, DC, with no money or support. They attempt suicide but are saved by a brave local police officer. The story about them appears in the newspaper, and a generous citizen offers help for them to finish their education. One day in 1907, Oksun and Ongnam read a newspaper article about "The Great Change in Korea," i.e., the abdication of throne by Gojong, ending five hundred years of monarchic rule. With great hopes for a modern civilized nation, the two siblings return to Korea to enlist their services. The entire village turns out for the rare spectacle of two modern siblings returning home from America. At the sight of her grown children, their mother suddenly recovers her lost mind. The next day, they escort their mother to a nearby temple to pray for their father's soul. During prayer, they are suddenly accosted by a mob of several hundred people denouncing Japan for the abdication of the Korean emperor. Suspecting the siblings of espionage for the royal police, they take them hostage while their mother prays to Buddha for their safety. The story ends on a cliffhanger.

As a literary and dramatic work, *Eunsegye* represents a crossroads of genre formation in Korean storytelling. Most artifacts and details of the 1908 Huidae premiere are lost, save for Part One of the novel, which also served as the playscript.[21] It would be a boon to know what role the pansori singers involved in the production played, who played the major and minor characters, and in what way the two parts of the play were staged. Andrew Killick surmises that Yi Injik gained familiarity with dramatic *shinpa* through his studies in Japan.[22] Yi envisioned pansori singers as exceptionally suited to his dramaturgy, and the pansori stage as an ideal platform for his politics.[23] The novel's opening lines convey an austere naturalism commonly employed by writers of the early modern period:

> Winter evening chilly air, sky turning bluer as if freshly coated, the sun sinks down as the north wind blows and a black patch of cloud rises from behind the faraway hill. Clouds gather upon clouds, behind, beside and below, blackening the blue sky and everything between heaven and earth. Snowflakes swirl downward, like falling pear blossoms or waltzing branches of willow. They silently

descend and melt away. The thin flurries thicken to a downpour dousing the atmosphere and shrouding the earth, tumbling steadily like rice powder sifted through a thickly woven strainer. The earth under the sky becomes a white rice-cake batter.[24]

Yi Injik's world of silver shines with new ideas and the allure of progress, all overlaid with the stark, funereal colors of winter. The granularity of description is characteristic of modern realist writing, using the national language of Hangeul to convey, among other things, sensory affect. His tone departs the prosodic world of pansori narrative singing, adopting a realist loquaciousness typical of modern descriptive writing or poetry recitation. For comparison, this is an introductory narration from the pansori *Song of Heungbo*:

Our Eastern nation is the country of virtuous people and ethics. Even in a township of ten households or less there live exemplary loyalists, and even children of seven years of age practice filial devotion. So how could there be even a single derelict among us? Still, even in the legendary eras of Yo and Sun there were four demons. Even in Confucius' time there lived the nefarious master thief Do Cheok. Perhaps inherent dispositions cannot be remedied. During the middle era, somewhere in the middle of Gyeongsang, Jeolla, and Chungcheong province there lived two brothers, Heungbo the younger and Nolbo the older.[25]

In contrast to the didacticism of pansori, Yi Injik's passage verbosely details the weather. The didactic aspect of pansori narration is straightforward and direct, delivering the collective voice of pansori tradition, while Yi's narration is the voice of the individual "author." In this sense, the playscript of *Eunsegye* could hardly be a product of pansori tradition but a literary opus credited to an individual playwright. At this time, playscripts were a new dramatic genre that differentiated new drama from old drama.[26]

On the other hand, from the point of view of *changgeuk* experimentation, *Eunsegye* was a successful production for a start, by virtue of the original pansori choral song the villagers sing after Choe Byeongdo is released from prison to die at home. It is a poignant song of social justice expressing their collective indignation toward the corrupt and cruel magistrate, in pansori. The song is a creative adaptation of folk and pansori tunes, including the *Farmers' Ballad* and a funeral procession chant interspersed with the original lyrics:

> Sir Choe of our village, a bit of scrooge, never did any wrong. Having more than the rest of us, he was taken to the courthouse to be beaten and still locked in cangue over half a year, *Yeo-o-heo, yeo-o-heo, eo-yeora sangsadiya.*

> Fellow farmers, listen to me. If you have money left of the harvest and expenditures, don't even think of saving but drink, gamble, and spend it all. When they extort everything we have, the worst you do is being rich, *Yeo-o-heo, yeo-o-heo, eo-yeora sangsadiya.*

> The sun falls behind the west mountain. Take another bundle of rice seedlings and divide it evenly. Let's do one more round of transplanting, *Yeo-o-heo, yeo-o-heo, eo-yeora sangsadiya.*

Anger and resentment are momentarily given to reenergizing laughter and mirth:

> Hey, Auntie over there, some dirt got on the back of your skirt. Lift, bunch it up and out of your way so you can work more securely, this is your labor of survival, so don't be shy about showing your thighs a little, *Yeo-o-heo, yeo-o-heo, eo-yeora sangsadiya.*

Interpolated in the next lyric is the ghostly image of Chunhyang in her prison cell resembling the image of the dying man:

Hair uncombed, sticky, and disheveled, covering his eyes and ears, his ghostly appearance is bloodcurdling even in dream, *Yeo-o-heo, yeo-o-heo, eo-yeora sangsadiya.*

Like a Greek Chorus witnessing an unfolding tragedy, the village community chants on:

An educated gentleman with impeccable elocution, Sir Choe told me in person the governor is destroying our nation. Enraged, Sir Choe was grinding his teeth and coughing out blood as he lamented the state of our people. Beaten so severely and bearing such murderous pain, he still cares only about our nation, *Yeo-o-heo, yeo-o-heo, eo-yeora sangsadiya.*

Come the day we get the news of Sir Choe's end, let as many of us as possible go and claim his remains, and bring him back on a stretcher with utmost care, *Yeo-o-heo, yeo-o-heo, eo-yeora sangsadiya.*

Let us be the pallbearers at his burial procession. We'll rest his casket on the funerary dais and lift it on our shoulders with due ceremony. We'll mourn and chant the dirge as best as we ever could, *Yeo-o-heo, yeo-o-heo, eo-yeora sangsadiya.*

At the mounting of his grave, we'll hold up the tamper and rammer the earth, *Yeo-o-heo, yeo-o-heo, eo-yeora sangsadiya.*

In conclusion, due to the paucity of evidential records, closer understanding of the experimental nature of the *Eunsegye* production remains difficult. Nevertheless, the tone of the narrative and lyric contents from the pages of its remaining playscript yields a limited understanding of what challenges the production must have met in pioneering a dramatic modernization. The negotiation between Korean oral tradition and "new" dramatic trends then started continues today, particularly in the popularization of pansori and *changgeuk*.

Encountering *Shinpa*, "New Style"

The *Eunsegye* production had promised a modern drama that would speak more than sing. Unfortunately, the creative impetus faltered with the spiraling debilitation of the Joseon state. The writer, Yi Injik, entered into politics with the pro-Japanese minister Yi Wanyong to support the Japanese annexation of Korea. Among dramatists of the day, enthusiasm for *changgeuk* fluctuated with the advent of *shinpa*. As the first iteration of "new style," *shinpa* was the Korean avatar of *shimpa*, the Japanese emulation of Western realism departing from the age-old *kabuki* act representative of the military regime of Tokugawa Shogunate (1603–1868). Starting as a theatre of political awareness in 1888, *shimpa* evolved as commercial entertainment drama of true crime and detective stories or tragic family or love stories for the most part.

Soon after entering Korean soil around 1910, *shinpa* occupied the center of a debate on whether it should be the standard for not only the true modernization of Korean traditional plays but also for their eventual construction of the new civilization.[27] Against the current of nationalist awareness unwilling to abandon native resources so callously, robust indigenization of *shinpa* proceeded, buoyed by the protection and support of the colonizers and their sympathizers, and boosted by the changing cultural appetite for newness among the colonial subjects. The feeling of desperation at the traumatic loss of nation brought radical thoughts and finger-pointing even at their own heritage, as the age-old disdain for indigenous Korean storytelling blatantly resurfaced in support of *shinpa*: Yi Haejo (1869–1927), the Enlightenment writer and journalist, does precisely that in his *shinsoseol* (new novel) titled *Jayujong* (*Freedom Bell*, 1910):

Could you learn politics by watching the story of Chunhyang? Would you understand law from Shim Cheong? Or morality from the story of Hong Giltong?[28] Let me tell you: the tale of Chunhyang is a textbook on obscenity, Shim Cheong is a handbook of misery, Hong Giltong is the very manual of absurdity ... every philandering man and pornographic woman in Korea is practically born under the influence of these stories![29]

The antithetical propaganda spelled out by an influential intellectual against Korea's most beloved stories was pouring cold water on the nascent *changgeuk* experiments. On the other hand, *shinpa*, bone fide "new drama," was growing its readership and fandom with advanced stage conventions and modern stories, languages, and imagination. The stage manpower was also growing: there were sixteen Japanese emigrant theatres in Seoul providing up-to-date programming from Japan. Performances in these venues typically featured traveling artists in the absence of in-house performers.[30] Koreans who found employment as stage assistants in the Japanese theatres acquired the acting techniques and stage conventions to fashion its Korean counterpart. Furthermore, *shinpa* provided Korean audiences and readers with the drama of life they had never imagined as options. For example, could the audience members, male and female, have thought in their wildest imagination of a story of a woman working as a school principal ordering her husband around to cook rice and massage her feet? The earliest known *shinpa* play, *Byeongja Samin* (Patients Three) by Jo Junghwan (1884–1947), is a poignant social commentary disguised as comedic entertainment deconstructing the traditional notion of patriarchy. An adaptation of *Huigeuk Useung-Yeolpae* (Comedy of the Survival of the Fittest) by Ito Otzu (伊東櫻州), a comedy of errors, was serialized in the *Maeil shinbo* during November 17–December 25, 1912. The four-act play juxtaposes three professional females holding superior positions and intellectual faculties and their comparatively inept husbands in slapstick farce, revolting against Confucian male supremacy to the point of absurdity. The dramatis personae showcases no paragon of filiality or chastity but a motley crew of ordinary people with exaggerated flaws, if not banality. The props are meager household items, and the characters are neither heroes nor heroines, adding to the story's modernistic semblance. The play opens with Jeong Pilsu on stage, complaining about his lot:[31]

Excerpt from *Byeongja Samin* (*Patients Three*)

Act One
Scene One
Characters
Yi Okcha, *schoolteacher*
Jeong Pilsu, *Yi Okcha's husband*
Updong Omma, *grain-store owner*
The living quarters of the home of Schoolteacher Yi Okcha. In the kitchen, rice cooking pots, pans, and sundry utensils are strewn about. Jeong Pilsu, Yi Okcha's husband, is busy tending the cooking rice by fanning the kitchen hearth.

Jeong Ah, this world is strange. I should've stayed in the backwoods of Gangweondo, tending my crops and laying low. Now what the hell am I doing here? When we came up to Seoul, the two of us were hand in hand and looking forward to a great future. Surviving on just water, we graduated school together and took the teaching certificate exam together. To my great misfortune, my wife passed and became a teacher, and I failed and became a custodial servant in her school, what the hell is this? At school, everyone, even my own wife, calls me "Hey Servant, hey Servant, hey hey!" running me on errands like I were an ox or a horse. I get so tired, I need to rest—but at home I have to cook! How rotten is my fate! I bet there's no other man living as a servant to his own wife![32]

In this opening scene, the grain-store owner Updong Omma enters to collect money owed from Yi Okcha and Jeong Pilsu. After Jeong laments his sorry situation and inability to pay up, Updong Omma leaves without collecting her due and further, promising Jeong that she will order soup for them on her way back home.

Updong Omma exits Stage Right. The rice was burned during the conversation with Updong Omma, and Jeong Pilsu is now flustered and worried that he will get another scolding from his wife. On the *hanamichi* (Japanese-style thrust stage conventionally used in kabuki plays) appears Yi Okcha, twenty or twenty-one years of age, Jeong Pilsu's wife and principal of a girls' high school, wearing a black skirt, hisashigami hairstyle (square box-style cut, presumably introduced from Japan) and carrying a bookbag, enters through the gate.

Okcha Smell, the rice is burnt! (*Sniffs.*)

Jeong Madam, thou art home! Thou likest rice scorched at the bottom, so I intentionally overcooked a little.

Okcha How many times do I have to teach you that if you overcook rice, you get less cooked rice? You don't listen, do you?

Jeong It just . . . happened so fast . . . (*Scratches head.*)

Okcha What happened so fast, huh? Hurry up and take these shoes off my feet, hurry!

Jeong Yes, yes, Ma'am, yes!

Okcha Stop repeating "yes," Dummy! Take them off my feet now!

He takes her shoes off. She sits on a floor cushion by the low table.[33]

Finding Modern Performative Identity

Shinpa was a major current of Korean dramatic modernity prior to the 1940s arrival of *shingeuk*, a newer "new drama" emulating European realism. While it lasted, the *shinpa* style of acting indelibly shaped the early modern Korean drama movement, including *changgeuk*. They were on the confluent course of dramatic modernization. Ryu Kyeong Ho goes so far as to speculate that with the momentum of changgeuk quickly ending with the *Eunsegye* production, it was *shinpa* that stepped up to the main field of Korean dramatic modernization.[34] As a result, the two genres came to share some structural and stylistic features, the concept of narrator who facilitates closer communication between the stage and the auditorium: the *byeonsa* in *shinpa* dramatically iterating the emotions and feelings of actors on stage, the *dochang* in *changgeuk* connecting the narrative disconnection by assuming the solo-pansori narrative presence between acts and scenes. *Changgeuk* actors also adopted the peculiar styles of overaction from *shinpa* actors who received such training from the Japanese *shimpa*. So much so that the term *shinpa-gatta* (acts like *shinpa*) serves as a metonym of the *shinpa*-like overacting some actors in both *changgeuk* and *shingeuk* used to practice.

Unlike other long-rooted traditional folk plays such as the itinerant *namsadang* play, regional mask dance drama, or pansori, *changgeuk* is a more recent innovation derivative of the tradition of pansori. With no preexisting format to which to adhere, *changgeuk* started and continues as an open chapter of creative possibility. The fluidity of its performative identity is traced in its polyonymy: at its beginning in the 1900s, it was the one and only *shin-yeongeuk*, new drama; when *shinpa* took root in the 1910s, it slipped to *gu-yeonggeuk* (old drama) or *gupageuk* (old style drama); in the 1920s–30s when music became a genre separate from drama, it came to be known as *gageuk* or *changgeuk*.[35] Both mean "singing drama," but *changgeuk* applies to the pansori-specific singing drama, leading to the speculation that those in music and drama were separating *changgeuk* from the general notion of singing drama borne of Western scale, tone, and style. Second, the term "changgeuk" in the 1930s was broadly applied to include pansori singing as well.

Contrary to the assumption that traditional Korean plays declined following Japan's annexation of Korea, pansori and *changgeuk* thrived in the 1910s, with the performers organizing themselves as performing troupes: a number of Gisaeng Johap Yeonjuhoe (gisaeng's performance unions) cropped up, starting 1914, and the mostly male Gyeongseong Gupa Baeu Johap (Gyeongseong [old name of Seoul] traditional actors' union) came a year later. They presented wider varieties of traditional and newly choreographed dances, songs, instrumental plays, pansori, and other dramatic plays.[36] Their traditional performative skills branded as *gugeuk* (old drama) discovered the momentum for new dramatic possibilities. In competition with other forms of "new drama" such as *shinpa*, the performers of traditional plays cultivated their modern traditional performative identity for pansori and *changgeuk*.

By the time *shingeuk*, the next wave of "new drama," arrived, realist play-acting was a standard convention for Western-trained Korean intellectuals and writers. The new dramatic intellectualism of their generation was influenced by Western literature and art. As offspring of *yangban* or the gentry, many new dramatists inhabited a different lifeworld from professional *gwangdae*, who were further disparaged for their connection to traditional performance. Paradoxically, modernist works from this milieu had the same dramatic playfulness as that of the plebeian *gwangdae*, differing only in their respective cultural orientation.

Modern Korean drama developed as a binary between *yeongeuk* and *yeonhui*. *Yeongeuk* (演劇, theatre, play, drama) refers to spoken plays emulating European realism, contemporary styles, and stage *mise-en-scène*. In contrast, *yeonhui* (演戲, display of playful talent) includes indigenous music-based enactments by traditionally trained singers and musicians and are synonymous with *jeontonggeuk* (traditional play), *gugeuk* (old drama), or *gukkeuk* (national drama). These monikers reflect a general disdain toward traditional drama, which connoted provinciality and obsoleteness.

Under these conditions, traditional plays, including pansori, nevertheless continued to facilitate modern and contemporary Korean theatre-making as a whole. *Changgeuk* (singing theatre) was one outcome of modern theatre "that does not sing,"[37] as the task of modernization was entrusted to vocalists and musicians who were the closest Korean counterpart to dramatists. If the *shin-yeongeuk* movement localized cosmopolitan dramatic conventions, *changgeuk* was the dramatic innovation from indigenous tradition. Its extenuation as modern experiment has sustained the schools of pansori singing as *sine qua non*. One hundred and twenty years later, the confluence of pansori and *changgeuk* adds creativity to *yeongeuk* and other genres of music, dance drama, and film.

As artistic novelties, *shinpa* and subsequent new forms, including film, grew in popularity, eclipsing *changgeuk*. With the subsequent decline in cultural purchase, *changgeuk* artists relinquished claims on new drama instead to reclassify the genre as a traditional performance medium.[38] *Changgeuk* prior to *shinpa* was more in line with the singing-dominant Chinese opera with hardly a dialog, but the 1916 production of *Heungbo* incorporated sets, backdrops, and prop displays under the influence of *shinpa*.[39] Contemporary *changgeuk* has superseded the dominant influence of *shinpa* and is established as an intercultural theatre of pansori tradition.

Champions of *Changgeuk*

The linkage of *changgeuk* to pansori was in part due to key pansori practitioner-masters and patrons, including members of the now deposed royal family. Emperor Gojong (1852–1919) upheld his father Daeweongun's legacy of patronizing favorite singers. Jeong Noshik and Pak Hwang documented the oral histories of the time's *eojeon-gwangdae* (royal singers).[40] Graced with political titles, pansori singers continually improved their craft even in the face of imminent national doom. They included the iconic Kim Changhwan (1854–1927), who served as artistic director of the Weongaksa Theatre and led the major performance tours around the country. With the fall of the Korean Empire, he retired to his hometown but remained a loyal subject by observing the three-year mourning following the death of His Majesty in 1919. The princely Yi Dongbaek (1867–1949), master of *Junggoche*-style singing, was particularly favored by Gojong, who granted him the Lordship of Tongjeongdaebu. This was the highest honor given to a *gwangdae*. Gang Yonghwan, a critical contributor to *changgeuk*, and Kim Chaeman (1865–1911), similarly enjoyed Gojong's support.

Another royal *gwangdae* was Song Mangap (1865–1939), the great-grandnephew of Song Heunglok, the nineteenth-century King of Singing. As heir to the "King," Mangap flamboyantly took a separatist path to form his own style. The explosive popularity of his self-made style among the "lowly" *gwangdae* and *gisaeng* was an affront to stalwart practitioners of canonical pansori. His distraught father is said to have attempted to poison him for his lack of filial piety in choosing the *gwangdae* path.[41] Their story is not the only tale of attempted filicide in pansori subculture, and no record of actual offspring-killing exists. In the 1993 feature film titled *Seopyeonche*, based on the fictional work of the novelist Yi Cheongjun, a failed pansori singer deliberately blinds his talented adoptive daughter so she could gain a deeper *han* or sadness in *sori*. These stories exist to highlight the perseverance and sacrifice demanded of pansori singers.

As a result of Song Mangap's excommunication from his renowned family, he could freely traverse different regions across the country to draw from and in turn influence other styles. In North Jeollado, Master of *dongpyeonche* Jeon Doseong (1864–1944) was enjoying the patronage of Governor Yi Jaegak, who appreciated his more traditional style of singing.[42] Jeon enjoyed a friendly rivalry with the pansori maverick Song Mangap. Governor Yi hosted a singing match between his protégé Jeon and Song. Siding with Jeon's purist reverence for the tradition, the governor admonished Song on abandoning the dignified singing deserving of nobleman's ear and family expectations to pursue fame, even for having too many students.[43] In addition to a robust transmission of his singing, Jeon's in-depth ethnographic and critical knowledge made an invaluable contribution to the oral history of pansori, documented verbatim in the *Joseon changgeuksa*.

Koreans on the threshold of modernity experienced new disparities in cultural production and consumption. Unlike the theatregoers of cosmopolitan Seoul after the taste of the "new," rural Koreans still delighted in the "old" entertainment by sojourning traditional *gwangdae*. In pansori, fewer young men were joining schools while the increasing number of women trainees began redefining its gender expectations, buoyed by the 1909 abolition of the government-controlled *gisaeng* recruitment system. Still marginal, the *gisaeng* profession was becoming more a matter of choice than a mandate of inheritance. Many from the households of southern provincial *danggol* or heritage shamans (as opposed to northern shamans, who received spirit-possession) instead chose to earn their living as *gisaeng*.[44] These adaptations were possible because both *gisaeng* and *danggol* were performing artists, and the nature of performance was largely commutable between the sacred and secular domains.

The participation of women in *changgeuk* and performance tours also led to increases in gender-crossing performances. Historically, female performance roles often required creative adjustments. To illustrate, a performance company was inaugurated in Gwangju in 1912 without a female singer to play the title role of Chunhyang or the supporting role of Chunhyang's mother, Weolmae. Two male singers instead played these roles, and the resulting performance was highly acclaimed. The first female performers to star in Weongaksa productions were Heo Geumpa and Gang Sohyang.[45] The next generation of women singers included: Bae Seolhyang (1895–

1938), wife and disciple of Jang Pangae; Kim Chohyang (1900–83), student of Kim Changhwan and Song Mangap; Kim Nokchu (1896–1923), disciple of Kim Jeongmun; and Yi Hwajungseon (1898–1943), a teenage bride who left her marriage and home to study with Song Mangap after seeing him perform. The stars of the following generation, Pak Nokchu (1906–79), Kim Yeoran (1907–83), Pak Choweol (1913–83), and Kim Sohui (1917–95), were the living national treasures when I began learning pansori in the 1970s.

In 1933, leading singers and musicians founded the Joseon Seongak Yeonguhoe (Association for Korean Vocal Music Study). Its 1935 inaugural performance of the *changgeuk Chunhyang* in Seoul featured the innovation of an orchestral music ensemble, including strings and flute in addition to drum.[46] Scripted with lengthened dialogs, the *changgeuk* premiere and extended tours were a welcome respite for nostalgic Koreans yearning for their national performing arts, particularly rural Koreans who had grown up in farming villages. This time, novelty and authenticity of traditional singing reconstituted a collective ethnic memory of a time before colonization.

Notwithstanding the growing sophistication of stage *mise-en-scène*, *changgeuk* productions had to combine two seemingly antithetical modalities, storytelling and story-enacting. In modern dramatic production, actor preparation typically builds on memorization of assigned lines for scheduled rehearsals, then unlearning them for the next production. Memorizing what is so disposable seems to have posed an existential discomfort for pansori singers trained in lifelong embodiment and improvisation. There arose occasions where a singer playing a character reverted to the storyteller role, causing his counterpart to scramble to their feet. An anecdote from the 1935 Joseon Seongak Yeonguhoe production of *Shim Cheong*, recounted in Pak Hwang's *200 Years History of Pansori* (*Pansori ibaengnyeonsa*), illustrates the conflicts that sometimes arose between classical pansori training and modern *changgeuk* innovation. Jeong Jeongnyeol, cast as Blindman

Shim, had fallen ill. The distinguished pansori Master Kim Changnyong stepped in as a substitute without memorizing the given lines. In the story, Shim falls into an icy stream and is rescued by a monk passing by. When Pak Nokchu's Shim Cheong rushed in showering her hypothermic father with worried pity, she found the actor Kim fanning himself with the grandiose persona of a pansori singer. The auditorium bubbled with mirth at the sudden comedy of error. Pak attempted a discreet whisper to prompt Kim to stop fanning himself. Kim, unprepared for the make-believe aspect of *yeongeuk*, continued to fan himself. Pak tried again but to no avail, and continued with her memorized lines, "Father, where and how did you fall in the water? You're soaked to the bone, how frozen you are! Please get out of the wet jacket and put on this one instead!" The frozen man kept fanning himself, and his desperate daughter frantically implores him to please lose the fan. The senior singer, miffed, disregarded Pak. He later apologized.[47]

Sizable *changgeuk* companies hit the road with new and classical repertoires, traveling throughout Korea and through Manchuria's Korean community. In the days ahead of the 1941 surprise attack on Pearl Harbor, Japan was intensifying its censorship on all facets of Korean cultural life. Complying with the new decree banning the use of the Korean language, singers on stage had to observe the new rule of rendering pansori in Japanese. Opium addiction was a rampant phenomenon in artist circles, coinciding with the passing of a high number of senior singers. Some historians explain the spread of addiction in the Korean art communities as part of Japan's program of cultural annihilation in Korea.[48] During the Asia–Pacific War (1941–5), no *sori* or *gisaeng* school was spared the devastation of opium addiction,[49] and singers were lost to conscription, illness, imprisonment, or escape.[50]

As *changgeuk* productions used more verisimilar enactment, *sori* singing was compromised by the waxing dialogs and theatrical actions that had greater appeal. Despite criticisms of *changgeukcho*, *changgeuk*-style singing or speaking, as corruptions of serious pansori, the shift from "telling" to "showing" energized the quest for novelty. One resultant innovation was *yeoseong gukkeuk*, all-women *changgeuk*. The genre emerged in 1948 and thrived despite war and devastation, and remained a popular form into the 1950s. All fifteen female *changgeuk* companies on the Ministry of Education registry during 1955–8 were robustly producing repertoires adapted from legends, folk and historical tales, and gripping love stories. The main players included Pak Nokchu, Pak Gwihui, Im Chunhaeng, Kim Sohui, and Kim Gyeonghui, with whom I first began studying pansori in the summer of 1974. In its heyday, all-women *changgeuk* was bitterly condemned for critically undermining the mixed-gender *changgeuk*. The animosity from other artists stemmed in part from their frequent monopoly over performance venues. Along with the nine registered all-women *nongaktan*, itinerant outdoor percussion troupes, *yeoseong gukkeuk-dan* (companies) would occupy most of the available indoor and outdoor performance spaces in all the major cities.[51] While the mixed-gender *changgeuk* retained the classical standard of pansori singing as its distinguishing feature, the *yeoseong gukkeuk-dan* aggressively marketed themselves with new materials, emboldened cross-gender acting, and dominated performance spaces. Refusing to stay within the shadow of male artist troupes, the all-women troupes radically transformed expectations of women *gugak* artists. From the perspective of colonial discourse, Homi Bhabha explains fixity as an ideological construction of otherness: "Fixity, as the sign of cultural/historical/racial difference in the discourse of colonialism, is a paradoxical mode of representation: it connotes rigidity and an unchanging order as well as disorder, degeneracy and daemonic repetition."[52] Under the banner of "all-women *changgeuk*," women artists challenged the fixity of patriarchal discourse, exercising innovation to secure their place in a highly competitive entertainment scene.

Contrary to the views of some orthodox practitioners, the mid-century decline of *changgeuk* was not solely attributable to the alleged predatory monopoly of the all-women troupes.

At the national level, a Western-aspirational transformation of Korean culture was underway. Mainstream Korean theatre typically built on translation, adaptation, or emulation of imported plays. In general, American musicals, ballet, and European operas formed highbrow culture, while indigenous music, drama, and storytelling were again considered outmoded. Performance traditions endured due to the intervention of such organizations as the National Center for Traditional Performing Arts (aka National Gugak Center) inaugurated during the Korean War (1950–3), or the National Changgeuk Company founded in 1961 under the umbrella of the National Theater. Some criticisms of *changgeuk* index supposed deficiencies in style and substance, citing its imitativeness of *shinpa* and paucity of semantic and musical content.[53] Such criticisms of *changgeuk* reflect a relative intolerance of its processual development and generic ambiguity, which predated the Western-derived frames of critique. *Gugak* scholarship today takes up the question of *weonhyeong* (archetype) for *changgeuk*. Given its syncretic developmental history, the cultural politics of *weonhyeong* recall Bhabha's caution about tradition as a restaging of disparate cultural pasts.[54] The search for the urtext of *changgeuk* allows for a reconceptualization of Korean theatre history. One may well question, however, what elisions are required for its construction.

PART THREE

Beyond the Twentieth Century

FIGURE 4 *An illustration of pansori recording. Artist: Hugo Campos.*

5

Preservation and Reinvention, Mutually

More than fifty years have passed since pansori was first taken up in Korean modern literary scholarship. The 1984 inauguration of the Pansori Hakhoe (Association of Pansori Study) has furthered inquiry into pansori music, drama, literature, and theatre. With the 1962 inauguration of the National Intangible Cultural Heritage system (*Muhyeong Munhwajae*), pansori was among the first designations and received UNESCO Intangible Cultural Heritage of Humanity status in 2003. The Gugak FM broadcast launched in 2001 promotes public education of traditional music through mass media accessible around the world. In the teaching and learning of pansori, traditional oral mnemonic transmission has not been replaced but instead technologically enhanced. Although Western Art musical staff notation has been introduced, its use is mainly limited to academic discourses and experimental adaptations of Western tonal structures.

Politics and Poetics of Preservation

Being a pansori *boyuja* (holder of intangible cultural asset) is a lifetime responsibility and honor. To illustrate, the *boyuja* seat for the *Song of Shim Cheong* was vacant since the death in

2017 of the former *boyuja* Seong Changsun. It was not until 2020 that Kim Youngja and Chung Hoisuk were newly designated: eligible singers among the next generation must wait for the next vacancy due to a death or other unfortunate cancellation. Within pansori subculture, the internal politics of designation are fiercely competitive and demand both perfectionism and conformism of initiates.[1] Some of those who do not achieve national-level consideration strive for the secondary honor termed *jibang munhwajae*, "local cultural property." As of 2013, a total of 31 local cultural properties had been bestowed, all to female artists.[2] While the bottleneck-system of transmission compounded with exorbitant fees for lessons may add to the notion of pansori as cultural treasure, it can also stifle creativity and the discovery of new talent.

The holder designation is often the site of clashing politics and poetics, with impassioned debates over who deserves to be the next *ingan munhwajae*, "human cultural heritage" or "living national treasure." Some researchers advocate retitling these designations, from "holder of intangible cultural asset" to "human cultural heritage," because the public is more habituated to the term.[3] This identification process has its downsides, however, as it tends to diffuse the goal of transmission of the art and craft of pansori into a contest of ethics or even smear campaign tactics.

The first cohort of designated holders of pansori were: Pak Choweol (박초월) for *Sugungga*; Kim Yeoran (김여란) and Kim Sohui (김소희) for *Chunhyangga*; Pak Nokchu (박녹주) for *Heungboga*; Kim Yeonsu (김연수) for *Chunhyangga*; Chung Kwonjin (정권진) for *Shimchongga*; Pak Bongsul (박봉술) and Pak Dongjin (박동진) for *Jeokpyeokka*; and Kim Myeonghwan (김명환) for *Gopeop* (pansori drumming). After the Hanguk Gugak Hyeophoe (Association for Korean Traditional Music, formed in 1962 to protect and nurture traditional Korean performing arts following the passing of the Cultural Heritage Protection Act of Korea) designates the "preserver" or "holder" (*boyuja* 보유자), the preserver in turn designates two initiates (*jeonsusaeng* 전수생) to receive the *boyuja*'s *sori*; upon completion of the five-year term, the trainees give a formal audition to become *isuja* (이수자), the graduates. To train in pansori, five years are generally enough just to achieve a novice level. The duration of *isuja* training may have presupposed that *jeonsusaeng* initiates were already substantially trained or at least acclimated to pansori through hereditary or geo-cultural ties.

Over fifty years later, the Cultural Heritage Administration (문화재청) has been actively designating new preservers to propel a more vigorous transmission of pansori. The new group of preservers designated in 2020 include: Chung Hoisuk (정회석 1963–) for *Shimchongga*; Kim Youngja (김영자 1951–) and Kim Suyeon (김수연 1948–) for *Sugungga*; Chung Sunim (정순임 1942–) and Yi Nancho (이난초 1959–) for *Heungboga*; and Kim Ilgu (김일구 1940–) and Yun Jincheol (윤진철 1965–) for *Jeokpyeokka*. In 2022, Ahn Sook Sun (안숙선 1948–) was designated for *Chunhyangga*, and Kim Cheongman (김청만 1946–) was designated for drum accompaniment.

Ecology of Giving and Receiving *Sori*

Published with a royal mandate in 1493, *Akhak Gwebeom* (Illustrated Text on Traditional Music) documents the Joseon court performance protocols of pitch, notation, instrumentation, costumes, and props. It is the authoritative reference for Korean court music performance. The transmission of folk music with hardly a standard system of notation or state mandate depended on mnemonic repetition, embodiment, and improvisational adjustment. The pedagogy of pansori is an oral exchange typically between two humans, the transmitter and the recipient. The teacher with the drum and the learner with the writing plus recording gears sit on the floor facing one another. Transmission of *sori* is a deeply interpersonal exchange. The teacher breaks down the lines into ingestible bits for the learner to listen, understand, remember, and reproduce. Where the reception gets difficult, the teacher divides lines into smaller units. As a pansori learner, I interpreted the vocal semantics of my teacher's nuanced "vowel plays" as a discovery of order in chaos. Since the early 1980s, the majority of learners have been recording their lessons, with increasingly sophisticated technology. Singers would also commission professional-quality recordings of their singing. These were often gifts to visitors, especially to researchers or journalists. Cassette tape-recordings have changed to digital copies (CD, MP3) more recently.

Transmission of musical knowledge from teacher to student, irrespective of genre, is a complex process involving mental, physical, and emotional faculties, although the process may be able to follow a bit of a more predictable path if embedded in a shared notation system. Without the intervening culture of notational or other codified standards in place, learning *sori* enters a more personal discovery zone of giving and receiving with nature guiding the way. The ultimate goal is to tame the self by bridging mind and body. The forefathers of pansori befriended ways of nature in forming methodologies and aesthetics of *sori*. The learners of today smartly combine technology with traditional methods.

The Learner's *Sorichaek*

If the system of *boyuja* designation presented an inscription of national identification onto particular artistic practices and their individual practitioners, another, more personal and micro-centered, practice of signification originating in pansori schools has been just as critical to preservation. Learner's *sorichaek*, "book of *sori*," is not a grand-scale public manifesto but an individuated manual for reproduction of the memory of your teacher's *sori*. It is the learner's private reservoir of teacher's musical sensitivity, narrative interpretation, and vocal habits as you perceive, like the sketch maps we used to draw for finding places before the age of "smart."

The pedagogical functionality of *sorichaek* along with the personal intimacy it installs between the two voices, of teacher and learner, invokes Ong's conceptualization of the relation between cognition and writing as a "secondary modeling system."[4] Further, the auditory component of language is essential for the written model to be felicitous: "Thought is nested in speech, not in texts . . . It is impossible for script to be more than marks on a surface unless it is used by a conscious human being as a cue to sounded words."[5] Writing has come a long way in restructuring the human consciousnesses that no longer "grow out of simply natural powers but out of these powers structured, directly or indirectly, by the technology of writing."[6] For Saussure, writing was intricately bound to semiotic structures. He observes that: "writing, though unrelated to its inner system, is used continually to represent language. We cannot simply disregard it. We must be acquainted with its usefulness, shortcomings, and dangers."[7] The enduring validity of both Ong and Saussure's theories is clear in pansori studies, given that traditional orality has come to adopt modern literacy and technology for identification and transmission. There are consequences to disturbing the ecology of oral transmission. Take *sanjo* for instance, a major instrumental genre translated as "scattered melody" for its improvisational nature. Jocelyn Clark points to how *sanjo* as a university curriculum changed forever from adapting to the systemic culture of transcription for pedagogy and publication. "The result was a kind of bifurcated system that sent *sanjo*'s transmitted traditions and its players traveling down different channels of the same river."[8]

Today's pansori teacher generously shares print materials specific to the lessons, or even makes printshop-bound workbooks containing the entire text. The digitalization of pansori instructional materials progresses in the age of smartphones toward the obsolescence of handwritten annotation. In the mid-1970s, a lesson routinely began with transcribing into a blank notebook page the teacher's verbally delivered lesson content. It has become more common for teachers to distribute printed materials, especially with group lessons. This practice would seem to improve the efficiency of the lessons. However, it precludes the original practice of the learners' own text-making and lesson transcription, which further enhance textual-acoustic entrainment.

Mountain Study

After exiting your teacher's studio, where in the densely populated urban setting could you go to drill the recent lesson and polish your *sori* without inviting unwanted attention? Korean urbanization since the 1970s has been synonymous with high-rise condo living, where heightened intolerance of sound other than your own became the daily source of contentiousness among neighboring units. Some trainees and practitioners of pansori today stretch their means to install a *bangeum-booth*, soundproofed indoor booth. Like glass mancaves or she-sheds, the *bangeum-booth* models have different price points and features such as electricity, ventilation, Wi-Fi, and other bells and whistles. It may reduce neighbor conflict, however, the soundscape of *sori* in these socio-physical capsules is isolated and disconnected.

In the past, a person showing promise was entrained in *sori* as soon as he could talk and was sent in early adolescence to a mountain hermitage for concentrated self-training.[9] In the early nineteenth century, the future master singers Song Heunglok and Mo Heunggap left home at that age and trained in the mountains for ten years, respectively. Their contemporary Yeom Gyedal, who came from a poverty-stricken household, entered the mountain at age eighteen as a temple servant and practiced singing between chores for seven years.[10] There is no record of female singers completing mountain study in past centuries, possibly due to the infeasibility of such an arrangement for women.

The committed among singers carried the mountain study tradition well into the twentieth century. Some singers, such as my teacher, had their training interrupted by the chaos of the Korean War. His father was Grandmaster Jeong Eungmin. His farmhouse in Boseong was the birthplace of *Gangsanche-Boseongsori*. Aspiring male and female practitioners came from around the country in the hopes of studying under him. They stayed at or near the teacher's house, learning, practicing, helping with chores, and being part of the family. The story goes that during daily practice, some of the learners would beat a tree trunk with their drumsticks for the rhythm. Unable to withstand years of the daily beatings, the trees perished.[11]

The expansive Korean mountainside, with its gorges, peaks, waterfalls, and solitude, defined the culture *sori* training that took place in the solitude of nature. Free from distractions or blockages, a hermit trainee uninhibitedly sought their voice amidst thunderous waterfalls, echoing caves, and soaring peaks. Today, with its learner population spreading beyond traditional kinship circles and elevated as a higher-education academic program, pansori schools offer *san-kongbu*, "mountain study" over the summer vacation as a month-long *sori* training camp in the mountain. While visiting Korea in summer 1993, I was invited to Master Pak Yangdok's camp at one of the hermitages of the Hwaeomsa Temple in the Jirisan Mountain. Trainees breakfasted in the silent temple dining-hall before dispersing to individual lessons with their teacher, then to each person's chosen place in the surrounding mountainside. Jirisan is the third highest mountain in the Korean Peninsula and the second highest in South Korea, and has an enduring significance in indigenous geomancy. Today's *san-kongbu* has maintained the kernel of voice training through their encounter with the natural world, albeit in a highly abbreviated form and with modern technology.[12]

Polishing *Sori* (*Sori Dakki*)

In his *Survey of Vocal Music*, Pak Heonbong recounts the spartan training practices notorious of pansori: "scale your voice from low to high while expanding horizontally till you're hoarse and inaudible . . . Continue the process for years despite occasional vocal-cord bleedings until your voice returns expressive and strong enough to sing for hours at a stretch."[13]

The standard process of "polishing sori," according to the testimonies of old-time masters, involved physiological and psychological commitment of the whole self. There are somewhat incredulous—totally unbelievable as well— narratives of bleeding vocal cords. More than one master singer has told me of their experiencing this condition, which would imply a painstakingly refined sori. One documented anecdote tells of the near-death experience of the nineteenth-century singer Bang Manchun of Haemi, South Chungcheong Province, known to have created his *junggoche*-style songs of *Shim Cheong* and *Jeokpyeok*. At age eleven, Bang entered the mountain and crafted his *sori* into his mid-twenties. While staying at a temple in Bongsan, Hwanghae Province, his vocal cords had expanded beyond repair from over-training and gave out at last. Out of utter frustration one day, he held onto the column of the Buddha Hall and gave out a yell with his last ounce of strength and then collapsed. A temple servant gathering firewood in the mountain heard a thunderous crash and bolted down to investigate. The temple was standing as before, except it was the loud announcement of the triumphant return of the singer's voice.[14]

In 1993, several Korean performing artists, including Master Pak Dongjin (1916–2003), visited the University of Hawai'i at Manoa and Hilo campuses for a performance tour. I accompanied them as interpreter. During the tour, Pak described an emergency home remedy extracted from outhouse contents that was used to resuscitate singers from extreme physical exhaustion: "putting my idling years behind, I applied myself to recovering my *sori*-voice, practicing deep into the night and often forgetful of eating, sleeping, or resting. I fell terribly ill from overexertion, and at the death's door it was that cure that brought me back."[15] Jeong Jeongnyeol (1876–1938), who left some of his lasting *deoneum* in the *Song of Chunhyang*, speaks of the harrowing experiences of his predecessors choosing the path to become true singers of pansori over death:

> In the old times, a serious learner would enter the mountain at least once a year for 100-day discipline. From the fatigue of practice your belly, face, hands, feet, and throat swell up, and you cough up blood ... you must overcome these symptoms and continue singing. If you give up and faint, you won't be able to sing again ... Today we barely sing for thirty minutes at a time. Then, pansori meant several hours of singing practically the whole story.[16]

Sori as Measure of Humanity

Just as fame or talent alone does not ensure stage appeal in acting, in singing the vocal quality or skill does not necessarily translate to appeal as the work could be "technically excellent but dull and vaguely soporific," according to Reynaldo Hahn:

> These singers not only do not feel what they are singing, they do not think as they sing, and that is why they fail to move the listener; their singing is inept and inexpressive ... If the words describe a state of mind, the singer must delve into his own experience, must search inwardly for all that is deeply felt and human, and must create in his own mind the very attitude he wishes to convey—he must experience, at that moment, the emotion he seeks to express.[17]

Sori may be described as a narrative voice channeling a better, concentrated, and organized human consciousness, as emphasized in the motto, "right mind, right tone" (정심정음 *Jeong-shim jeong-eum*),[18] or a distillation of humanity situated in an ethical and aesthetic matrix. If you wish to be a good singer, you must first be a good person, as my teacher reminded us. The *sori* reveals the truth of the singer's psyche and storyteller-self. This is a tall order, and the singers may not be able to deliver it routinely, just as the actors in every rehearsal or show cannot be expected to suspend or empty the self to be filled with fresh contents.[19] Nevertheless, pansori singers assume a symbiotic reflection of their humanity and the humanity of their narrative as performative truths.

Reinvention, the Counterpoint to Preservation

Amidst a fluid topography of popular culture and entertainment, efforts by pansori singers to keep pace with the trends of modernization began early in the twentieth century. Their vision of modernity evolved as the Korean phenomenon of intercultural globalism thereafter. Bhabha describes the globalization of local culture as contingent and liminal.[20] The designation of pansori as an archetypal treasure somewhat insulates it from change, but pansori as a living performativity synchronizes with time. In this part, I discuss examples of the intercultural reinvention of pansori over the past century. Experiments include newly composed or creatively adapted *changgeuk* and *pansori*; alternative pop pansori crossover or hybrid hip-hop; and contemporary theatre production where pansori enters as a key intercultural element. Owing to the close connection between pansori and *changgeuk*, these formats are intermixed and interchangeable, often invalidating any fixed boundaries. I present them as a raw set of concepts to help facilitate the discourse of new pansori as it relates to these genres.

Kim Gyutaek's Satiric Adaptations

Seoul in the 1920s was in a tide of modern influence. Storytelling, including pansori narrative as popular entertainment, found new venues as newspaper and magazine cartoon serials and phonograph albums. Kim Gyutaek, the author of *Modern Shim Cheong* and *Modern Chunhyang*, found humor and satire in framing the classical storytelling in "modern." It "reveals the commercial entertainment culture and poverty in cities by complexly shaping the urbanization process and existing local culture."[21] For example, the character of Shim Cheong is cast as a rubber-factory worker leaving for Harbin to dance in a club to raise the three hundred won her father needs. In Kim's parody, Shim Cheong is not a naive village girl but a would-be cosmopolitan who envies her friend's savvy on which of the city's pubs to sell gum in: "I never attended school, so no one will hire me as a shopkeeper. Instead of abacus, if they let me do mental arithmetic, I know I can be hired. I hear a new rubber shoes factory opened in Pyongyang, but that's too far from home."[22] The poetry of Shim Cheong's filiality gives way to the matters of survival of the urban poor.

Similarly, Kim Gyutaek's *Modern Chunhyang* deconstructs the narrative for parody and comedic effect. In the classical *Song of Chunhyang*, Mongnyong is captivated by Chunhyang's beauty and visits her house. He is led into her boudoir and looks around, and the following song in the *semachi* beat reveals her refined taste in art and literature:

> On the east wall, the ancient duke of Ju, Gang-Taegong, wishing to meet King Mun, waits with his fishing rod hung on the Wi River.
>
> On the west wall, four white-haired hermits of Sang Mountain around a checkerboard, one holding a white stone, another holding a black stone, anxious to score a winning move while appearing blasé. Another old man is being scolded for kibitzing and embarrassed.
>
> On the south wall, the two sworn brothers Gwan U and Jang Bi are lost in archery practice. *Ttuk! Sururururu—!* Arrow flies off! Bull's eye! It hits the flying goose, round and round it swirls down.
>
> On the north wall, by the rivers of So and Sang after the night rain, moon rises on Dongjeong Lake, and through the ethereal bamboo grove the two wives of Emperor Sun

dressed in white plucking the 25-string zithers resting obliquely on their knees, *Seul-gi-deong dung-deong!*

On her reading desk, Chunhyang's own handwritten resolution to serve one and only one husband reads thus: "Plant bamboo after spring rain, burn incense and read deep into the night." She has the legendary brush stroke of Wang Huiji![23]

In his illustration of Modern Chunhyang's first night with Mongnyong, Kim Gyutaek leaves nothing to the imagination: photos of Charlie Chaplin and silent screen goddess Clara Bow adorn the wall by the make-up table. Holding a guitar, Chunhyang leans seductively on Mongnyong with a deck of flower cards strewn before her.[24] Concerned about Mongnyong's new love interest hindering his studies, his father summons him:

Father Boy, you think I don't know what you're up to? What sort of woman is Chunhyang, tell me everything!

Son Definitely a modern, Father.

Father I don't know what "modern" is, but wouldn't such a "hi-color" girl ruin our household?

Son Not at all, Father, I guarantee you![25]

"Modern" in Kim's *Modern Chunhyang* is not just a new world but a form of social capital that could challenge or even supersede age-old class distinctions. In this version, the son Mongnyong could persuade his father of Chunhyang's suitability as a partner by explaining her comportment as modern. The fusion of classical storytelling with the modern apparatus of serialized newsprint would have provided novel excitement in the literary imagination of the reading public.

Intercultural Theatre of Indigeneity

Strictly speaking, reinvention involves incorporation of unknown into known forms or vice versa, and artistic reinvention similarly draws on earlier material. In the second half of the twentieth century, South Korea under President Park Chunghee accomplished the economic *hangangeui gijeok* (Miracle on the Han River), which was a first step in promoting national culture to global audiences. The result of Park's centralized global cultural initiative was a staging of "national culture" that fragmented and homogenized extant heritages in the name of a unary cultural product. The economic boom sponsored a national culture-building project alongside a disparate array of discourses and influences, an effect theorized by Bhabha.[26] In *gugak* and pansori, the intangible cultural assets system also laid the foundation for reinvention of the traditional legacies inherited.

The intercultural theatre movement has been a search for "'authentic,' real experience elsewhere than in Western cultures."[27] The movement often leads to indigenous rituals or folk performative traditions from around the globe that inspire theatrical reinventions in the mainstream. Korean ritual performance quickly gained traction in modern world theatre innovations. One memorable instance was the opening of the *Symposia on Korean Kut and P'ansori* at the Lincoln Center, which I attended in 2003. Senior Mudang Kim Geumhwa, holder of the Northwestern Haesukut ocean ritual, led her troupe in staging the full spectacle of the opening *kut* ritual, replete with a whole roasted pig speared on the shaman's trident at stage center and Kim riding the *jaktu* (shaman blades) before a rapt New York audience. The ritual show was followed by the *Obatang* pansori performance by five masters, each performing a story.

Contrary to assumptions of the envisioned past as finished and done, pansori's developmental path continues. At the folkloric nexus of sacred and secular, it became canon and precipitated the Korean modern theatre experiment. Today, pansori continues to adapt and be adapted. In the 1990s farmers' anti-globalization protest against the threat to domestic ecologies of production and consumption, the idiom *shintoburi*, "A person and its native soil should be one, not separate two," circulated among renewed appreciation for domestic farm and cultural produce. The late Pak Dongjin was featured in a 1992 public service announcement (CF) famously pansoritizing the catchphrase, *Urigeoseun joeungeosiyeo*, "Our products are the good ones," embedding a powerful association between pansori and national consciousness across the nation.

The Korean playwrights and directors of the early 1970s were mindful of global trends incorporating the syntax and semiotics of indigenous folk performances into contemporary theatre, largely dealing with death, dying, and healing. Playwright Oh Taeseok incorporates Korean indigenous performances into his "metacultural theatre." By means of the "poetic rhythm of indigenous Korean narrative," Oh participates in contemporary Korean dialogue with its cultural inheritance.[28] One of his earlier plays, the surrealist *Grass Tomb* (*Chobun*) of 1973 restages the forgotten indigenous burial rites of the southern Korean islands. In the 1974 *Birth Cord* (*Tae*), Oh portrays the human survival instinct amid one of the most gruesome political purges in the history of Joseon. In his remake of the Shim Cheong story titled, *Why Did Shim Cheong Plunge into the Sea Twice?*, Oh brings Shim Cheong back to the troubled human realm in the absurd company of the Dragon King. As Kim Gyutaek in the colonial era had done in his *Modern Shim Cheong*, Oh replaces the mythological dimension of the original Shim Cheong with a depressing social reality, revealing his view of Korean history as "essentially tragic."[29]

> He is a committed avant-gardist who mines Korea's cultural and theatrical traditions, not so much to preserve them as to interrogate them in the light of contemporary social conditions and post-Artaudian aesthetics. His recent plays are highly original and often disturbing explorations of his country in the context of several cultures—ancient and modern, Eastern and Western—which have both nourished and ravished it.[30]

The *changgeuk* of the later twentieth century were largely adaptations of canonical pansori with minimal alteration to its storytelling scheme. Their especial fidelity to orthodox pansori necessitated an insider knowledge of pansori singing that was rare among modern theatre directors. In the wake of cultural internationalization buoyed by the 1988 Seoul Olympics, the National Changgeuk Company began inviting domestic and foreign theatre directors in anticipation of their contemporary interpretations and expressions. For the 110th anniversary of the history of *changgeuk*, the company produced a scenographic operatic adaptation of *Sugungga*, titled *Mr. Rabbit and the Dragon King* (2011), under the direction of the German opera director Achim Freyer. The director shared these reflections on the project:

> Pansori is not known in countries other than Korea yet, and I have been told that it is a genre that only a small number of people enjoy in Korea. Korea has a great number of traditional cultures to maintain and promote. They should not stay in museums.[31]

In *A Different Chunhyang* (*Dareun Chunhyang*, 2014), the American director Andrei Serban jazzed up pansori with postmodern settings, *mise-en-scène*, and costuming: "Like Shakespeare's stories, you can turn the story upside down, improvise and do the craziest experiments to recreate."[32] The Be-Se-To (Beijing–Seoul–Tokyo) Theatre Festival (2000–) presented a novel East Asian collaboration on adapting the story of Chunhyang to Beijing opera, *changgeuk*, and *kabuki*. Euripides' *Medea* as the 2013 *changgeuk* premiere was an example of global theatrical modernization involving both Greek and Korean traditions. Greek tragedy and *changgeuk* have much in common, both composed of songs and dialogues, affecting the senses of sight and hearing.[33] An official custodian of the theatrical pansori, the National Changgeuk Company today partners with the other branches of the National Theater of Korea in cultivating the national soft power under the banner, Gukka Brand Gongyeon Saeop (National Brand Performance Project).

"Singer in the Gully" and the Creation of New Pansori

As the iconic status of pansori sedimented into Korean national culture, enthusiasm grew among the middle-class urban public. In the capitol city of Seoul alone, major universities, including Seoul National, Ewha, Chungang, and Korean National University of Arts, mitigated the age-old cultural marginalization of Korean traditional music through the development of curricula in Korean music. Keith Howard notes that "A similar circular mode of exchange actually characterizes much Western music in Korea," studying with the best professors, giving them gifts and payments, selling their concert tickets, "in what is essentially a 'master–servant relationship.'"[34]

Outside the highly politicized appellation of human national treasure designations granted to a chosen few, many in various stages of learning and competence engage in creative works reflective of their own cross-cultural sensibilities contemporary to *hallyu* (Korean wave), hip-hop or K-pop. Heather Willoughby examines such innovations in pansori as a juxtaposition of traditional pansori texts with new musical accompaniments and altogether original pansori compositions.[35] Subjects for original composition exceed the original folkloric corpus to include characters from online games, children's dinosaur song, a confectionary village of Korean snacks, and the crowd's rhythmic chant of *Dae—hanminguk!* at the memorable World Cup 2002. Willoughby observes that while traditional pansori has both humor and pathos called *han*, the new pansori lacks the emotional depth and is unable to mount as a masterpiece, "concentrating on only the lighter more jovial aspects of life."[36]

In the 1980s, innovation in *gugak* coalesced around the efforts of youthful practitioners (*jeolmeun gugak-in*) with the vision of globalization (*segyehwa*) and popularization (*daejunghwa*). Though invested in traditional arts, the younger generation tended to eschew norms around deference to elders. Observing the time's momentous expansion in new music, Hilary Finchum-Sung explicates the new musical variety:

gugak-style arrangement of Euro-American pop or classical melodies, creation of *gugak* pop songs and light music, academic or classical *gugak* played in popular music style, fusion, and crossover, "the hallmark of young kugak."[37] R. Anderson Sutton describes this convergence as a place of hope, "a kind of intentional cultural impurity ... an important site in the creative struggle for the future of 'Korean Music.'"[38]

From the margins of orthodox pansori in the twenty-first century, the new *changgeuk* pansori captivated national venues. The old terminology of *ttorang gwangdae*, "singer in the gully," resurfaced, not as the traditional derogatory "singer without pedigree," but as vogue nomenclature for creators of new pansori. It should be noted that many performers in this cohort had thespian training and sought to build their dramatic profile by means of pansori. The winner of the Ttorang Gwangdae Contest 2005, Kim Myeongja explains:

Ttorang may be a tiny gully but necessary, they were the singers in the village gatherings and events without being onerous ... new pansori is created with content familiar to the contemporary audience ... I hope it serves as the steppingstone for reaching the tradition itself. If ttorang gwangdae spreads *sori* in every village, the *pan* resuscitates, so does pansori. In this sense, new pansori is a restorative genre for the culture of the *pan*.[39]

Where pedigree is less of an issue, the singer could more freely express the self, and the "singers in the gully" indeed provided a more carefree pansori singing, contributing to widening the audience base.[40] The peripheral existence of *ttorang gwangdae* may in fact have been a serendipitous locus of reinvention, and the 2001 inauguration of the Ttorang Gwangdae Contest was an attempt to resurrect the freer-flowing imaginations and creativities of the traditional *ttorang gwangdae*. The annual event contends to recapture the dynamics of popular appeal of pansori allegedly shrunk in its canonization process: "Easy pansori, friendly pansori, recovery of the *pan* not confined to 'stage,' the mental attitude of the traditional *ttorang gwangdae* with which to locate the pansori of today ... improvisational, satiric, humorous, original, and keep the amateurism afloat!"[41]

The amateurism of the traditional singer in the gully is elegantly transformed as the artistic capacity to create new pansori today. It incentivizes collaboration between the members of experimental theatre and younger-generation pansori singers keen on reclaiming the popular appeal of pansori. After six decades of protective care in pursuit of its "archetype," pansori shows a surer promise of sustainability to meet the innovative need of our time. Richard Bauman, in conceptualizing folklore, posits two views: a romantic view of tradition as the collective, ready-made, stereotyped as opposed to the more recent performance-centered approaches emphasizing individuality and creativity.[42] The contemporary *changgeuk* personalizes various directorial visions and approaches in meshing pansori with theatre, dance, storytelling, and technology. The lavish publicities and media coverages they receive melt down the existing class or genre divisions between pansori and *changgeuk*, mainstream and margin, or traditional and contemporary. On the influence of K-pop in the popularization of pansori, Anna Yates-Lu aptly concludes that *changgeuk* plays a major role in supporting young singers in contemporary Korea.[43] *Changgeuk* provides them with opportunities to perform while being on a payroll. The young singers reciprocate with the K-pop culture and energy the production can tap into, if that is part of the popularization scheme.

New *Changgeuk*: Ongoing Innovation in Pansori

Today, pansori continues to serve as a wellspring for innovation in the constellation of theatrical schools, venues, and movements. One example is in the work of singer-director Ji Gihak, who led the group Michin Gwangdae (Mad Singers) in the 2021 *saepansori* (new pansori) theatrical adaptation of Hwang

Sunmi's 2000 allegorical novel *Madangeul naon amtark* (*The Hen Who Dreamed She Could Fly*). Ji conceptualizes this adaptation as an inquiry of *je* (school), *badi* (style), and *deoneum* (idiosyncratic composition of a master singer). Not just another adaptation of pansori for popular entertainment, the production was a musicological study of pansori, featuring four singers taking turns to demonstrate each one's school and style. External theatrics such as lighting, costume, or set were minimized, and the performers engaged the audience by adding dramatic and comic relief.

> Director Go Seonung tweaked the Heungbo narrative, Music Director Yi Jaram modified its sori, and the Changgeuk Heungbo-ssi, beyond anything you can imagine, is born ... middle-age viewers enjoy the pansori while the younger generations immerse themselves to the beat as if listening to a rap![44]

The splashy promotion by the National Theater of the 2018 National Changgeuk Company production of *Heungbo-ssi* added for the audience "fresh shock of narrative reversal, repositioning, paralleling."[45] For example, when the starving Heungbo needs urgent rescue, an extraterrestrial being appears in place of the original mendicant monk. The relationship of Heungbo and Nolbo is transposed into family secrets typical of a modern family drama: the adopted Heungbo gives up his first-son privileges to appease the biological son Nolbo. Modifications to the existing narrative structure allow for exciting dramatic twists and subventions of audience anticipation, and the new *changgeuk* joins in such playfulness.

While *changgeuk* based on classical pansori celebrates familiar narratives of heroism and virtue, contemporary creative *changgeuk* instead trends toward a novelization of pansori about ordinary characters, actions, and situations. *Omae Arirang* (*Mother's Arirang*, 2013) produced by the Jeonbuk Provincial Changgeuk Company, dramatizes a real-life contemporary story. Scripted by Pak Seonghwan and adapted and directed by Ju Hojong, the plot unfolds like a standard K-drama (popular soap opera that has gained international viewership): during the Korean War, the protagonist is separated from her son and lives a difficult life. Near the end of her life, she is at last reunited with her son, and she dies shortly thereafter. The tragedy borne by private citizens against the backdrop of the Korean national tragedy still produces strong empathy, affirmed by audience tears and cheers for the protagonist.

In the twenty-first century, the long-held claim of Korean monoracial homogeneity was fraying at the seams under the weight of globalization. The alleged racial and ethnic purity of the Korean populace is demythologized by a rise in *damunhwa gajeong* (multicultural families). Men from rural or working-class backgrounds are at a perceived disadvantage in a hyper-competitive, materialistic marriage industry. International marriages are thus on the rise. Scripted by Jeong Gyeongjin and directed by Ryu Jangyeong, *Huong's Hope Diary* (2016) produced by the Jeonnam Provincial Changgeuk Company builds on the challenges of transnational marriage. The Korean onion farmer Samsik brings home his Vietnamese wife Huong. Huong's father in Vietnam still carries a deep scar from the wartime cruelties allegedly committed by Korean troops fighting alongside the US troops during the Vietnam War (1955–75). On the other hand, Samsik's grandfather in Korea is proud of having raised his family by tilling the land he had purchased with savings from fighting the same war. Samsik falls into internet gambling, and his mother blames Huong for it, but Huong forgives Samsik. Samsik's grandfather dies, and his spirit appears to ask for forgiveness for the victims of the Vietnam War. The play ends with everyone singing songs of hope.[46]

New Pansori, from Heroic to Satiric to Novelic

New pansori repertoires are called *changjak pansori* (creative pansori) or *saepansori* (new pansori). These terminologies are tautological in that all inherited and newfangled pansori narratives are new creations of one time or another. Introducing pansori in these contrastive terms may amplify the stereotypical notion of pansori as an aged phenomenon already at birth just as Athena sprang out of Zeus' skull fully grown. The new solo-story singing pieces, referred to from here on as "new pansori," are in essence contemporary iterations of an enduring pansori tradition.

Yeolsaga (Songs of the Patriots)

The new pansori of the mid-to-later twentieth century builds on the unfolding political reality of the nation, from praise for national heroes to denunciations of power and corruption. At the close of the Asia–Pacific War and Japan's surrender, the *Yeolsaga* (Songs of the Patriots), songs of four national heroes who perished while fighting for the Korean independence gained popularity. The more recently discovered *Yeoksaga* (Songs of History) chronicles heroic events and deeds in the larger Korean history,[47] including the sixteenth-century Admiral Yi Sunshin, whose fleet successfully repelled the Hideyoshi Invasion in 1597. Pansori historian Bae Yeon Hyung locates these affectively charged and entertaining narratives in a nation-building discourse: such tales of national pride and perseverance "stepped into the role of social education in the post-independence, postwar reconstruction of nation in schools, military foxhole circuits, and private and public institutions."[48]

The authorship of the text and *deoneum* of *Yeolsaga* is unknown, except it is most closely associated with the name Pak Dongsil, who migrated to North Korea in the 1950s. Pansori musicologist Yoo Yeongdae observes that following Korea's 1945 liberation, *Yeolsaga* spread, like popular music of the time, in a cathartic torrent of patriotic sentiment after decades of colonial censorship.[49] In form, the four vignettes are like miniature pansori: they speak in the language of pansori in expressing sorrow, loneliness, despair, or loyalty to the nation in their respective storytelling. I introduce these four heroes of the *Yeolsaga* in chronological order. Yi Jun and his company traveled to the Netherlands to deliver Gojong's secret appeal that Korea had never agreed to Japan's protectorate treaty of 1905 and needed the help of the world gathered at the Second Hague Peace Conference of 1906. At the Hague, they were denied entrance to the conference room, and all efforts failed. Yi Chun died of grief there. The *Song of Ahn Junggeun* (1879–1910) is a dramatization of Ahn's assassination of the Japanese Government-General of Korea Ito Hirobumi at Harbin Train Station (1909), and his arrest and execution. The *Song of Yu Gwansun* recounts the tragically abridged life story of Yu Gwansun (1902–20), a female high school student who co-organized the March First National Independence Movement in 1919 and was tortured to death in prison.[50] Yun Bonggil (1908–32) was a poet, educator, and independence activist who was executed after carrying out the assassination of influential Japanese persons in Shanghai. The pathos of *han* structures *Yeolsaga*, building on discrete episodes of heroism and martyrdom to elicit a response of sorrowful indignation.

Ojeok (The Five Bandits)

In the 1970s, the Republic of Korea was a scene of continual protest and state reprisals, with flying rocks, Molotov cocktails, and tear gas. President Park Chunghee's "Crush Communism" (*Myeolgong*) and Yushin Constitutional Reformation of 1972 met with sustained protests from democracy activists. The National Democratic Youth Students Alliance (*Mincheonghangnyeon*) and the National Revolutionary Party (*Inhyeoktang*) at the helm intensified resistance and street demonstrations. Inequality, corruption, dictatorship, and a most contradictory term of democracy were the catchphrases for the parroting students and workers that in turn provided a facade for the ceaseless attempts to destroy, truth be told, mostly by the communist North of the South. To protect the national security of the fledgling republic, the state arrested 180 members of the Alliance and carried out the extreme measure of executing eight of them. Against such backdrop appeared

Ojeok, "Five Crooks," a sardonic narrative poem written in the tone of pansori by the activist poet Kim Jiha and sung by the activist singer Im Jintaek." The poem sweepingly condemns the establishment corruption of *jaebeol* conglomerates, National Assembly members, high-ranking officials, generals, and cabinet and deputy ministers. Kim employs parody and burlesque in his famous description of their national thievery promenade, reminiscent of the corrupt new magistrate's scandalous gisaeng pageantry from the *Song of Chunhyang*.

Entering the new millennia, singers with diverse sociocultural exposures and training push the existing boundaries of pansori to challenge new transnational thematic and narrative possibilities: Park In-Hye's monodramatic pansori, *Pilgyeongsa Bartleby*, is based on Herman Melville's story of Wall Street, *Bartleby, the Scrivener*; Jung Eun-hye's *Dante-eui singok* is an avant-garde pansori version of *La Divina Commedia*. Considering that modern and contemporary Korean theatre has long invested in translated or adopted foreign plays, the new trend of pansoritizing non-Korean materials is hardly coincidental. Yi Jaram's *Sacheon-ga* is a pansori adaptation of Brecht's *The Good Woman of Setzuan*. Sundeok, alter ego of Brecht's Shen Te of our time, works diligently to remain kind and good, but there are hardships and prejudices blocking her way. The interference takes acrimonious physical and material tropes of prejudice such as Koreans' hypersensitivity toward weight, especially of females, leading to blatant discrimination against overweight women in workplaces. For Sundeok, the USD20,000 gross national product and the dreamlike apartment units are fanciful but unattainable aspirations.

In *Dongmul nongjang* (2019), an adaptation of George Orwell's *Animal Farm*, Jang Seo-Yoon casts into the folkloric acoustics of pansori singing Orwell's prominent revelation of the corruptive nature of power. The universal adaptability of the novel's theme finds a compelling new host in the folkloric pansori representative of the vicious cycle of backbreaking work and exploitation that turns the wheel of life and death. Jang's singing style comfortably adheres to the original convention, i.e., standing stage middle with a fan alternating between *aniri* and *sori* avoiding unnecessary movements, yet her pansori communicates comfortably with her contemporary audience. No visible efforts to look "new" except her costume: black slacks and boots, the brown Picasso-esque half-jacket dramatically tailored to cover only her right torso and arm over her pink *jeogori* blouse. Onstage, Jang is flanked by two musicians, one to her left handling several drums including the *buk*, the other to her right on several strings including guitar and *geomungo* zither. Her work echoes Shin Jaehyo's framework for pansori aesthetics: they are transposable and also universal, requiring singer presence, taut narrative, well-executed *sori*, and appropriate gesturing.

The above introduced samples are but a few representations of the robust productions of new pansori in Korea today. They indicate larger trends in the intercultural theatre of pansori. Female singers constitute the majority in the field, perhaps in proportion to the dominance of female singers in pansori singing today. Second, the typical grouping of a female singer with several male musicians aligns with the format of Korean shamanic ritual, one of the performative origins of pansori. Third, new solo-pansori is typically developed as a one-person production, where the singer creates or adapts the narrative, composes music to the songs, collaborates with the musicians, and performs it on stage. Insofar as the process conjures the nomadic image of the traditional *gwangdae* singer and drummer together sustaining the entire system of ecology of pansori production and consumption, the new pansori is in many senses a continuation of tradition.

Pansori in the Circuitry of "K-Sound"

Korean traditional singing and storytelling has left its enduring tune for all seasons and weathers. They anchor the contemporary search for a Korean intercultural voice via emulation, deconstruction, and modification. They are the living and nurturing progenitors actively shaping their postmodern acoustic posterity.

Onstage2.0, inaugurated in 2010 as a discovery channel of hidden indie music talents in Korea, has staged over 600 groups since inception. Its signature skeletal Square Stage, resembling a postmodern version of the *pan*, traditional off-the-cuff stage within the stage, has become the ultimate dream venue among the Korean contemporary musicians. In 2019, it featured several crossover *gugak* groups that have since soared to colossal popularity as the face of the Korea Tourism Organization's Feel the Rhythm of Korea project, widely viewed and shared across social media platforms. Ak-Dan-Gwang-Chil (ADG7), formed in 2015, turns heads with its colorful sights and sounds of the Northwestern Korean shamanic ritual and folk singing. Leenalchi, multi-vocal "modern-look" pansori remixed with funky hip-hop and borrowing the name of the nineteenth-century pansori virtuoso Yi Nalchi, has created waves with their adaptations from *Song of the Water Palace (Sugungga): Yakseongga* (Song of Medicines), *Eoryudogam* (Fish Map), and *Beom naryo onda* (Tiger Comes Down), among others. The vocal and instrumental ensemble synthesize with the movement of the Ambiguous Dance Company founded in 2007. The Company employs pastiche in the spectacle, blending traditional and modern cultural geographies. Creatively repurposing traditional primary colors, patterns, and accessories, the Ambiguous Dance Company aligns choreographic and sartorial bricolage.

Pansori has also been detected in the crime thriller genre. The new pansori, *Tamjeong Baek Yeongho-Gyeongseong Chugyeok-dieon* (Detective Baek Yeongho's Seoul Chase), has received considerable state and corporate sponsorship to be promoted as "pansori drama" (*pansori-geuk*) and "detective pansori novel" (*tamjeong soseol pansori*). The publicity statement reads: "Money, power, infatuation, intrigues! Chase, tackle, strike, mow down the criminals within the Four Great Gates of Gyeongseong (older name for Seoul)! Directed by Choe Yongseok of the Badaksori! October 20–21, 2022." "Badaksori," literally "bottom-sori," is a term of formulaic self-deprecation. Some singers outside the mainstream would identify their craft as *badaksori*. In claiming an outcast or abject position, they would be free of stylistic constraints and expectations, and thus able to explore the world of *sori* unconstrainedly. *Badaksori* art is reminiscent of Grotowski's poor theatre, which draws on the transformative power of minimalism in technical design and *mise-en-scène*. This detective pansori production reflects the popular culture industry's abiding enthusiasm for and colonization of pansori. Appealing to popular fascination with graphic depictions of crime and punishment, the play's promotional phrase reads: "In a package from an unknown, a finger!" In this case, pansori, a metonym for neo-Confucian social propriety, serves as the backdrop to a lurid, titillating scenario between *femme fatale* and detective.

6

Singing Who You Are: An Autoethnography

In performance, "knowing" necessitates embodiment. As Tami Spry observes, "practice is connection, meaning making, socioculturally entrenched, and life-giving ... a process of discovering relationships particularly between seemingly disparate places and spaces, peoples and ideas."[1] For Spry and other scholars of autoethnography, the researcher's embodied practice is integral to knowledge production and the discernment of relationships and sense-making in a particular context. In this chapter, I apply an autoethnographic lens to my own embodied knowledge of pansori transmission, preservation, and innovation.

Reinventing Text, Context, Performance

In 1974, when I first encountered the pansori world as a postgraduate living in Seoul, everyday Koreans' attitudes about *gugak* vacillated between prejudicial and exoticist. As discussed earlier, pansori has roots in the outcast classes of performers, entertainers, and shamans. For the urban middle class who had little to no firsthand experience of the genre, pansori continued to be strange and undesirable. My encounter with pansori happened because of a detour outside of my own social orbit. I was not alone in seeking out pansori studies as a cultural outsider, as did other learners without heritage knowledge of the arts and had no expectation to acquire skills and techniques reserved for insiders.

Attending middle and high school for girls in 1960s Seoul, I learned Euro-American art songs and scaling practices from Frantz Wüllner's *Chorübungen* for smooth tonal transition between the natural voice and falsetto. My voice was curiously untrainable, and I developed a profound level of insecurity in music class. Instead, I continued to find joy in singing along with American pop songs airing on the Armed Forces of Korean Network (AFKN) Radio. During university studies in English, I participated in American musical theatre productions and even tried my hand at singer-songwriting. A young composer debuted my voice in his record, *Kim Euicheol noraemoeum* (*Kim Euicheol Song Collection*, Seongeumsa, 1974), but in the era's political unrest and censorship, the album was summarily banned at the time of release. The official reason given for the ban was my "insufficient vocal skill" (*changpeop misuk*). I did get my justice a quarter of a century too late, as the record was "unlocked" and available to national and social media channels. The once condemned voice of mine was discovered by groups of "mania" (loanword for dedicated groups of people sharing a "maniacal" fondness for something). It is now "preserved" due to their listening.

In the spring of 1974, Ms. Kim Gyeonghui, who in her prime was recognized for her outstanding male impersonation in the *Yeoseong gukkeuk* (all-women *changgeuk*) genre, was teaching pansori in the storage room of her famous sister Kim Sohui's studio across from the Secret Garden Palace. A close friend of mine sharing a similar thespian interest had recently found pansori and invited me to come along, so began my journey with pansori. I was aware that a husky contralto is preferred in pansori, and my voice did not disappoint even as I frequently lost it. The voice of Ms. Kim was superlatively husky and low-pitched, simultaneously wonderful and painful in proximity to Louis Armstrong's gravelly voice. *Pyeonsichun*,

A Slice of Spring, was the first song she taught me, modeling a genderless voice. The beginning lines are translated here:

> The affairs of this world, all for naught.
> Do you not see the peach blossoms in the east garden fade?
> Lady of the Pleasure House, listen.
> A man's life work is measured against the fleeting time,
> River winds eastward, waves rush on,
> Whitewater creeks reach the east sea, to return when?
> The rays of sun setting over Ox Mountain are tears of Gyeonggong of Je,[2]
> Autumn Wind Song on Bun River is the sorrow of Emperor Muje of Han[3]
> Cuckoo crying tears of blood, what grieves you so?
> . . .
> Barely awake from the youth-dream, deeper is the sorrow of gone grey.[4]

Ms. Kim's guttural vocals, commingling with the torrential monsoon rain striking her window, formed a lasting acoustic memory for me. Pansori made me aware of temporalities and history that had vanished from my lifeworld. In *A Slice of Spring*, Duke Je is a vainglorious and extravagant person and an incompetent ruler. His faithful adviser An Ja did his utmost to guide his lord truthfully, even giving up his life to do so. On the Ox Mountain at sunset, Je lamented An's passing, "Whosoever would correct me now that he's gone?!"[5] As a learner, I was also rediscovering history through music. My new adventure ended due to an unexpected conflict of interest: after a week of lessons, Ms. Kim asked for my long black hair to turn it into a *darae*, a traditional wig thickener for her thinning hair, or *tchok*, chignon-like bun for pansori performance. I was not ready to part with my hair, however. Though I was something of a rebel, I was a product of the teaching, *shinchebalbu sujibumo* (Protect your constitution, hair, and epidermis as they were given by your parents). After she told me about her most unusual dream, in which I had cut my hair and given it to her, I left with my hair intact.

Though her request seemed unusual, it may have reflected the sort of gift-exchange culture that she was part of. In lessons, a *sori* teacher gives to another person part of her painstakingly cultivated voice. In the larger context of Korean culture, teachers are regarded with deference to some extent because of the belief that they are selflessly imparting something precious to the learner. The teacher's *sori* is akin to authorship or intellectual property systematically valued in academe. Lacking such institutional protections on her personal asset, the student's hair for wig-making may have seemed like a reasonable request, especially since I was making the most of her giving. Just as my voice-receiving could not be calculated monetarily, her voice-giving was not simply reducible to lesson-fee money.

The legacy of class division endured in the world of pansori and *gugak* as a whole expanded to the diasporic communities of artists living outside of Korea. In Honolulu, where I relocated shortly after being initiated into pansori, I met Master Ji Yeonghui (1909–80), the 1973 designated *boyuja* of *sinawi* music, and his wife, Master Seong Geumyeon (1923–83),[6] the 1968 *boyuja* of *gayageum* zither. The couple had immigrated to Honolulu in 1974, and were consequently made to relinquish their titles, which was a great loss for the Korean *gugak* community of the time. It was in Honolulu, during my graduate studies, that I met Masters Ji and Seong, who welcomed me to their house. Along with the music and songs of *gugak*, Master Seong's delicious *pagimchi* (green onion kimchi) nourished me with the flavors of home. I feel eternally grateful to them for guiding me to Master Chung Kwonjin when I expressed my interest to learn pansori during the summer of 1976. Their advice to me, however, was to stop at my current level of training, lest I be perceived as a *gisaeng*. Though I had set out to learn the art forms rather than engage in the cultural politics around performer castes, I was confronted with the complex cultural hierarchy imposed on pansori and those who learn and practice it.

In the summer of 1976, while heading into my second year of MFA in stage directing at the University of Hawai'i, I had a fresh vision of defining Korean theatre in pansori. With a personal introduction from the masters Ji Yeonghui and Seong Geumyeon, I went to Korea to seek the tutelage of Master Chung Kwonjin. At the time, Master Chung was leading the pansori curriculum at the Gugak Yesul Hakkyo, a secondary *gugak* conservatory school in Seoul, attended mostly by the children of professional traditional musicians. In the large training room in the basement of the building, I received Master Chung's *sori* training, sometimes joined by an entire class of pupils or a few other adult disciples. My teacher started me with the warm-up song, *Jinguk Myeongsan*, "Mountains of National Peace and Prosperity," a panegyric on the auspicious energy of the mountains surrounding the old Seoul. I was pleasantly surprised that the Samgak Mountain, honored as the "Northern Master" (*Bukchu*) in the song, was the stationary hill that was always standing in the background of the house I grew up in! And the line, "Naksan mountains left is the dragon, Inwang Mountain right is the tiger" (*jwaryong Naksan, uho Inwang*) are the same locations where as a little girl I followed my older sisters and friends to pick mountain herbs and greens in spring, wash clothes by streamsides in summer, gather acorns in autumn, and ride the rickety sleigh my brother fashioned for me over the carpet of snow. Those hills were de facto giver of energy for the whole nation! The final cautionary message in the song was also inspirational: when you pass middle age, stop chasing fame and fortune but secure a small corner in nature, a retreat where you can enjoy music and poetry in the company of like-minded friends. When I could begin to sing Jinguk Myeongsan without opening my *sorichaek*, Master Chung started me on the Kim Sejong-style *Song of Chunhyang*. In 1979, I moved back to Korea with the intention to go deeper into pansori singing. One day, my teacher had me switch to learning the *Song of Shim Cheong*, for a reason.

The *boyuja* of the *Song of Shim Cheong* in the style of *Gangsanche Poseong Sori* (1970), Chung Kwonjin had the progressive vision of bringing pansori out of the societal margins by introducing intellectual discourse on the artform. In selecting his trainees, he attempted to combine performative and intellectual strengths to complement one another. In 1981, he announced his two *jeonsusaeng* (new trainees): Han Seonha, already an accomplished singer from a prominent *gugak* family and, to my great surprise, myself. However, the Korean Traditional Music Association (*Gugak Hyeophoe*) disqualified me because of my citizenship status: I had just been naturalized a US citizen and therefore had to relinquish my Korean nationality according to the Korean Ministry of Justice' ordinance. Retrospectively, this roadblock may have helped shape my research and performance from a more independent angle, and my teacher would be happy to know that pansori did become a serious discourse in the arts and humanities globally just as he had envisioned. Today, the Korean government continues to support *gugak* as part of its initiative to define national culture in *hallyu*. *Gugak* resources are also growing in the Korean diasporic communities outside Korea. In 2014, the Korean government bestowed ten overseas *gugak* performers the title, *Haeoe Myeongye Jeonseungja*, "Honorary Overseas Transmitter." These designees "fulfill the important mission of representing hallyu in traditional culture."[7] The symbolic capital of honorary designations reflects the difference between academic and artistic worlds. Honorary designations for *gugak* artists accord them with important, albeit subordinate, credentials with which to marshal critical resources for their projects. The ten overseas honorees include Ji Yunja of Los Angeles for gayageum, Han Changhyeon of Vancouver, Canada, for Songpa Sandae mask dance drama, and Kang Daeseung (d. 2022) for *Gangnyeong* mask dance drama and folk percussion.

Oral transmission of *sori* from teacher to disciple parallels the parent–child dynamic of the unconditional sharing of deeply embedded knowledge to the next generation. I had been a clumsy learner, solely dependent on the daily "lessons" when my teacher passed away in 1986. Feeling underequipped for independent training, I sought lessons from several teachers of distinction: *Dongpyeonche*-style *Song of Heungbo* from Han Nongseon, Boseongsori-style *Song of Chunhyang* from Sung Uhyang, and *Seopyeonche*-style *Song of the Water Palace* from Pak Yangdeok. They afforded me a valuable experience of their schools and individual styles as well as priceless oral histories. These exposures also helped me hone my independent learner skills to build on what I had learned before my teacher's premature passing: it was a short ten years under his tutelage, but long enough for me to acquire the core cognizance for moving on. I reorganized my learning kit into a set of cassette tapes of my teacher's *sori* and volumes of my old *sorichaek*.

Making Translingual Voice Literature

My personal journey with pansori was developing as a hybrid of research and performance. Back at the University of Hawaiʻi graduate program with pansori as my dissertation topic, I had the opportunity to perform on a few occasions, and they were less than gratifying. The main reason was the difficulty of communicating the narrative content of pansori to the audience during performance. Contrary to the view among those who trust pansori should simply be appreciated as a vocal theatricality and requires no logocentric interpretation, my work builds on the literary understanding of the *saseol*. Rather than pigeonholing pansori as a mere theatrical acoustics, I had my work cut out for me: performative delimitation of an audience's comprehension of the lyrical content of pansori without resorting to subtitles. Through trial and error, I created a bilingual pansori where English *aniri* and original *sori* alternately interpret and illustrate one another.

In my bilingual pansori experimentation, I was searching for a communication alternative to the noisy and cumbersome subtitle screening that distracted the audience's attention away from the performance on stage. More recently, I returned to the use of subtitles thanks to the ready accessibility of presentation slide software. From the perspective of the audience, they can engage in two activities concurrently, i.e., listen to the singing while reading its content in either Korean or English translation. Members of my audience reassure me that this confluence of audiovisual reading and listening is pleasantly engaging with hardly a dull moment.

"Pansori Performance Art," Cheong's Death

In the summer of 1987, the Batangkol Art Center in Seoul produced the nine-day Festival of Death as a gesture of mourning the casualties of political crossfire. I was entrusted with producing a stage play that resulted in the *changgeuk*-style pansori, *Cheong-eui jugeum* (Cheong's Death) adapted from the *Song of Shim Cheong*.[8] The cast and musicians were made up of traditional Korean music majors and established or training singers. In scripting and directing, I focused on the ongoing challenge of *changgeuk*, i.e., making the old storytelling engaging: Shim Cheong's death by drowning would imply a different cause and effect, necessitating different trials and errors.

I still recall, thirty-five years later, the uncomfortable mix of shock and laughter from the audience when they saw the departing soul of Cheong's mother on stage, played by me, making her final goodbye. I had recontextualized a village funeral procession with the casket adorned with flowers and mounted on the shoulders of male villagers. The conventional procession chanting the *manga*, death chant, starts from the home of the deceased, makes the final walk through the village, out onto the road and up the hill where the grave is prepared. In my minimalist production, I tied the ends of four long muslin straps around the waist of the deceased, played by me, and cast the other ends over the shoulders of four pallbearers to hold. This may have been a staging most of the theatregoers that evening had not seen before, hence the strange sense of alienation transmitted through their laughter and shock. I also added new details to the storyline for dramatic effect. For example, in the original story, a mendicant monk on his return to the monastery finds Blindman Shim drowning in the icy stream. In this play, three monks—a senior monk, junior monk, and child monk—travel together. Assuming they are alone in the empty mountain, they crack jokes, sing pleasurable songs, and gambol while boldly addressing the audience, and the child monk amuses himself by imitating them. Their unmonastic behavior staged boisterous gaiety before the story's turn toward loss and death.

Pak Heungbo Traverses the Diaspora

On January 13, 1903, a ship carrying the first Koreans contracted to work on the sugar plantations in Hawai'i entered Honolulu Harbor. On January 13, 2003, the Koreans in Hawai'i celebrated the centennial anniversary of Korean immigration to America. For the opening ceremony, the younger members of the preparation committee recommended my bilingual pansori performance, and encountered objections from the senior members who thought pansori to be "long and boring." I later learned the younger members vouched for me to give a "rock pansori." I was clueless as to what I could do to match that expectation. The history of the displacement and relocation of the first Koreans in Hawai'i gave me a place to start: homeless Pak Heungbo, being driven out of his home by his older brother Nolbo, was among the first arrivals in Hawai'i. The result was the monodrama, *Centennial Pansori: In 1903, Pak Heungbo Went to Hawai'i*, drafted and performed at the celebration.

Familiar folk and pansori singing punctuating the storytelling underscored the hardships of displacement, relocation, and "the multi-generation making of community in their home away from home."[9] These interpolated songs echoed the communal journey of the Korean diaspora on the sugar plantation: a doleful *Arirang* in the voices of those cast out of their homes and lands to the Manchurian wasteland echoes Heungbo's eviction and departure to Hawai'i. Heungbo's passage across the Pacific recalls Shim Cheong's voyage to her drowning. More celebratory moments in the repertoire include the *Milling Song* for the first sugar harvest, the *Love Song of Chunhyang* for the nuptial union of Heungbo and his Picture Bride, and the Korean-Hawai'ian *Gourd Song* duet promising a happy future with plentiful *kokua*, the Hawai'ian term for the spirit of kindness. Props established the local intercultural setting of the *pansori* adaptation: a gourd dipper for travel, a white apron invoking the memory of the hardworking Korean women of the plantations, and also to be improvised as the iconic veil/headcover for the Picture Bride impersonation, a bouquet for Heungbo's wedding, and a rope for the gourd sawing. Ironically, the most challenging prop to obtain was a pair of sugarcane plants I needed for the *Milling Song*. While sugarcane was a widely cultivated cash crop in the early twentieth century, the state of Hawai'i was in the process of eradicating all sugar farming. A storekeeper at the Honolulu Downtown marketplace cut two for me that were still growing in her grandpa's backyard. An old friend let me borrow his pair of leather work gloves for protection from the sugarcane splinters during the show. I will introduce one of my original lyrics adapted to the tune of *Nongbuga*, Farmers' Ballad:

Centennial Pansori: *In 1903, Pak Heungbo Went to Hawai'i*

Refrain: *Oyeo yeoheo yeoheoru sangsadwiyeo* . . .

Over the majestic Ko'olau towering like serrated blade
Rain wind blows to cool our sweaty backs
Surf roars and crashes into the shore,
The willowy sugarcanes dance *salpuri*
Evening glow spreads, stars come out.
I light my pipe and gaze at the North Sea
I miss my loving family,
I miss my home far far away.

Refrain: *Oyeo yeoheo yeoheoru sangsadwiyeo.*[10]

In 1937, Pak Heungbo went to Almaty

In 2007, Pak Heungbo reincarnates as folkloric testimony of another Korean diaspora, the Goryeo Saram of Kazakhstan. *Pak Heungbo Went to Almaty* is a two-act storytelling play dedicated to "The Trials and Triumphs of the Korean Diaspora of Central Asia," in collaboration with the Korean Theatre of Kazakhstan, performed on July 14, 2007. Act One retells the history of Korean migration to the Russian Far East and their deportation in 1937. More than 2,800 Korean leaders and intellectuals were executed, and 172,000 Koreans were forced to travel in rusty old livestock cars:

> Asking the moon and the stars through the holes in the ceiling, "Why?"
> Chilled to the marrow by the Siberian winter cold,
> With clothing and food to last a month and no more,
> Caring for the sick, the elderly, the children, and the pregnant,
> All headed west to the abysmal depths of the unknown,
> Many perished during the ride,
> Many more died where their rides ended.[11]

The Heungbo narrative spans many nodes of modern Korean diasporas. Though non-fictional, these stories are no less captivating. In the story of Hawai'i, a fictional character is set up as a first Korean settled in a sugar plantation, blending fictitious character into the historic setting. In *Pak Heungbo Went to Almaty*, Heungbo is part of the Korean migration story in Central Asia. The train's arrival in Kazakhstan is cued by the strumming of the Kazakh dombra. The narrative highlights the ethnic kinship between Koreans and Kazakhs, as this was not just the story of Korean forced resettlement but the start of friendship between the two communities. In the story, I specified the Altaic kinship Koreans share with the Kazakhs, reminding one that it is not only a story of Korean resettlers but also of the Kazakhs welcoming them. The Koreans are known to be good farmers, so good they turned the wastelands of the Russian Far East into fertile farmlands. Farming meant survival but also the salvaging of hope for a livable future. I wrote a lyric of crops in two parts: recitative then shifts to jajinmori. *The Song of Crops* is in energizing hip-hop style, dispelling the gloom of what history was experienced. I mixed both vegetables universally used as well as those specific to Korean cuisine:

The Song of Crops

(*In recitative*)
Tilled and sowed, planted and transplanted,
weeded and watered and harvested crops.

Sori (*Jajinmori*)
Rice, cotton, sugar beets, turnips,
Peppers, onions, taros, pumpkins,
Eggplants, cucumbers, cabbages, chives,
Lettuces, carrots, kkaennip, ssukkat,
Gosari, doraji, dallae, naengi ... (*Actors chime in*)[12]

The day after the performance marking the 70th Anniversary of the Korean Diaspora of Central Asia, delegates from Uzbekistan approached me with an invitation to stage another version of the Korean deportation to Uzbekistan. The capital, Tashkent, is home to another Goryeo Saram diaspora resulting from the same forced migration.

English Pansori: *When Tiger Smoked Its Pipe*

The pansori adaptation I have developed is sometimes referred to as "English pansori," but it is more accurately described as bilingual interpretive pansori. It is not singing pansori in English translation, but rather finding ways to deliver the meaning of the lyric in English *aniri* in combination with singing in the original *sori*. In the autumn of 2003, the Honolulu

Theatre for Youth joined the centennial celebration of Korean immigration to America with the production *When Tiger Smoked Its Pipe*, an omnibus-style play adapted by the novelist Nora Okja Keller from three Korean folk tales. The director Mark Lutwak invited me to help realize his vision of a pansori-style narrator for the play. I was given a month-long residency to develop the script into a pansori-like play and the leading actor to a pansori-narrator. I combed the script for points of conversion to pansori format, composing them into *sori* and teaching the actor to sing them well enough for an impressionistic creation of the pansori ambience. My understanding was that we were designing a play for the mostly primary school-age children from around the Isle, so this pansori project did not oblige a national treasure-grade singing and composition. In other words, our goal was for a main actor to "act" the part of pansori singer/storyteller for the local children.

Composing pansori in English made me aware of the indivisible connection between the *sori* and its original language art. Second, a lyric originally written in English and sung in the style of pansori should still bespeak the syntactics or semantics of English. In other words, the art of that language expression is implicated in the new equation. This is a different labor from translating the existing pansori repertoire, as many people have inquired. In this case, the labor involves putting the English translation into the already set music of the existing song. In composing new music to the lyric already written in English, you have a bit more freedom to play with the English language art marrying a new singing style of pansori.

Postmodern *Shim Cheong*

Shim Cheong: A Korean Folktale (2003), a collaboration with the California State University Northridge Theatre Department, premiered at the Paul Getty Center, October 24–25 and was restaged at the National Theater of Korea, November 19–23. Dismissing the written script, the play developed as a loosely constructed impressionist play with human collages of Korea interspersed with the story of Shim Cheong. The cast and crew animated those elements of the narrative that they individually found most resonant, including dream sequences, filial piety, sacrifice, Karma, unsolved suicide, and other national trauma as well as the aggrandized image of the Demilitarized Zone (DMZ) between the Koreas.

In my role as pansori narrator, I was to join the often-desultory enactment of current occurrences in Korea to the structured poetics of pansori *Shim Cheong*. The staging of the classic confrontation and skirmishes at the DMZ enters the folkloric reality of the birth, life, and death of Shim Cheong. Death marks the beginning of Shim Cheong's journey to the other world and the dystopic reality of the divided Korea. In autumn 2003, the alleged suicide of a *jaebeol* CEO, Hyundai's Jung Mong-heon, was a frequent topic in public discourse.[13] In the play, the stage character of Jung Mong-heon accompanies Shim Cheong to their falling deaths as the stage blackout cuts stops the frenzied drumming. This experimental work alerted me to how folkloric traditions and historical imaginations are borderless for better or worse, and I happened to have been part of this story of *Shim Cheong* through the intercultural prism of Korean political images.

Fox Hunt, Historical *Inhyeonggeuk* (Doll Theater)

Playing make-believe with dolls was one of my favorite "dramatic" activities when growing up. Half a century later, I did just that with Kathy Foley, scholar and puppeteer in the Indonesian Wayang tradition and my graduate school classmate. It started with combining puppetry with pansori to tell stories of women in Korean history. The first version was *Intertwined Lives, Korean and Western Women*, and the first reading was held at the Art-Theatre-Community, University of California Santa Cruz, on March 7, 2009. It progressed to *Fox Hunt and the Death of a Queen*, recounting the tragic assassination of Empress Min, wife of Gojong. *Fox Hunt* premiered at the East-West Center at the University of Hawai'i on September 30, 2012.

Two female voices interlace throughout the narration: the firsthand recount by the British traveler Isabella Bird Bishop (1831–1904), and a Korean storysinger. The feud between Gojong's queen and father endangered Korea as colonial powers competed for hegemony over the peninsula. It was alleged that Japan received the tacit approval of Empress Min's father-in-law and political adversary, the Regent Daewongun, to carry out her assassination in the early hours of October 8, 1895, an action they coded as "The Operation Fox Hunt."

Fox Hunt narrated the end of Joseon with minimal theatricality. Though dolls and puppets were used, the grim subject matter required a non-fiction documentary style. Two storytellers respectively delivered investigative details from their contrasting perspectives, using vocalization and movement that train the audience attention on the doll characters. For the royal trio, Queen Min, King Gojong, Prince Daeweongun, I visualized sedentary images of their alter egos, i.e., dolls seated, standing, or barely moving in their magnificent royal attires while plotting revenge or defense. The hallmark of Korean aristocratic behavior is precisely their ability to act unruffled and composed. The aria for the queen in her moment of doubts, fear, and insecurity was an original composition:

Aniri:
I fought hard with all my charm, shrewdness, sagacity, and power
for the safety and dignity of my husband and son, and for the downfall of my Father-in-law!
My life was a battle!
I constantly evoked the aid of sorcerers and shamans,
in dread the son of a concubine would be declared heir to the throne.
I prayed hard for the safety of Korea.[14]

Sori (*semachi*):

I pray, I pray, Benevolent Being I pray before you.
Heaven, Earth, Lord of the Devas, Help me!
The fate of the nation is hanging by a thread,
Toxic politicians and heinous sons everywhere,
I'm just a woman confined deep within the palace walls, how could I endure it?
O Bright Heaven, take pity on us
Light the future days of Joseon![15]

Aniri:

I lived in ceaseless anxiety about my only remaining son's health.
Could foreigners help me?!
Potions from the Western doctors seemed magical.
Dr. Allen saved my cousin's life after the assassination attempt at the Post Office.
Mrs. Underwood and her new friend Mrs. Bishop seemed to be better healers than many of our medical kisaeng.
"Who's out there?
Send for Mrs. Isabella Bird Bishop,
Tell her I am inviting her over tea."[16]

The stationary power of the doll gaze was a fitting illustration of royal composure, and I sewed the iconic royal garments for the three dolls as featured in historic photos. Kathy's Wayang-inspired movements during the scene of assassination were climactic. We constructed a miniature funeral bier and casket for the queen-doll, and the funeral parade led by the master chanter Cho Ohwhan and chimed by the attendant members of the campus community was a memorable community event not too shabby for the soul of an empress.

While each production was a reinvention, they also drew on tradition in ways that would be acceptable to artists within the *gugak* sphere and intercultural settings. Each experiment was done from a clean slate with no precedence, and none of them has been restaged or reworked yet. When restagings occur, they will more likely remain in transcultural settings removed from the originary contexts of gugak, and their theatre of voice, drum, and listening would be continuously inflected by a wider range of intercultural mediations.

Adaptive experiments such as the ones I have recounted here take place against the backdrop of *hallyu* as a determining influence on theatrical imagination today. Along with rapid-trending music and televisual K-culture that saturates available media circuits, the refrigerator commercials, automobile logos, tourism, foodways, smartphones, and other cross-marketed products are sedimented into audience expectations as they encounter pansori today. After one performance, a professional singer approached me with the idea of her bilingual interpretive pansori in French. Although she did not speak French, she conveyed her passion for such a project. Pansori may not be as transposable as other Korean popular cultural products, for instance hit pop songs in new linguistic territory. Nevertheless, the singer's creative proposal suggests future confluences for *gugak* in *hallyu*. Even the seemingly mundane technology such as slide presentation software has transformed pansori literacy in the form of subtitles flowing with the singing for global audiences, as proven by the bilingual interpretative productions I have described in this chapter.

There are voices in the fields of performance leery of the shape, size, and utility of subtitles, and the film director Bong Joon-Ho in his Oscars Best Picture acceptance speech for *Parasite* is subtly apologetic of subtitles: "Once you overcome the one-inch-tall barrier of subtitles, you will be introduced to so many more amazing films."[17] All forms of communication lingual or metalingual, physical or metaphysical, and with or without subtitles are susceptible to failure. When there is failure, subtitles should not be singled out as the sole culprit. To be fair, subtitles are there to serve as the minimum necessary communication. Far from endangering cultural performance traditions, digitalization has the potential to broaden their availability in public discourse. These are authentic combinations of technology and literacy where the audience can anchor their reading, listening, and imagination. All combined, it is high time for extending this interpretive transnational pansori into more than one language territory.

Conclusion

Pansori is a living tradition of epic narrative. It is still learned and performed, galvanizing discourse on the relationship between storytelling and its temporality. Today's pansori is the outcome of three centuries of a dramatic journey from archaic and later subaltern origins to protection and anointment as national treasure. Pansori singers are also amply represented in *hallyu* cultural production and popular entertainment culture. Many new forms of pansori grow out of the singers' need to inhabit the popular cultural sphere, and so the libretti, melodies, and rhythms cannot stay long in their formal encasement.

The question of popularity and reinvention of pansori test the validity of the modernity–tradition binary. Is tradition antithetical to modernity, or does tradition root the popular cultures of our present? Individual artists differ in their conceptualization of tradition and the acceptable parameters of innovation. For those who regard pansori as not just an adaptable formula for reinvention but also an expression of human subjectivity, the voice of pansori offers a thread of continuity through at times labyrinthine societal disruption. The institutionalization of pansori has created financial pressures: as star performers gain celebrity regard and command exorbitant tuition rates, they retain authority over interpretation. Despite this social capital, pansori celebrities often defer to the directorial management of media companies in the final interpretation. Outside of commercialized orthodoxy, adherents of *Badaksori* (akin to Grotowski's "poor theatre") exercise more liberal choices in their adaptations of pansori, being already alienated from the exclusive society of prospective future *boyuja*.

Pansori tradition could be the platform for Bhabha's ideological construction of otherness or fixity. In this scenario, the intercultural experiment of pansori would be more grounded as the "traditional voice." On the other hand, if tradition is an ambiguous or culturally constructed entity, one might feel freer to roam the boundaries of the tradition. In Korea's rapid modernization, pansori was sometimes viewed and drafted to represent not only the past but also the misery of class hierarchies of the past (and present). Reduced to tradition, pansori also symbolizes *han*, alleged ethnic sorrow of injustice. Alternatively, pansori narratives metonymize class struggle. Mock or even real street funerary processions are a manufactured vehicle for organized protest today in collective expressions of *han*. Most directly, the traditional–modern distinction is apparent in acoustic difference: the pansori singer's vocal inflections are found nowhere else in contemporary Korean performing arts. Although pansori training is exoticized for the alleged extremes of self-injury (bleeding vocal cords), one could find parallels in the punishing routines of would-be K-pop performers, who may be expected to undergo surgical body modification and extreme dieting to conform to management standards. Despite the otherness conventionally associated with pansori in the Korean performing arts, it is moving toward incorporation into mainstream popular culture.

Arnold van Gennep views the processual phenomenon of cultural transformation as three phases of the rite of passage, i.e., separation, transition, then reincorporation, "a stage further along life's culturally prefabricated road."[1] The subject separated from the norm or familiar ground enters or exits to the "limen," threshold or marginal space which Victor Turner characterizes as "a period or area of ambiguity"[2] before being resituated. For pansori, its perpetuation requires more than technical considerations, given the changes to fundamental aspects of narratives. The embodiment of vocal techniques and skills by necessity implicates cognitive awareness of the poetic reality from the past. At this juncture, consciousness connects with tradition in new iterations of theatrical imagination.

As with Korea's other intangible cultural treasures, government intervention ensured the continuation of pansori. Along with institutional procedures, structures, and funding, individual singers' dedication to maintain the arts despite the growing pull of mainstream, commercial, and global popular culture has ensured a robust ecology of well-trained and educated younger-generation singers continuing the work of preservation and reinvention, creating new stories, genres, and circulations in the shifting popular cultural atmosphere.

Interculturalism is now a standard in world theatre. Already three decades ago, researchers observed artists inclined toward formal experimentation drawing closer to Japanese aesthetics while those politically engaged turn to Latin American, Indian, Southeast Asian, and African.[3] Among the performances that could be included as Korean theatre, *kut*, shaman ritual performance, has been a popular genre for its spiritual spectacle and charismatic music and dance. There are multiple ways of telling a story, including folkloric storytelling, stage drama, and film. The storytelling art of pansori involves the human musical voice that has been trained to function as dramatic expression. Where the arts of speaking, writing, and social interaction are augmented or displaced by technological innovation, the dramatist's craft offers one hope of retaining humanity's most intrinsic expressive art—storytelling. Finally, what does the theatre of pansori, an oral literature from Korea's more ecocentric past, afford to a technocratic civilization now confronted with serious questions about survivance? I hope artists and audiences of the future discover in pansori a technology of theatrical imagination "to remain human in a machine universe."[4]

NOTES

Preface

1 Albert B. Lord, *The Singer of Tales* (Cambridge, MA: Harvard University Press, 1960).

2 In Shakespeare's *As You Like It*, Act Two, Scene Five, the forest is the site of a convergence between characters who survive difficult situations and find healing.

Introduction

1 Walter J. Ong, *Orality and Literacy: The Technologizing of the Word* (London: Routledge, 1982), 7.

2 Ibid., 32.

3 Elizabeth Eklund, "Memory and Enshrining Writing: Rethinking the Ethnocentrism Imbedded in Written vs. Oral Traditions," *Arizona Anthropologist*, 28 (2017): 76.

4 Margaret Mead MacDonald, "Editor's Note," in Margaret Read MacDonald (eds.), *Traditional Storytelling Today: An International Sourcebook* (Chicago, IL: Fitzroy Dearborn Publishers, 1999), xiii–xiv.

5 Mikhail Bakhtin, *The Dialogic Imagination*, edited by Michael Holquist, translated by Caryl Emerson and Michael Holquist (Austin, TX: University of Texas Press, 1981), xix.

6 Marshall R. Pihl, *The Korean Singer of Tales* (Cambridge, MA: Harvard University Press, 1994), 3.

7 Gang Hanyeong (1966), in Seo Daeseok, "Issues in Pansori Research," *Seoul Journal of Korean Studies*, 1 (1988): 114.

8 Ong, *Orality and Literacy*, 77.

9   Kyung Moon Hwang, *A History of Korea* (New York: Palgrave MacMillan, 2010), 69–70.
10 In his treatise, *Hunminjeongeum: Teaching People the Correct Sound Transcription.*
11 Ki-baik Lee, *A New History of Korea*, translated by Edward W. Wagner with Edward J. Shultz (Cambridge, MA: Harvard University Press, 1984), 192.
12 Ibid., 192–3.
13 三國志演義 *Samgukjiyeoneui*, fourteenth-century martial novel by Luo Guanzhong of Ming, based on the record of the war among the Three Kingdoms (魏 Wi, 蜀 Chok, 吳 O) by the historian 陳壽 Jinsoo (233–97) of West Jin 西晉 (Seo Jin).
14 三顧草廬 (*Samgo choryeo*), originated from this anecdote of Yu Bi, it is a metaphor for exercising patience and humility if to acquire a person of talent or opportunity.
15 Jack Goody and Ian Watt, "The Consequences of Literacy," *Comparative Studies in Society and History*, 5, 3 (1963): 307.
16 Ong, *Orality and Literacy*, 46.
17 Ibid., 80–1.
18 Lee, *A New History of Korea*, 32–3.
19 Pihl, *Korean Singer of Tales*, 17–18.
20 Kyung Moon Hwang, *A History of Korea*, 45.
21 Lee, *A New History of Korea*, 188.
22 Cho Dong-il, "Two Stages of Transition from Premodern to Modern in Korean Literature," paper presented at the Pacific Rim Korean Studies Conference, Honolulu, Hawai'i, 1992, 3.
23 Bakhtin, *The Dialogic Imagination*, 15.
24 Robert Scholes and Robert Kellogg, *The Nature of Narrative* (London: Oxford University Press, 1966), 11.
25 *Sugungga* (*Song of the Underwater Palace*), Traditional.
26 Included in *Gyeongsudang jeongo*(警修堂全藁, *Entire Collection of the Writings of Gyeongsudang*, 1812), Gyeongsudang was Shin Wi's pen name.
27 In Chan E. Park, *Voices from the Straw Mat: Toward an Ethnography of Korean Story Singing* (Honolulu, HI: University of Hawai'i Press, 2003), 57.

28 Plato, "The Republic: Book III," *Complete Works of Plato*, edited by John M. Cooper (Indianapolis, IN: Hackett, 1997), 400a–402c.

29 Aristotle, "Book Eight, Part Five," *Politics*, translated by Benjamin Jowett, *Internet Classics Archive* (n.d.), available online: http://classics.mit.edu/Aristotle/politics.8.eight.html (accessed March 15, 2023).

30 Confucian teachings of balancing music and ceremony, explicated in vol. 19 of *Akki* (樂記 Record of Music) in *Yegi* (樂記 Book of Ceremonies or Rites), one of the foundation texts of Confucian study that Korea imported during the Three Kingdoms (Goguryeo, Baekche, Silla) era.

31 Ibid.

32 Aristotle, "Book I," *Poetics*, translated by S. H. Butcher, *Internet Classics Archive* (n.d.), available online: http://classics.mit.edu/Aristotle/poetics.1.1.html (accessed March 15, 2023).

33 O'Shea, Suzanne, and Miroslav Holub, "Interview with Miroslav Holub," *Poetry Ireland Review*, 30 (1990): 70.

34 Bae Yeon-hyung, "Pansori yupa-eui gaenyeom-gwa hyeonsil (Study of the Concept and Reality of Pansori Faction)," *Pansori yeongu* (*Journal of Pansori*), 52 (2021): 39–84.

Chapter 1

1 A tactician in the final years of the Warring States (476–221 BCE), Beomnyeo (范蠡) helped avenge Gucheon (句踐, d. 464 BCE), king of Weol (越), by killing Bucha (夫差, d. 473 BCE), king of O (吳).

2 Chok (蜀) is an ancient kingdom situated in today's Sichuan. The phrase is from the poem, "Difficulty of the Shu Road" by Li Po (李白, 701–61).

3 From a song from *Sugungga* (Song of the Water Palace). Hare escapes death from Dragon King's Water Palace and urges Turtle to bring him back to the Land without delay.

4 Phrase from *Daemong* (大夢 Great dream) by Chegal Gongmyeong (諸葛孔明), strategician to Yu Bi (劉備).

5 *Gwang-pung-je-weol* (光風霽月, Clear wind and bright moon after rain), a metaphoric term for lofty personality or well-regulated world, is credited to Hwang Jeonggyeon (黃庭堅), Northern Song poet (960–1127), in his praise of his contemporary scholar/philosopher Ju Doni (周敦頤).

6 *Yeonbi-eoyak*, abbreviation of *Yeonbi yeocheon eoyak uyeon* (鳶飛戾天 魚躍于淵) from the *Book of Odes*.

7 Traditional.

8 Traditional.

9 Pihl, *Korean Singer of Tales*, 60.

10 From the Jeolla regional shamanic chant (*ssitkimkut*), no identified composer.

11 A famous love poem adapted from the Joseon Poetess Hwang Jini (1506–67).

12 District of many ministerial mansions adjacent to the Joseon-era royal palace and today's presidential Blue House. A dignified *yangban* gentleman may not have been inclined nor expected to free a kite stuck in a tree.

13 Traditional.

14 John Stanley, *Classical Music* (London: Mitchell Beazley, 1994), 260.

15 Richard Miller, *The Structure of Singing* (New York: Schirmer, 1986), 150.

16 Pak Heonbong, *Changak daegang* (*Survey of Vocal Music*) (Seoul: Gugak yesul hakkyo chulpanbu, 1966), 71–2.

17 Cheon Idu quoted in Yi Bohyung, "Hanguk eumak-eui 'sigimsae' yeongu bangbeop siron: minsok eumak-eul jungsimeuro," *Eumaktan*, 13 (1999): 5.

18 Yi Bohyung, ibid.

19 Refer to Heonbong, *Changak daegang*, 71.

20 Park, *Voices from the Straw Mat*, 204.

21 Zeami Motokiyo, "Fushikaden (Style and the Flower)," *On the Art of the Nō Drama: The Major Treatises of Zeami*, translated by J. Thomas Rimer and Yamazaki Masakazu (Princeton, NJ: Princeton University Press, 1984), 27–30.

22 Zeami Motokiyo, "Shikadō (True Path to the Flower)," ibid., 66.

23 Jeong Noshik, "Shin Manyeop," in *Joseon changgeuksa* (History of Korean Singing Drama) (Seoul: Joseon ilbosa, 1940), p. 42.

24 Yi Gukja, *Pansori yesul mihak* (Seoul: Nanam shinseo, 1989), 157.

25 Sug-bae Kim in his article, "Joong-goje Pansori and Park Dong-jin's Pansori," establishes the geographic importance of Chungcheong province, home of many Junggoche-style singers including Park's teachers. In *Pansori yeongu* (*Journal of Pansori*), 49 (2020): 47–80.

26 Park, *Voices from the Straw Mat*, 180.

27 Gang Hanyong (ed.), *Shin Jaehyo pansori saseol-jip* (Collection of Shin Jaehyo's Pansori Libretti) (Seoul: Minjung sogwan, 1971), 13.

28 Gang Hanyong, ibid., 669.

29 Heonbong, *Changak daegang*, 68; also in Jeong Byeonguk, *Hanguk-eui pansori* (Korean pansori) (Seoul: Jimmundang, 1981), 62; also in Noshik, *Joseon Changgeuksa*, 25–8.

30 Traditional, Taught to me by Master Chung Kwonjin. Translated byPark, *Voices from the Straw Mat*, 183–4.

Chapter 2

1 Iryeon, *Samguk Yusa* (Memorabilia of the Three Kingdoms), Book One, originally published in 1281 (original publisher unknown, reprinted by Choe Namseon, Seoul: Minjung Seogwan, 1969).

2 Choe Donghyeon, *Pansori yeongu* (*Journal of Pansori*) (Seoul: Munhak Academisa, 1991), 155.

3 Yu Giryong, "Pansori 8 myeongchang-gwa jeonseungja-deul (Eight Pansori Virtuosos and Transmitters)," in *Pansori-eui ihae* (Understanding Pansori), edited by Cho Dongil and Kim Heunggyu (Seoul: Changjak-kwa bipyeongsa, 1978), 161–2.

4 Yu Giryong, ibid.

5 Park, *Voices from the Straw Mat*, 3.

6 Ilsan, the artistic name of the late Kim Myonghwan.

7 Noshik, *Joseon changgeuksa*, 34.
8 Jeong Byeongheon, "Pansori-eui hyeongseonggwa byeonmo" (Formation and Transition of Pansori), in Gang Hanyeong (ed.), *Pansori* (Seoul: Shina chulpansa, 1988), 247–76, at 261.
9 Park, *Voices from the Straw Mat*, 176.
10 Ibid., 108–9.
11 Mihaly Csikszentmihalyi, *Flow: The Psychology of Optimal Experience* (New York: Harper & Row, 1990), 67.

Chapter 3

1 Cited in Kim Heunggyu, "Pansori ui sahoe jeok seonggyeok kwa geu byeonmo (Pansori's Social Characteristics and Change)," in Jeong Yang and Choe Donghyeon (eds.), *Pansori ui batang gwa areumdaum* (The Characteristics and Beauty of Pansori) (Seoul: Indong, 1986), 115.
2 In *Akchang deungnok* (Certified Record of Music Management), 56b–57a (22 October, 1657), cited in Peter Lee, *Sourcebook of Korean Civilization*, revised edition, vol. 2 (New York: Columbia University Press, 1996), 246–7.
3 Yi Hyegu, "Chapter 18: Song Manjae eui Gwanuhui (Gwanuhui by Song Manjae)," in *Hanguk eumak yeongu, Gungmin eumak yeonguhoe* (1957). In 1955, Yi Hyegu discovered it in the Taksamungo section at Yonsei University Library, Seoul.
4 Customarily referred to as *Manhwabon Chunhyangga*.
5 Kim Donguk, *Chunhyangjeon yeongu* (Study of the *Tale of Chunhyang*) (Seoul: Yonsei University, 1965), 75–7.
6 "廣寒樓前烏鵲橋 吾是牽牛織女爾." Gyeonu and Jingnyeo, Altair and Vega, are the celestial lovers in Korean mythology, in Yu Jinhan's *Manhwabon Chunhyangga*, in Kim Donguk (1965), 167.
7 Yu Geum, in *Gajeong mungyeon lok* (Records of Family Experiences). 先考癸酉春南遊湖南 歷觀其山川文物 其翌年春還家 作春香歌一篇 而卒被時儒之. I take this opportunity to correct my earlier mention that Yu was "stationed" in Jeolla Province, in Park, *Voices from the Straw Mat*.

8 Pihl, *Korean Singer of Tales*, 33.
9 Introduced with annotation in Hanyeong's *Shin Jaehyo pansori saseol-jip*.
10 There is thought to have been a Korean (*hangul*) handwritten manuscript. Kim Sambul's 1950 annotated version is included in Jeong Choong Kweon, "*Onggojip taryeong* (Ballad of the Curmudgeon)," in *Encyclopedia of Korean Folk Culture* (Seoul: National Folk Museum of Korea), available online: https://folkency.nfm.go.kr/kr/topic/detail/1152 (accessed April 2, 2023).
11 Wanne J. Joe, *Traditional Korea: A Cultural History* (Seoul: ChungAng University Press, 1972), 427.
12 Ibid., 425.
13 Lee, *A New History of Korea*, 261.
14 Also see Pak Hwang, *Pansori ibaengnyeonsa* (Two-Hundred Year History of Pansori) (Seoul: Sasang sahoe yeonguso [Ideology and Society Research Institute], 1987), 112.
15 Hanyeong, *Shin Jaehyo pansori saseol-jip*, 1.
16 Pihl, *Korean Singer of Tales*, 96–7.
17 Ibid., 97.
18 Ibid., 98.
19 Ibid.
20 Shin Jaehyo, *Dorihwaga* (Song of Peach and Plum Blossoms), in Hanyeong, *Shin Jaehyo pansori saseol-jip*, 687–9.
21 Pihl, *Korean Singer of Tales*, 101.
22 Translated in Pihl, *Korean Singer of Tales*, 101. The letter had been in the safekeeping of Shin Jaehyo's great-grandson. It was published in Gang Hanyeong, "Pansori-ui iron (Theory of Pansori)." See Gang, *Gugeo gungmunhak* (The Korean Language and Literature), 49–50 (September 1970): 13.
23 Pihl, *Korean Singer of Tales*, 100.
24 Ibid., 32–3.
25 In Noshik, *Joseon changgeuksa*, 17–18.
26 Cho Dongil, *Hanguk munhak tongsa III*, 178, translated and cited by Pihl (1994), 34.
27 Pihl (1994), 34.

28 Noshik, 30–1, translated and cited in Pihl, *Korean Singer of Tales*, 34–5.
29 Pihl, *Korean Singer of Tales*, 35.
30 Ibid., 32–3.
31 Ibid.
32 Shin Jaehyo, *Gwangdaega* (Song of Gwangdae), in Hanyeong, *Shin Jaehyo pansori saseol-jip*, 669–70. Pihl's translation can be found in his *Korean Singer of Tales* (1994).
33 Yi Bohyeong, "Pansori-ran mueosinya? (What is Pansori?)," in *The Deep-Rooted Three Pansori Collection: Chunhyang-Ga Song by Sang-Hyon Cho, with Drum Accompaniment by Myong Hwan Kim* (Seoul: Korean Britannica Corporation, 1982), 17–21.
34 Noshik, *Joseon changgeuksa*, 74.
35 They are: *Sansi cheonglam* 山市 晴嵐, "Haze shimmer on mountain village"; *Eochon seokcho* 漁村夕照, "Fishing village in sunset"; *Weonpo gwibeom* 遠浦歸帆, "Boat returns to harbor afar"; *Sosang yau* 瀟湘夜雨, "Night rain on So & Sang river"; *Yeonsa manjong* 煙寺晚鍾, "Foggy temple, evening bell"; *Dongjeong chuweol* 洞庭秋月, "Dongjeong Lake, autumn moon"; *Pyeongsa nagan* 平沙落雁, "Geese fall on sand bank"; *Gangcheon moseol* 江天暮雪, "Evening snowfall on river."
36 Noshik, *Joseon changgeuksa*, 76.
37 Nipponophone 6131, in 1913, reproduced in mid-1920.
38 Noshik, *Joseon changgeuksa*, 18–20.
39 Traditional, popularized by Gweon Samdeuk. I learned it from Han Nongseon.
40 Prehistoric legendary king who invented the fishing net and the Eight Trigrams for divination.
41 From 鳶飛戾天 魚躍于淵 in *Sigyeong* (C. Xijing 詩經, Book of Poetry), "Kite is circling the sky, fish are jumping in the pond." This expression in the song describes the kite following its routine, while Nolbo, eager to catch a swallow, is startled and all ears.
42 火及棟梁 燕雀何知, from a divination in the *Tojeong bigyeol*, annual fortune people in Korea read. "Fire reaches the girder,

but how would swallows and sparrows in the nest at the tip of the eaves know it?" If a person is so divined, he must be careful from the beginning of the year.

43 Noshik, *Joseon changgeuksa*, 24.
44 Traditional, popularized by Song Mangap. I learned it from Master Chung Kwonjin.
45 Noshik, *Joseon changgeuksa*, 43.
46 *Ibyeolga* (Parting Song), Traditional. I learned this song from Master Chung Kwonjin.
47 A nineteenth-century painting by an anonymous artist, the work is a ten-panel panorama that includes a painting of a pansori performance along the Daedong River, currently in the Seoul National University Museum.
48 This version of the traditional song is credited to Mo Heunggap, in Noshik, *Joseon changgeuksa*, 28.
49 Traditional, Boseongsori version.
50 In Noshik, *Joseon changgeuksa*, 234–9.
51 Part of a poem ascribed to An Minyeong (1816–unknown), singer and co-compiler of the poetic songbook titled *Gagok weollyu* (歌曲源流, 1876), with his teacher Pak Hyogwan. Includes 26 of his own works among more than 800 songs.
52 *Nyang* is a unit of Old Korean coinage; one *nyang* is about 37.5 g, and equivalent to ten *don*.
53 Kim Sejong quoted in Noshik, *Joseon changgeuksa*, 63–5.
54 Ibid.
55 Ibid.
56 Traditional, I learned it from Master Chung Kwonjin.

Chapter 4

1 Michael J. Pettid, "Introduction," in Michael J. Pettid (ed.), *Silvery World and Other Stories: Anthology of Korean Literature* (Ithaca, NY: Cornell University Press, 2019), 17.

2 See Julia Kristeva, *Powers of Horror: An Essay on Abjection*, translated by Leon Roudiez (New York: Columbia University Press, 1982).

3 Kelly Oliver, *The Colonization of Psychic Space: A Psychoanalytic Social Theory of Oppression* (Minneapolis, MN: University of Minnesota Press, 2004), 83.

4 Yeonho and Sangu, *Wuri yeongeuk 100 nyeon* (*100 Years of Our Drama and Theatre*) (Seoul: Hyeonamsa, 2000), 26.

5 Ibid., 28–9.

6 Iyagi gyeongyeong yeonguso, "Gwanghwamun negeori 'ginyeombijeon'-eul asyimnika? (Do You Know the History of the 'Memorial Monument' on the Gwanhwamun Intersection?)," online editorial, July 20, 2016, available at: http://www.storybiz.co.kr/?p=13657 (March 10, 2023).

7 Gweon Dohui, "Daehan Jegukki hwangsil geukchangeui daejung geukchang euroeui jeonhwan gwajeonge daehan yeongu (Study of the Transformation of the Royal Theatre into Popular Theatre during the Days of the Great Korean Empire)," *Gugakwon nonmunjip* (*Journal of National Gugak Center, JKTPA*), 32 (2015): 97–120, at 99.

8 From an article in *Daehan Maeilsinbo* (Daily Newspaper), July 3, 1909.

9 Yi Duhyeon, *Hanguk shingeuksa yeongu* (Study of Korean New Drama) (Seoul: Seoul National University Press, 1966); Yeonho and Sangu, *Wuri yeongeuk 100 nyeon*; Pak Hwang, *Pansori ibaengnyeonsa*.

10 Pak Hwang, *Pansori ibaengnyeonsa*, 139.

11 Pak Hwang, *Changgeuksa yeongu* (Study of the History of Singing Drama) (Seoul: Paengnok chulpansa, 1976), 64.

12 Pak Hwang, *Pansori ibaengnyeonsa*, 143–4.

13 Ibid.

14 Yu Minyeong, "Changgeuk," in *Encyclopedia of Korean Culture*, Academy of Korean Studies, 1995, available online: http://encykorea.aks.ac.kr/Contents/Item/E005534 (March 13, 2023).

15 Pak Hwang, *Pansori ibaengnyeonsa*, 142.

NOTES

16 Two-part novel published by Dongmunsa in 1908. Part Two is missing and is not available to contemporary readers.
17 *Hwangseong Shinmun*, July 28, 1908.
18 Lee Jinhyoung introduces the poet and literary critic Im Hwa in, "Hybridity, and the Anti-Colonial Politics," *Kritika Kultura*, 30 (2018): 261.
19 Ibid., 260.
20 Sora Kim Russell's translation of the novel *Silvery World* by Yi Injik (1862–1916), in Pettid (ed.), *Silvery World and Other Stories*, 27–144. Translated excerpts and summary narratives are my own. The original text of *Eunsegye* is in the public domain.
21 The cover page of a copy of the novel shows in handwriting *shin-yeongeuk* ("new theatre").
22 Killick (2010), 62.
23 Ibid.
24 Chan E. Park, Translation from Yi Injik, *Eunsegye*, 1908, Public Domain.
25 Chan E. Park, Translation of *Song of Heungbo*, Traditional. I learned the song from Han Nongseon, 1993.
26 See Kim Kiran, "A Study on the Yeun-Se-Gae (Eunsegye), the First 'Shin-yeun-Guik (New Theatre, 신연극)' Performance in Korea," *Hanguk geundae munhak yeongu*, no. 16 (2007).
27 Yeonho and Sangu, *Wuri yeongeuk 100 nyeon*, 54.
28 Hong Giltong-jeon written by Heo Gyun (1569–1618), about the difficult life of the illegitimately born Giltong. Through miraculous good fortune and his own valorous conduct, he eventually becomes king.
29 Yi Haejo, *Jayujong* (Liberty Bell) (Seoul: Gwanghakseopo, 1910), Public Domain, 23.
30 Lee Jisun, "Aspects of the Traditional Japanese Performances in Japanese Theatres in Seoul between 1900s and 1910s," *Gugakweon nonmunjip* (*JKTPA*), 31 (2015).
31 Chan Park, translation of Jo Junghwan, *Byeongja Samin* (병자삼인), Maeil Shinbo November 17, 1912–December 25, 1912 edition, Public Domain, 3–5.

32 Ibid.

33 Ibid., 84–99.

34 Ryu Kyeong Ho (유경호), "A Comparative Study on Acting Types of Chang-keuk & Shinpa-keuk," *Pansori yeongu* (*Journal of Pansori*), 34 (2012): 106–42, at 113–14.

35 Baek Hyeonmi (백현미), *Hanguk changgeuksa yeongu* (Study of the History of Korean Changgeuk) (Seoul: Taehaksa, 1997), 24–5.

36 Ibid., 114–15.

37 Yu Minyeong, *Hanguk hyeondae huigoksa* (History of Modern Korean Drama) (Seoul: Hongseong shinseo, 1982), 22.

38 Killick (2010), 76.

39 Pak Hwang, *Pansori ibaengnyeonsa*, 172.

40 Ibid., 152–67.

41 Noshik, *Joseon changgeuksa*, 184; also in Pak Hwang, *Pansori ibaengnyeonsa*, 154.

42 Pak Hwang, *Pansori ibaengnyeonsa*, 165–6.

43 Ibid.

44 Son Taedo, "Yeoseong gukkeuk (Women's National Drama)," in *Encyclopedia of Korean Folk Culture*, National Folk Museum of Korea, n.d., available online: https://folkency.nfm.go.kr/topic/detail/6304 (accessed March 5, 2023).

45 In Pak Hwang, *Pansori ibaengnyeonsa*, 167.

46 Ibid., 206–7.

47 Ibid., 208–9.

48 Ibid., 217.

49 Ibid., 219.

50 Ibid., 239–40.

51 Ibid., 293.

52 Homi K. Bhabha, *The Location of Culture* (London: Routledge, 1994), 66.

53 Yu Minyeong, "Changgeuk."

54 Bhabha, ibid., 2.

Chapter 5

1 Yoo Youngdai, "Pansori jeonseung hyeonhwanggwa bojon bangan (Current Status of the Traditions of Pansori and the Means of Preservation)," *Pansori yeongu (Journal of Pansori)*, 36 (2014): 352.

2 Ibid., 366.

3 Song Mi-Sook, "A Study on the Title and the Selection of Important Intangible Cultural Asset Learners," *Urichumgwa gwahak gisul* (Our National Dance and Science and Technology), 9, 1 (2013): 9–31.

4 Walter Ong cites Jurij Lotman, *The Structure of the Artistic Text*, translated by Ronald Vroon (Ann Arbor, MI: University of Michigan Press, 1977), in *Orality and Literacy* (1982), 75.

5 Ong (1982), 74–5.

6 Ibid., 77.

7 Ferdinand de Saussure, *Course in General Linguistics*, edited by Charles Bally and Albert Sechehaye in collaboration with Albert Riedlinger, translated with an introduction and notes by Wade Baskin (New York: McGraw-Hill Book Company, 1959), 23.

8 Jocelyn Clark, "*Sanjo* for *Sanjo*'s Sake: Weaving the Living Tradition," in R. Anderson Sutton (ed.), *Perspectives on Korean Music: Sanjo and Issues of Improvisation in Musical Traditions of Asia*, Volume 1 – Fall 2010 (Seoul: Ministry of Culture, Sports and Tourism Republic of Korea, Fall 2010), 77–91, 85.

9 Pak Hwang, *Pansori ibaengnyeonsa*, 78.

10 Ibid., 78–80.

11 This is an anecdote that circulated among Master Chung's students and was told to me as I trained in his school.

12 Park, *Voices from the Straw Mat*, 162.

13 Heonbong, *Changak daegang*, 70.

14 Pak Hwang, *Pansori ibaengnyeonsa*, 104–5.

15 Comment by Pak Dongjin (1916–2003), in Honolulu, 1993.

16 Jeong Jeongnyeol interview in *Maeil shinbo*, May 5, 1937, in Choi Hyejin, "Study on Critical References in Relation to

Modern Pansori (근대판소리비평자료의 검토)," *Pansori yeongu* (*Journal of Pansori*), 38 (2014): 145.

17 Reynaldo Hahn, *On Singers and Singing*, translated by Léopold Simoneau, O.C. (Portland, OR: Amadeus Press, 1990), 121.

18 Epigram from the *Gangsanche Poseongsori* school, transmitted by Chung Kwonjin.

19 John Lutterbie, "Neuroscience and Creativity in the Rehearsal Process," in Bruce McConachie and F. Elizabeth Hart (eds.), *Performance and Cognition: Theatre Studies and the Cognitive Turn* (New York: Routledge, 2006), 149.

20 Bhabha, *Location of Culture*, 216.

21 Seo Yu Kyung, "A Study on the Reflection of City Culture in the Modern Reproductions of Pansori Works," *Pansori yeongu* (*Journal of Pansori*), 41 (2016): 116.

22 Shim Cheong's monologue from Kim Gyutaek's *Modern Shim Cheong*, in Kyung, ibid., 120.

23 In *Song of Chunhyang*, Traditional. I learned this from Master Chung Kwonjin.

24 Writing and illustration by Kim Gyutaek, serialized in the *Jeilseon Magazine*, November 1932–March 1933. Photo at: parkseokhwan.com.

25 From *Modern Chunhyang Jeon*, Episode 21, in Seo Eun-young, "The Laughter and Aesthetics of Korea Manwha in 1920–30s," *Korean Cartoon and Animation Studies*, 46 (2017): 170.

26 Bhabha, *Location of Culture*, 216.

27 Bonnie Marranca and Gautam Dasgupta, "Preface," in Bonnie Marranca and Gautam Dasgupta (eds.), *Interculturalism and Performance* (New York: PAJ Publications, 1991), 15.

28 Ah-jeong Kim, and R. B. Graves, *The Metacultural Theatre of Oh Taeseok* (Honolulu, HI: University of Hawai'i Press, 1999), 2.

29 Ibid., 3.

30 Ibid.

31 Achim Freyer at Press Conference, *The Korea Herald*, Reporter: Park Min-young, March 29, 2011.

32 Andrei Serban at Press Conference, appeared in the *Korea Herald*, November 5, 2014.

33 Choe Keysook, "The Meeting of Changgeuk and Greek Tragedy: Transcultural and Transhistorical Practice of Korean Pansori-Changgeuk and the Case of Medea," *Korea Journal*, 56, 4 (2016): 67.

34 Keith Howard (2018), 210–11, cites from Nicholas Harkness, *Songs of Seoul: An Ethnography of Voice and Voicing in Christian South Korea* (Berkeley, Los Angeles, CA, and London: University of California Press, 2014), 150–7, 175–81.

35 Heather A. Willoughby, "Melding Past and Present: Korean Identities in Contemporary P'ansori Performances," *Journal of Musicology* 音.樂.學, 18, 1 (2010): 202–6.

36 Ibid.

37 Hilary Vanessa Finchum-Sung, "Designing a Fresh Tradition: Young Gugak and Sonic Imaginings for a Progressive Korea," *The World of Music (New Series)*, 1, 1 (2012): 124.

38 R. Anderson Sutton, "'Fusion' and Questions of Korean Cultural Identity in Music,'" *Korean Studies*, 35 (2011): 4.

39 "*Dongne sorikkun 'Ttorang Gwangdae'* (Village Pansori Singer in the Gully)," Saepansori gwangdae Kim Myeongja interview by Jeon Hyeyoung (2005).

40 Kim Kee Hyung, "The Character and the Modern Transformation of the 'Ddorang Kwangdae,'" *Pansori yeongu (Journal of Pansori)*, 18 (2004): 7–23.

41 Translated excerpt from the pamphlet for the Second Annual Ttorang Gwangdae Contest, in Kim Kee Hyung, "The Character," 14–15.

42 Richard Bauman, "Folklore," in Richard Bauman (eds.), *Folklore, Cultural Performances, and Popular Entertainments* (Oxford: Oxford University Press, 1992), 32 3.

43 Ana Yates-Lu, "When K-Pop and Kugak Meet: Popularising P'ansori in Modern Korea," *Yearbook for Traditional Music*, 51 (2019): 53.

44 Gwak Byeong Chang, "Performance Strategy of New Pansori 'Leafie, a Hen into the Wild,'" *Pansori yeongu (Journal of Pansori)*, 52 (2020): 184.

45 Gwak Byeong-Chang, "Key Elements of Minhwa in Go Seon-woong's Changgeuk," *Pansori yeongu* (*Journal of Pansori*), 50 (2020): 101.

46 See *Huong-eui huimang ilgi* (Huong's Hope Diary), in Gwak Byeong Chang, "The Originality and Modernity Revealed in Two 'Creative Chang-geuk' – Focused on 'Mother's Arirang' and 'Huong's Hope Diary,'" *Pansori yeongu* (*Journal of Pansori*), 46 (2018): 89–133.

47 Bae Yeon Hyung, in "A Study on Song Yeong-Seok's Pansori, Yeoksa-ga," introduces Song and his work originally published in *Hwajeong Gayojip* (1957), *Pansori yeongu* (*Journal of Pansori*), 45 (2018): 116.

48 Bae Yeon Hyung, "A Study on Song Yeong-Seok's Pansori, Yeoksa-ga," 88.

49 Yoo Yeongdae, "Changjak pansori Yeolsaga'e daehayeo (About the Creative Pansori Yeolsaga)," *Pansori yeongu* (*Journal of Pansori*), 3 (1992): 370–2, 371.

50 Translated from Jeong Sunim's version of the *Yu Gwansun Yeolsaga* (c. 1945).

51 Kim Jiha, "Five Bandits," in *Sasanggye* (World of Ideology) (Seoul: Gungmin Sasang Yeonguweon (Center for Research of National Ideology), Ministry of Culture and Education, May 1970), page numbers unknown.

Chapter 6

1 Tami Spry, "Autoethnography and the Other: Performative Embodiment and a Bid for Utopia," in Norman K. Denzin and Yvonna S. Lincoln (eds.), *The Sage Handbook of Qualitative Research*, 5th ed. (Thousand Oaks, CA: Sage, 2017), 643–4.

2 Duke Jing of Qi, ruled the State of Qi, 547–490 BCE.

3 Emperor Wu of Han, reigned 141–87 BCE.

4 Traditional song that was popularized by the performances of Im Bangul (1904–61).

5 *Anja Chunchu*, 晏子春秋, Book One. 及晏子卒, 公出屛而立曰：嗚呼! 昔者從夫子而游公阜, 夫子一日而三責我, 今誰責寡人哉?

6 The title of "Master" is gender neutral, indicating mastery in a performing art tradition.

7 Jeong Sukhui, "To Be Selected as Overseas Honorary Transmitter" (해외 명예전승자' 에 뽑혀), *The Korea Times*, June 19, 2014.

8 Yeongeuk. Muyong. Misul. Eumak eui "Hanmadang" / Jugeum juje "haengdong yesulche" (Grand Stage of Theatre. Dance. Fine Art. Music / Performance Art on the Theme of Death), *The JoongAng*, July 22, 1987.

9 Lyrics by Chan E. Park, "In 1903, Pak Heungbo Went to Hawai'i," in Nora Okja Keller, Brenda Kwon, Sun Namkung, Gary Park, and Kathy Song (eds.), *Yobo: Korean American Writing in Hawai'i* (Honolulu, HI: Bamboo Ridge Press, 2003), 23.

10 Refrain from *Farmers' Ballad*, a traditional song. Adapted by Chan E. Park.

11 Lyrics by Chan E. Park.

12 Lyrics by Chan E. Park.

13 Jeong was reported to have committed suicide by jumping from his twelfth-story office after facing prosecution for illegal financial activities involving the North Korean state. Seoul, "Hyundai Boss Jumps to His Death," *Guardian*, August 4, 2003, available online: https://www.theguardian.com/world/2003/aug/04/northkorea (accessed March 2, 2023).

14 Lyrics by Kathy Foley, from unpublished script by Kathy Foley and Chan E. Park.

15 Lyrics by Chan E. Park, ibid.

16 Lyrics by Kathy Foley, ibid.

17 In Jieun Kiaer and Loli Kim, "One-Inch-Tall Barrier of Subtitles: Translating Invisibility in *Parasite*," in Youna Kim (ed.), *The Soft Power of the Korean Wave: Parasite, BTS and Drama* (London: Routledge, 2022), 90.

Conclusion

1 Cited in Victor Turner, *From Ritual to Theatre: The Human Seriousness of Play* (New York: PAJ Publications, 1982), 24–5.
2 Ibid.
3 Marranca and Dasgupta, "Preface," 14.
4 Edward V. B. Miller, "Authoritarianism: The American Cults and Their Intellectual Antecedents" (PhD dissertation, University of Hawai'i, Honolulu, 1979), 368.

BIBLIOGRAPHY

Aristotle. "Section 1, Part I." *Poetics*. Translated by S. H. Butcher, *Internet Classics Archive*. c. 350 BCE. Available online: http://classics.mit.edu/Aristotle/poetics.1.1.html (accessed March 15, 2023).

Aristotle. "Book Eight, Part Five." *Politics*. Translated by Benjamin Jowett, *Internet Classics Archive*, c. 350 BCE. Available online: http://classics.mit.edu/Aristotle/politics.8.eight.html (accessed March 15, 2023).

Associated Press. "Hyundai Boss Jumps to His Death." *Guardian*, August 4, 2003. Available online: https://www.theguardian.com/world/2003/aug/04/northkorea (accessed January 3, 2023).

Author Unknown. "Yeongeuk. Muyong. Misul. Eumak eui 'Hanmadang' / Jugeum juje 'haengdong yesulche' (Grand Stage of Theatre. Dance. Fine Art. Music / Performance Art on the theme of Death)." The JoongAng. July 22, 1987. Available online: https://www.joongang.co.kr/article/2109705#home (accessed January 5, 2023).

Bae, Yeon-Hyung. "A Study on Song Yeong-Seok's Pansori, Yeoksa-ga ('A Chant on Korean History')." *Pansori yeongu* (*Journal of Pansori*), 45 (2018): 87–117.

Bae, Yeon-Hyung. "Pansori yupa-eui gaenyeom-gwa hyeonsil" (Study of the Concept and Reality of Pansori Faction). *Pansori yeongu* (*Journal of Pansori*), 52 (2021): 39–84.

Baek Hyeonmi (백현미). *Hanguk changgeuksa yeongu* (Study of the History of Korean Canggeuk). Seoul: Taehaksa, 1997.

Bakhtin, Mikhail M. *The Dialogic Imagination*. Edited by Michael Holquist and translated by Caryl Emerson and Michael Holquist. Austin, TX: University of Texas Press, 1981.

Bauman, Richard. "Folklore." In Richard Bauman (ed.), *Folklore, Cultural Performances, and Popular Entertainments*, 29–40. Oxford: Oxford University Press, 1992.

Bauman, Richard, ed. *Folklore, Cultural Performances, and Popular Entertainments*. Oxford: Oxford University Press, 1992.

Bhabha, Homi K. *The Location of Culture*. London and New York: Routledge, 1994.

Cho, Dongil. *Hanguk munhak tongsa* (Comprehensive History of Korean Literature). Vol. 3. Seoul: Jisik saneopsa, 1989.

Cho, Dongil. "Two Stages of Transition from Premodern to Modern in Korean Literature." Paper presented at the Pacific Rim Korean Studies Conference, Honolulu, Hawai'i, 1992.

Choe, Donghyeon. *Pansori yeongu*. Seoul: Munhak Academisa, 1991.

Choe, Keysook. "The Meeting of Changgeuk and Greek Tragedy: Transcultural and Transhistorical Practice of Korean Pansori-Changgeuk and the Case of Medea." *Korea Journal*, 56, 4 (2016): 62–91.

Choi, Hyejin. "Study on Critical References in Relation to Modern Pansori." *Pansori yeongu* (*Journal of Pansori*), 38 (2014): 121–52.

Clark, Jocelyn. "*Sanjo* for *Sanjo*'s Sake: Weaving the Living Tradition." In R. Anderson Sutton (ed.), *Perspectives on Korean Music: Sanjo and Issues of Improvisation in Musical Traditions of Asia*. Volume 1 – Fall 2010, 77–91. Seoul: The Ministry of Culture, Sports and Tourism Republic of Korea.

Confucius (551–479 BCE). *Akki* (樂記 Record of Music) 19. In *Yegi* (禮記 *Book of Ceremonies*).

Csikszentmihalyi, Mihaly. *Flow: The Psychology of Optimal Experience*. New York: Harper & Row, 1990.

Cummings, Bruce. *Korea's Place in the Sun: A Modern History*. New York: W. W. Norton & Company, 2005.

Eklund, Elizabeth. "Memory and Enshrining Writing: Rethinking the Ethnocentrism Imbedded in Written vs. Oral Traditions." *Arizona Anthropologist*, 28 (2017): 76–87.

Finchum-Sung, Hilary Vanessa. "Designing a Fresh Tradition: Young Kugak and Sonic Imaginings for a Progressive Korea." *World of Music*, 1, 1 (2012): 121–44.

Gang, Hanyeong. "Pansori-eui iron" (Theory of Pansori). *Gugeo gungmunhak* (Study of Korean Language and Literature), 49–50 (1970): 9–16.

Gang, Hanyeong, ed. *Shin Jaehyo pansori saseoljip* (Collection of Shin Jaehyo's Pansori Libretti). Seoul: Minjung seogwan, 1971.

Goody, Jack, and Ian Watt. "The Consequences of Literacy." *Comparative Studies in Society and History*, 5, 3 (1963): 304–45.

Gwak, Byeong-Chang. "Key Elements of Minhwa in Go Seon-woong's Changgeuk." *Pansori yeongu (Journal of Pansori)*, 50 (2020): 75–120.

Gwak, Byeong-Chang. "Performance strategy of New Pansori 'Leafie, a Hen into the Wild.'" *Pansori yeongu (Journal of Pansori)*, 52 (2021): 143–84.

Gwak, Byeong-Chang. "The Originality and Modernity Revealed in Two 'Creative Chang-geuk' – Focused on 'Mother's arirang' and 'Huong's Hope Diary.'" *Pansori yeongu (Journal of Pansori)*, 46 (2018): 89–133.

Gweon, Dohui. "Daehan Jegukki hwangsil geukchang-eui daejung geukchang euro-eui jeonhwan gwajeong-e daehan yeongu" (Study of the Transformation of the Royal Theatre into Popular Theatre during the Days of the Great Korean Empire). *Gugakwon nonmunjip (Journal of National Gugak Center, JKTPA)*, 32 (2015): 97–120.

Gutmanis, June. *Na Pule Kahiko* (Ancient Hawai'ian Prayers). Honolulu, HI: Editions Limited, 1983, 66–7.

Hahn, Reynaldo. *On Singers and Singing*. Translated by Léopold Simoneau, O.C. Portland, OR: Amadeus Press, 1990.

Howard, Keith. "Chapter Ten. Korean Music: Definitions and Practices." In Reinhard Strohm (ed.), *Studies on a Global History of Music: A Balzan Musicology Project*, 198–219. London: Routledge, 2018.

Hwang, Kyung Moon. *A History of Korea*. New York: Palgrave MacMillan, 2010.

Hwang, Sun-Mi. *Madang-eul naon amtark* (Hen Who Dreamed She Could Fly). Seoul: Sagyejeol chulpansa, 2000.

Iryeon. *Samguk Yusa* (Memorabilia of the Three Kingdoms), Book One. Originally published in 1281. Original publisher unknown. Reprinted by Choe Namseon. Seoul: Minjung Seogwan, 1969.

Jeong, Byeongheon. "Pansori-eui hyeongseonggwa byeonmo" (Pansori Formation and Transition). In Gang Hanyeong (ed.), *Pansori*, 247–76. Seoul: Shina chulpansa, 1988.

Jeon, Hyeyoung. "Dongne sorikkun 'Ttorang Gwangdae'" (Village Pansori Singer in the Gully). Interview with Saepansori gwangdae Kim Myeongja. *Godae Sinmun*. September 26, 2005. Available

online: https://www.kunews.ac.kr/news/articleView.html?idxno= 6455 (accessed March 10, 2023).
Jeong, Byeonguk. *Hanguk-eui pansori* (Korean Pansori). Seoul: Jimmundang, 1981.
Jeong, Choong Kweon. "*Onggojip taryeong* (Ballad of the Curmudgeon)." *Encyclopedia of Korean Folk Culture*. Seoul: National Folk Museum of Korea, n.d. Available online: https://folkency.nfm.go.kr/kr/topic/detail/1152 (accessed April 2, 2023).
Jeong, Noshik, *Joseon changgeuksa* (History of Korean Singing Drama). Seoul: Joseon ilbosa, 1940.
Jeong, Sukhui. "To Be Selected as Overseas Honorary Transmitter (해외 명예전승자' 에 뽑혀)." *The Korea Times*. June 19, 2014.
Joe, Wanne J. *Traditional Korea: A Cultural History*. Seoul: ChungAng University Press, 1972.
Kiaer, Jieun, and Loli Kim. "One-Inch-Tall Barrier of Subtitles: Translating Invisibility in *Parasite*.' In Youna Kim (ed.), *The Soft Power of the Korean Wave: Parasite, BTS and Drama*, 90–103. London: Routledge, 2022.
Killick, Andrew. *In Search of Korean Traditional Opera: Discourses of Ch'anggŭk*. Honolulu, HI: University of Hawai'i Press, 2010.
Kim, Ah-jeong, and R. B. Graves. "Introduction." In *The Metacultural Theatre of Oh Taeseok*, 1–20. Honolulu, HI: University of Hawai'i Press, 1999.
Kim, Donguk. *Chunhyangjeon yeongu* (Study of the Tale of Chunhyang). Seoul: Yonsei University, 1965.
Kim, Heunggyu. "Pansori-eui sahoe-jeok seonggyeok-kwa geu byeonmo" (Pansori's Social Characteristics and Change). In Jeong Yang and Choe Donghyeon (eds.), *Pansori-eui batang-gwa areumdaum* (The Characteristics and Beauty of Pansori), 102–36. Seoul: Indong, 1986.
Kim, Kee Hyung. "The Character and the Modern Transformation of the "ddorang kwangdae.'" *Pansori yeongu* (*Journal of Pansori*), 18 (2004): 7–23.
Kim, Kiran. "A Study on the Yeun-Se-Gae (Eunsegye), the First 'Shin-yeun-Guik' (New-Theatre) Performance in Korea." *Hanguk munhak geundae yeongu*, 16 (2007): 195–241.
Kim, Sug-bae. "Jaonggoje Pansori and Park Dong-jin's Pansori." *Pansori yeongu* (*Journal of Pansori*), 49 (2020): 47–80.
Kristeva, Julia. *Powers of Horror: An Essay on Abjection*. Translated by Leon S. Roudiez. New York: Columbia University Press, 1982.

Lee, Jinhyoung. "Hybridity, and the Anti-Colonial Politics." *Kritika Kultura*, 30 (2018): 260–75.

Lee, Jisun (Yi Jiseon). "Aspects of the Traditional Japanese Performances in Japanese Theatres in Seoul between 1900s and 1910s." *Journal of National Gugak Center (JKTPA)*, 31 (2015): 145–90.

Lee, Ki-baik. *A New History of Korea*. Translated by Edward W. Wagner with Edward J. Shultz. Cambridge, MA: Harvard University Press, 1984.

Lee, Peter H. ed. *Sourcebook of Korean Civilization*. Vol. 2. New York: Columbia University Press, 1996.

Lord, Albert B. *The Singer of Tales*. Cambridge, MA: Harvard University Press, 1960.

Lutterbie, John. "Neuroscience and Creativity in the Rehearsal Process." In Bruce McConachie and F. Elizabeth Hart (eds.), *Performance and Cognition: Theatre Studies and the Cognitive Turn*, 149–66. London and New York: Routledge, 2006.

MacDonald, Margaret Mead. "Editor's Note." In Margaret Mead MacDonald (ed.), *Traditional Storytelling Today: An International Sourcebook*, xiii–xiv. Chicago, IL, and London: Fitzroy Dearborn Publishers, 1999.

Marranca, Bonnie, and Gautam Dasgupta. "Preface." In Bonnie Marranca and Gautam Dasgupta (eds.), *Interculturalism and Performance*, 9–23. New York: PAJ Publications, 1991.

Miller, Edward V. B. "Authoritarianism: The American Cults and Their Intellectual Antecedents." PhD diss., University of Hawai'i, Honolulu, HI, 1979.

Miller, Richard. *The Structure of Singing: System and Art in Vocal Technique*. 1st ed. New York: Schirmer Books, 1986.

Motokiyo, Zeami. "Fushikaden (Style and the Flower)." In *On the Art of the Nō Drama: The Major Treatises of Zeami*, translated by J. Thomas Rimer and Yamazaki Masakazu, 27–30. Princeton, NJ: Princeton University Press, 1984.

O'Shea, Suzanne, and Miroslave Holub. "Interview with Miroslav Holub." *The Poetry Ireland Review*, 30 (1990): 62–70.

Oliver, Kelly. *The Colonization of Psychic Space: A Psychoanalytic Social Theory of Oppression*. Minneapolis, MN: University of Minnesota Press, 2004.

Ong, Walter J. *Orality and Literacy: The Technogizing of the Word*. London and New York: Routledge, 1982.

Pak, Heonbong. *Changak daegang* (Survey of Vocal Music). Seoul: Gugak yesul hakkyo chulpanbu, 1966.

Pak, Hwang. *Changgeuksa yeongu* (Study of the History of Singing Drama). Seoul: Paengnok chulpansa, 1976.

Pak, Hwang. *Pansori ibaengnyeonsa* (Two-Hundred Year History of Pansori). Seoul: Sasang sahoe yeonguso (Ideology and Society Research Institute), 1987.

Park, Chan E. "In 1903, Pak Heungbo Went to Hawai'i." In Nora Okja Keller, Brenda Kwon, Sun Namkung, Gary Park, and Kathy Song (eds.), *Yobo: Korean American Writing in Hawai'i*, 23–34. Honolulu, HI: Bamboo Ridge Press, 2003.

Park, Chan E. *Voices from the Straw Mat: Toward an Ethnography of Korean Story Singing*. Honolulu, HI: University of Hawai'i Press, 2003.

Pettid, Michael J. "Introduction." In Michael J. Pettid (ed.), *Silvery World and Other Stories: Anthology of Korean Literature*, 1–26. Ithaca, NY: Cornell University Press, 2019.

Pihl, Marshall R. *The Korean Singer of Tales*. Cambridge, MA: Harvard University Press, 1994.

Plato. *Republic*. Book III, 400a–402c. *Complete Works of Plato*. Edited by John M. Cooper. Indianapolis, IN: Hackett Publishing, 1997.

Ryu, Kyeong Ho (유경호). "A Comparative Study on Acting Types of Chang-keuk and Shinpa-keuk." *Pansori yeongu* (*Journal of Pansori*), 34 (2012): 106–42.

Saussure, Ferdinand de. *Course in General Linguistics*. Edited by Charles Bally and Albert Sechehaye and translated by Wade Baskin. New York, Toronto, London: McGraw-Hill Book Company, 1959.

Scholes, Robert, and Robert Kellogg. *The Nature of Narrative*. London: Oxford University Press, 1966.

Seo, Daeseok. "Issues in Pansori Research." *Seoul Journal of Korean Studies*, 1 (1988): 113–25.

Seo, Eun-young. "1920–30 nyeondae Hanguk manhwa-eui useum-gwa mihak-jeok teukching" (The Laughter and Aesthetics of Korean Manhwa in 1920–30s). *Korean Cartoon and Animation Studies*, 46 (2017): 151–79.

Seo, Yeonho, and Yi Sangu. *Wuri yeongeuk 100 nyeon* (100 Years of Our Drama and Theatre). Seoul: Hyeonamsa, 2000.

Seo, Yukyung. "A Study on the Reflection of City Culture in the Modern Reproductions of Pansori Works." *Pansori yeongu* (*Journal of Pansori*), 41 (2016): 107–33.
Son, Taedo. "Yeoseong gukkeuk" (Women's National Drama). In *Encyclopedia of Korean Folk Culture* (n.d.). Seoul: National Folk Museum of Korea. Available online: https://folkency.nfm.go.kr/topic/detail/6304 (accessed March 5, 2023).
Song, Mi-Sook. "A Study on the Title and the Selection of Important Intangible Cultural Asset Learners." *Urichum-gwa gwahak gisul* (Our National Dance and Science and Technology), 9, 1 (2013): 9–31.
Spry, Tami. "Autoethnography and the Other: Performative Embodiment and a Bid for Utopia." In Norman K. Denzin and Yvonna S. Lincoln (eds.), *Sage Handbook of Qualitative Research*, 5th edn, 627–49. Thousand Oaks, CA: Sage, 2017.
Stanley, John. *Classical Music*. London: Mitchell Beazley, 1994.
Sutton, R. Anderson. "'Fusion' and Questions of Korean Cultural Identity in Music." *Korean Studies*, 35 (2011): 4–24.
Turner, Victor. *From Ritual to Theatre: The Human Seriousness of Play*. New York: PAJ Publications, 1982.
Willoughby, Heather A. "Melding Past and Present: Korean Identities in Contemporary P'ansori Performances." 音.樂.學 *Eum.ak.hak*, 18, 1 (2010): 187–220.
Yates-Lu, Anna. "When K-Pop and Kugak Meet: Popularising P'ansori in Modern Korea." *Yearbook for Traditional Music*, 51 (2019): 49–71.
Yi, Bohyung. "Hanguk eumak-eui 'sigimsae' yeongu bangbeop siron: minsok eumak-eul jungsimeuro (An Essay on the Method of *Sigimsae* Studies)." *Eumak rondan*, 13 (1999): 1–18.
Yi, Bohyung. "Pansori-ran mueosinya? (What is Pansori?)." In *The Deep-Rooted Three Pansori Collection; Chunhyang-Ga Song by Sang-Hyon Cho, with Drum Accompaniment by Myong Hwan Kim*. Korean Britannica Corporation, Seoul, Korea, a Subsidiary of Encyclopaedia Britannica, Inc., 1982, 17–21.
Yi, Duhyeon. *Hanguk shingeuksa yeongu* (Study of Korean New Drama). Seoul: Seoul National University Press, 1966.
Yi, Gukja, *Pansori yesul mihak* (Aesthetics of Pansori Art). Seoul: Nanam shinseo, 1989.
Yi, Haejo. *Jayujong* (Liberty Bell). Seoul: Gwanghakseopo, 1910.

Yi, Hyegu. *Hanguk eumak yeongu* (Study of Korean Music). Seoul: Gungmin eumak yeonguhoe, 1957.

Yi, Injik. "Silvery World." In *Silvery World and Other Stories*, translated by Sora Kim Russell and edited, annotated, and with an introduction by Michael J. Pettid, 27–144. Ithaca, NY: Cornell University Press, 2019.

Yoo, Youngdae. "Changjak pansori Yeolsaga-e daehayeo (About the Creative Pansori Yeolsaga)." *Pansori yeongu (Journal of Pansori)*, 3 (1992): 370–2.

Yoo, Youngdae. "Pansori jeonseung hyeonhwang-gwa bojon bangan" (Current Status of Pansori Tradition and Preservation). *Pansori yeongu (Journal of Pansori)*, 36 (2014): 351–87.

Yu, Giryong. "Pansori 8 myeongchang-gwa jeonseungja-deul (Eight Pansori Virtuosos and Transmitters)." In Cho Dongil and Kim Heunggyu (eds.), *Pansori-eui ihae* (Understanding Pansori), 145–63. Seoul: Changjak-kwa bipyeongsa, 1978.

Yu, Minyeong. "Changgeuk." In *Hanguk minjok munhwa dae baekkwa sajeon* (Encyclopedia of Korean Culture). The Academy of Korean Studies, 1995. Available online: http://encykorea.aks.ac.kr/Contents/Item/E005534 (accessed March 15, 2023).

Yu, Minyeong. *Hanguk hyeondae huigoksa* (History of Modern Korean Drama). Seoul: Hongseong shinseo, 1982.

INDEX

A Different Chunhyang
(Serban) 157
A Slice of Spring 171
aak (graceful music) 81
AFKN (Armed Forces of
Korean Network) Radio
170
Ak-Dan-Gwang-Chil (ADG7)
167
Akhak gwebeom (standard
music text) 120, 145
Ambiguous Dance Company
167
Anderson Sutton, R. 159
Andong Kim Clan 91
Animal Farm (Orwell) 165
aniri (stylized speaking) 25,
165–166, 175, 180
Arirang 177
Aristotle 22, 24–25, 119
Asia–Pacific War (1941–5) 138
'autotelic' experience 72

badaksori (*bottom-sori*)
167–168, 187–188
Bae Changho 6
Bae Seolhyang 136–137
Bae Yeon-Hyung 25, 163
Bae-bijang taryeong (Ballad of
Chief Deputy Bae) 88–89
Baennorae (boat song) 5
bak (rhythm) 54
Bakhtin, Mikhail 3, 17

Ballad of Birds 18
Bang Manchun 98, 150
bangeum-booths 148
bangseok (cushions) 20
Batangkol Art Center 176
Bauman, Richard 160
Be-Se-To Theatre Festival 157
Bhabha, Homi 139, 152, 155,
188
bigabi 102
Birth Cord (Oh Taeseok) 156
Bishop, Isabella Bird 118, 183
Bong Joon-Ho 185
Boseongsori-style 175
Bow, Clara 154
boxcar (notation) 26
boyuja (cultural asset holder)
143–146, 188
Brecht, Bertolt 165
buchae (folding fans) 19, 21
buchimsae (musical
composition) 55, 93
Buddhism 15–16, 83
buk 19, 56
bukchae 19
bunchang (divided role singing)
72, 119
Byeon Gangshoe Taryeong see
Garujigi Taryeong
(femme fatale)
Byeongja Samin (Jo Junghwan)
129–131
byeongpung (screen) 20

Cao Cao 11–12
Catholicism 81
Centennial Pansori 177
centripetal force (Bakhtin) 3
changgeuk Chunhyang 137
changgeuk (operatic pansori)
  birth of 118–121
  and *bunchang* 72
  champions of 134–140
  and Euripides' *Medea* 157
  experimentation 122, 126, 128–129, 152
  Heungbo-ssi 161
  introduction 115
  of later 20th Century 156–157
  new 159–162
  and seven *taryeong* 86
  and *shinpa* style 132–133
  and Song Heunglok 105
  supporting young singers 160
  thriving in 1910s 133–134
  and Young Eungmin 107
changgeukcho 138–139
changjak pansori (creative pansori) 162
Chaplin, Charlie 154
chemyon (face) 20
Cheolchong, King 91
cheondokut 37
Cheong-eui jugeum (Cheong's Death) 176
Cheuksin (outhouse activities) 14
China 84, 95
Cho, Master 48
Cho Sanghyun 48, 107
Choe Byeongdo Taryeong 121–122

Choe Seondal 2, 97
Choe Yongseok 167
Chông Noshik 98
Chorübungen (Wüllner) 170
chuimsae 20, 32
chuimsae gosu (experts) 20
Chunchu magazine 121
Chung Hoisuk 144
Chung Kwonjin, Master 39, 42, 45–49, 55, 76–77, 107, 172–174
Chungcheong people 47, 97
Chunhyang (film) 26, 31, 48, 157
Chunhyang story 94–95, 103–104, 108–109, 119, 129
Chunpung (spring wind) 102
Chuseok (Korean Thanksgiving) 10
Clark, Jocelyn 147
Columbia Records 26
Confucius/Confucianism 15, 18, 22–23, 83, 91, 96, 115, 130
Csikszentmihalyi, Mihaly 72
Cultural Heritage Administration 145
Cultural Heritage Protection Act 144–145

Daehan Jeguk (Great Korean Empire) 117
daehwachang (dialogic singing) see *bunchang* (divided role singing)
Daesaseup of Jeonju 92
damunhwa gajeong (multicultural families) 162

danga (song) 32–33, 95
danggol 136
Dangun 53
danjungmori see *eotchungmori* (asymmetrical jungmori)
Dante-eui singok (Jung Eun-hye) 165
Deep-Rooted Tree Pansori Collection 99
Deokchin Gongweon park 92
Deoksu Palace 118
deoneum (musical composition)
 female 110
 and Hwang Sunmi 161
 individual artistic contribution 44–46, 99–100, 113
 introduction 27, 32
 lyrical 102
 and Pak Yujeon 107
 and Song Heunglok 105
Detective Baek Yeongho's Seoul Chase (Tamjeong Baek Yeongho-Gyeongseong Chugyeok-dieon) 167
DMZ (Demilitarized Zone) 182
dochang (singer-storyteller) 120
Dongmul nongjang 165
Dongnip shinmun, Independence Paper 116
dongpyeonche (singing) 46, 105, 135, 175
Dorihwaga (film) 95
dotchari (mat) 20
Downtown, Changgeukkwan venue 119
Dragon in the well 14
drums 1, 3, 19, 27, 31, 52–56, 72, 76–77

Eklund, Elizabeth 2
Enlightenment school of learning 116
eojeon-gwangdae (royal singers) 134–135
eonmori (asymmetrical drive) 66
eonmun ilchi (speech/transcription) 115
eotchungmori (asymmetrical jungmori) 66, 72, 76–77
Eunsegye (Silver World) 115, 121–128, 132

Farmers' Ballad 126
Feel the Rhythm of Korea (project) 167
Festival of Death 176
Finchum-Sung, Hilary 158–159
Fish Map (Eoryudogam) 167
Five Narratives (Obatang) 6–12, 44, 87, 93
Five Professional Generations time 86
Foley, Kathy 182
Fox Hunt and the Death of a Queen 182–184
Freyer, Achim 157

Gabo Reformation (1894) 6, 115
gageuk (music/drama) 132
Gagok weollyu 111, 199n.51
Gang Hanyeong 47–48, 93
Gang Sohyang 136
Gang Yonghwan 119–121, 135
Gangneung Maehwa taryeong (Ballad of the Plum Blossom of Gangneung) 89
Gangnyeong Talchum (mask dance) 174

Gangsan village 106
Gangsanche Poseong Sori (song) 58, 173–174
Gangsanche (river/mountain style) 47, 106
Gangsanche-Boseongsori (singing style) 106–108, 149, 203n.11
Gangsangpungweol (Wind/Moon/River) 32–33
Garujigi Taryeong (femme fatale) 86–87
Gasa chunhyangga ibaekku 85
gasa style 14
Gashinseon taryeong (Ballad of the Fake Immortal) 90
gayageum 76, 103
gayageum byeongchang 103
Gentlemen's Excursion Team 116
Gilsori (road song) 5
gisaeng (female performers)
   and abolition of government-control 136
   author's experience 172
   description 81–82
   and *Gisaeng Roll Call* 109–110
   and Jin Chaeseon 94–95
   lewd acts 119
   and opium addiction 138
   and *Song of Chunhyang* 84–85
   and Song Mangap 135
Gisaeng jeomgo (roll call) 109–110
Gisaeng Johap Yeonjuhoe (performance unions) 133
gisaeng Maengnyeol 105
Go Seonung 161

Go Sugwan 21, 97
Go-Song-Yeom-Mo 97
Gojong, Emperor 91, 117, 121, 134–135, 164
The Good Woman of Setzuan (Brecht) 165
Goody, Jack 12
Goryeo Dynasty 16, 83, 102, 179–180, 198n.35
Gourd Song 178
Grass Tomb (Oh Taeseok) 156
Grotowski's poor theatre 168, 187–188
gu-soseol (classical novels) 14
gu-yeonggeuk (old drama) 132
gueum (mouth music) 15
Gugak FM (broadcast) 143
gugak (music) 25, 139–140, 159, 167, 169, 172, 174, 185
Gugak Yesul Hakkyo School 173
gugeuk (old drama) 133, 134
gujeonshimsu 13
Gukka Brand Gongyeon Saeop (National Brand Performance Project) 157
gukkeuk (national drama) 134
gungmun (national writing) 6
gupageuk (old style) 132
gwageo examination 82–83, 115
Gwak-ssi 63
Gwang-pung-je-weol 33, 194n.5
gwangdae (male performers)
   aristocratic 102–105
   bottom strata 81
   introduction 2
   and Jeong Jaegeun 107

lewd acts 119
and new dramatists 133
and new pansori 166
norms during Joseon 20–21
and rural Koreans 135
serving as teachers 98
and Shin Jaehyo 99
socially outcast 92
tightrope performing 83
and Yi Dongbaek 135
Gwangeuk jeolgu shibisu (Go Sugwan) 21
Gwanglok 105
Gwangmudae Hyeomnyulsa venue 119
Gwanuhui (Song Manjae) 83
Gweon Samdeuk 49–50, 103–104
Gwian (Jeon Gi) 103
gwimyeongchang (great singer) 2
gyemyeoncho 46–49
Gyeongbok Palace 93–95
Gyeongdeureum 50
gyeongdeureum-cho 50
Gyeonggi; ogu-kut 37
Gyeonggi Province 97
Gyeongseong Gupa Baeu Johap (traditional actors) 133

Ha Handam 2, 97
Haeoe Myeongye Jeonseungja, (Honorary Overseas Transmitter) 174
Hague Peace Conference (1906) 164
Hahn, Reynaldo 151
hallyu (Korean wave) 3, 158, 174, 185
han 43–44, 188
Han Dynasty 11–12

Han Nongseon 104, 175
Han Seongjun 55, 120–121
Han Seonha 174
hanbok 20
hancha script 5, 115
hangeul script 4–6, 25, 83, 115–116, 125
Hanguk Gugak Hyeophoe (Korean Traditional Music Association) 144–145
hanji (mulberry paper) 6
hanmun (logographic literacy) 5
hansi (poetry) 85
Hawai'i 177–179
Heo Geumpa 136
heung (spirit) 25
Heungbo 83, 134, 161, 178
Heungbo-ssi (production) 161
Heungboga 9
Heunglok 97
Heungseon Daeweongun, Prince 91–95, 102, 106–107, 109–110, 134
Hideyoshi Invasion (1597) 93, 163
History of Korean Singing Drama (Jeong Noshik) 98
hogeolche (heroic mode) 49–50, 104
hogeolche-Junggocho (style) 47
Holub, Miroslave 25
Hong Giltong 129, 210n.28
Hong Giltong-jeon 210n.28
Honolulu Theatre for Youth 180–181
Howard, Keith 158
Huidae auditorium 118–120, 124
   see also Weongaksa Theatre

Huigeuk Useung-Yeolpae (Ito Otzu) 129–130
Huong's Hope Diary (production) 162
Hwang Sunmi 160–161
Hwanin 53
Hwanung 53
hwaraengi 15
hwarang (flower youths) 15–16
hwimori (sweeping/vortexing) 66
hyangak (ritual music) 23
Hyeomnyulsa office 118

Ibyeolga (parting song) 50, 107
Il-gosu, yi-myeongchang 54
Ilsan 55, 76, 195n.6
Im Chunhaeng 139
Im Hwa 122
Im Jintaek 165
Im Kwon-taek 31
imyeon (interior dimension) 42–44, 49
ingan munhwajae (human cultural heritage) 144
Intertwined Lives, Korean and Western Women 182
ipchechang (three-dimensional singing) *see bunchang* (divided role singing)
Isan-jeosan see *Sacheolga* (song)
ishim-jeonshim 112
isuja 145
Ito Hirobumi 164
Ito Otzu 129

jaebeol conglomerates 165
jajinmori (frequent beat) 58, 76–77
jaktu (shaman blades) 155
Jang Pangae 105, 137

Jang Seo-Yoon 165–166
jangdan (long/short) 25, 27, 53–56, 76
janggo (drum) 38
Jangki taryeong (Ballad of the Pheasant) 89–90
Japan 116–119, 121, 128–129, 138
Japan–China conflict 90
Jayujong (Freedom Bell) (Yi Haejo) 128–129
Jebi nojeonggi (swallow's flight itinerary) 103
Jebiga (Song of Swallows) 104–105, 198–199nn.41-2
Jenkins, Henry 31
Jeokpyeok 150
Jeokpyeokka 11
Jeolla *muga* (shaman song) 66
Jeolla style 47, 97
Jeollado 97
Jeon Doseong 45, 97, 104, 135–136
Jeon Gi 103
Jeonbuk Provincial Changgeuk Company 161
Jeong Byeongheon 63
Jeong Chunpung 102–103, 107
Jeong Eungmin 107, 148
Jeong Gyeongjin 162
Jeong Hyeonseok 96, 197n.22
Jeong Jaegeun 107
Jeong Jeongnyeol 137–138, 150–151
Jeong Noshik 45, 63, 86, 97, 98, 106, 134–135
Jeong Yagyong 81
jeongak (court music) 23, 48, 81
jeongganbo (notation) 26
Jeongshim jeongeum 42

INDEX 223

Jeonju *daesaseup* competition 106
Jeonnam Provincial Changgeuk Company 162
jeonsusaeng (initiates) 145, 174
jeontonggeuk (traditional play) 134
Ji Gihak 160–161
Ji Yeonghui, Master 172–173
Jin Chaeseon 94–95, 109–110
Jindo islands 97
Jinguk myeongsan (song) 35, 173
jinogwi-kut (rite of passage) 37
Jinyang-jo (slow six-beat) 39, 63, 76
Jiri Mountain 46, 149
Jo Junghwan 129
Joseon changgeuksa (Noshik) 86, 136
Joseon dynasty
  absolute monarchy of 81
  court performance protocols 145
  and Daeweongun 93
  and Dangun the founder 53
  end of 183
  fall of 92
  introduction 5–6, 16, 20
  and narrative imagination 83
  political purges in 156
  pre-modern literature 122
  shaman culture in 37
  spiraling debilitation of 128
Joseon Seongak Yeonguhoe (Association Korean Vocal Music Study) 137
Josun Hotel 117
Jowang (kitchen god) 14
Ju Hojong 162
Jukchang manghye (song) 35

jul-gwangdae (tightrope) 83
Jung Eun-hye 165
Jung Mong-heon 182, 207n.13
junggoche (style singing) 47, 135, 150, 195n.25
jungin 93
jungjungmori (faster *jungmori*) 58, 105–106
jungjungmori jangdan 72
jungmori (12-beat cycle) 33, 58, 63, 66, 72, 76, 95, 104

K-culture 185
K-drama 162
K-pop 160, 188
K-sound 166–168
kabuki act 128
Kang Daeseung 174
Keller, Nora Okja 181
Kellogg, Robert 17
Killick, Andrew 124
Kim Chaeman 135
Kim Changhwan 118, 122, 135, 137
Kim Changnyong 104, 138
Kim Chohyang 137
Kim Euicheol noraemoeum (record) 170
Kim Geumhwa 155
Kim Gyeonghui 139, 170
Kim Gyutaek 152–154, 156
Kim Hongdo 82
Kim Jeongmun 105, 137
Kim Jiha 165
Kim Myeongja 159
Kim Myonghwan *see* Ilsan
Kim Nokchu 137
Kim Okkyun 122
Kim Sejong 107, 111–112
Kim Seongok 105

Kim Sohui 137, 139, 170–171
Kim Yeoran 137
Kim Youngja 144
Kim Yundeok 42
King of Sori (*Gawang*) 105–106
kkwaenggari (gong) 54
kokua 178
Korea Britannica Corporation 99
Korea and Her Neighbors (Bishop) 118
Korean court music 26
Korean Traditional Music Association 174
Korean War (1950–3) 6, 140, 148, 162
Korea–US Commercial Treaty 116
Koryo examination system 16
Kristeva, Julia 116
kut (healing ritual) 14, 38, 189
kwangdae (a singer) 3, 86, 96
Kwanghae, Prince 82

La Divina Commedia 165
Lee Jong-pil 95
Lee, Ki-baik 5
Leenalchi (modern look pansori) 167
Liu Bei 12
Lord, Albert 6
Love Song of Chunhyang 178
Lovers' Parting Song (*Ibyeolga*) 107
Luo Guanzhong 11
Lutwak, Mark 181

MacDonald, Margaret Mead 2
Madangeul naon amtark (*Hen Who Dreamed She Could Fly*) 161

Maeil shinbo 129
Manga (funeral dirge) 5, 176
Manhwajip (Yu Chinhan) 85
March First National Independence Movement (1919) 164
Medea (Euripides) 157
Melville, Herman 165
menari-che (provincial style) 49
Michin Gwangdae (the Mad Singers) 160–161
Milling Song 178
Min, Empress 183
Mo Heunggap 97, 108, 148
Modern Chunhyang (Kim Gyutaek) 152–153
Modern Shim Cheong (Kim Gyutaek) 152–153, 156
Mr. Rabbit and the Dragon King (Freyer) 157
mudang (Korean shamans) 14
 see also shamans
musok (ritual) 15
Musugi taryeong (Ballad of the Philanderer Musugi) 90
My Heart (film) 6
myeongchang (star singers) 92

Namsadang performance troupe 92
National Center for Traditional Performing Arts 140
National Changgeuk Company 86, 140, 157, 161
National Democratic Youth Students Alliance 164
National Intangible Cultural Heritage system 38, 143
National Revolutionary Party 164

Neo-Confucianism 5, 16, 23, 81–83, 88
  see also Confucius/Confucianism
nongaktan (all-women) 139
Nongbuga, Farmers' Ballad 5, 178
Northwestern Haesukut ocean ritual 155

Obatang (Gentlemen's Pansori) 6–7, 11, 16, 31, 88, 90–98, 155
Official Heo Eui, Royal Music Institute 82
Oh Taeseok 156
Ojeok (The Five Bandits) 164–166
Oliver, Kelly 116
Omae Arirang (Mother's Arirang) 161
Ong, Walter 1, 4, 147
Onggojip taryeong (Ballad of the Curmudgeon) 87–88, 197n.10
Onstage2.0 167
opium addiction 138
Orwell, George 165
O'Shea, Suzanne 25

Pak Choweol 137
Pak Dongjin, Master 150, 156
Pak Dongsil 163
Pak Gwihui 139
Pak Heonbong 149
Pak Heungbo 177–180
Pak Heungbo Went to Almaty (play) 179
Pak Hwang 134–135, 137
Pak Hyogwan 110, 199n.51

Pak Mansun 97
Pak Nokchu 104–105, 137, 139
Pak Seonghwan 161–162, 162
Pak Yangdok, Master 149, 175
Pak Yujeon 106–107
p'ansori (folk art) 3–4, 97–98, 155
Pansori Hakhoe (Association of Pansori Study) 143
Pansori ibaengnyeonsa (Pak Hwang) 137
Pansori Ilgop Madang 86
pansori requisites
  deugeum (vocal attainment) 94
  inmul (appearance) 94
  neoreumsae (accompanying gesture) 94
  saseol (narrative composition) 94
Park Chunghee, President 155, 164
Park Dongjin 47
Park In-Hye 165
Parry, Milman 6
Pearl Harbor 138
Pettid, Michael 115
Picture Bride 178
Pihl, Marshall 3, 37, 94, 97
Pilgyeongsa Bartleby (Park In-Hye) 165
Plato 22
Pungmul (farmers' band music) 54, 174
Pyeonsichun, A Slice of Spring (song) 170–171

Red Cliff, Yangzi River 12
Romance of Three Kingdoms 11
Russia 118

Ryu Jangyeong 162
Ryu Kyeong Ho 132

Sacheolga (song) 35–36
Sacheon-ga (Yi Jaram) 165
sadaebu (scholar-intellectuals) 27
saepansori (new pansori) 160–163
Samgak Mountain 173
samgang oryun 16, 23
Samil yuga (painting) 82
san-kongbu (mountain study) 149
Sang, land of 5
Sang river 102
sanjo (scattered melody) 147
Saseol (narrative) 99–100, 102, 175
Saseoljip collection (Jaehyo) 87
satiric adaptations 152–154
Saussure, Ferdinand de 147
Scholes, Robert 17
segyeong bonpuri 37
Sejong the Great, King 5–6, 115
Semachi (faster *jinyang*) 63, 66
semachi jangdan 66
Seomjin River 46
Seong Changsun 107, 144
Seong Geumnyeon, Master 76, 172–173, 207n.6
Seong Uhyang 107
seongeum (voice music) 27, 32, 41–43, 49, 63
Seopyeonche (film) 135
Seopyeonche (singing style) 46, 106
Seoul Olympics (1988) 157

Seoyugyeonmun, Travel Observations of the West (Yu Gilchun) 116
Serban, Andrei 157
shamans 2, 15–16, 37–38, 66, 81–82, 89, 136, 155, 166–167, 189
Shilla kingdom 15–16
Shim Cheong 1, 26, 31, 129, 137, 150, 176, 181–182
Shimcheongga 8
Shin Jaehyo 47, 50, 87, 91, 93–99, 102, 107, 109–110, 166
Shin Manyeop 45
Shin Wi 21, 97
Shin Yunbok 82
shin-soseol (new novel) 121–122, 128
shin-yeongeuk (new drama/theatre) 121, 132, 134
shingeuk (new drama) 132–133
shinmyeong (spirit) 25
shinpa (new style) 124, 128–134, 140
shinpa-gatta (acts like shinpa) 132
shintoburi 155–156
Shipchangga (Song of Ten Lashes) 103
siki-da (to compel) 42
Singer Song Heunglok 92
sinim changdan see Jeolla *muga* (shaman song)
Sinitic literacy 96
Sirhak philosophy 81
Skitcheneongju (house spirit) 14
Slice of Spring (song) 171, 206n.4
So river 102

sogak (crude music) 81
Song of Ahn Junggeun 164
Song of Chunhyang
 (Chunhyangga)
 domination of 84–85
 example of *hwimori* usage 66
 and *Gangsanche Boseongsori* repertoire 107–111, 113, 175
 and *han* 44
 introduction 5, 7–8, 18, 21
 and Jeong Jeongnyeol 150–151
 and Kim Jiha 165
 major repertoires of 99–100
 story of 153–154
 ujo and gyemyeoncho 47
 and Yi Mongnyong 50
The Song of Crops 180
Song Gideok 103
Song of Gwangdae (Gwangdaega) 50, 94
Song Gwangnok 55
Song of Heungbo (Heungboga) 9–10, 18, 66, 103–104, 125, 175
Song Heunglok 92, 97, 104–105, 135, 148
Song Mangap 104–105, 135–137
Song Manjae 82–83
Song of Medicines (*Yakseongga*) 19, 167
Song of the Red Cliff (Jeokpyeokka) 11–12, 18, 84, 94
Song of Shim Cheong (Shimcheongga) 5, 8–9, 18, 31, 49, 58, 72, 105, 143–144, 173–174

Song Uryong 105
Song of the Water Palace (Sugungga) 10–11, 18, 84, 105–106, 167, 175
Song of Yu Gwansun 164
sori buk (drum) 55–56
sori (singing)
 canonical five 86
 and *Dongmul nongjang* 165
 and English *aniri* 175, 180–181
 graphic linguistics of 111–113
 as measure of humanity 151–152
 and opium addiction 138
 oral transmission of 172
 and Pak Yujeon 107
 past importance of 148–149
 polishing 149–151
 projection onto visual realm 120
 and *Seopyeonche* 135
 and *sorichaek* 25
 teacher 172
 and teaching 26
 training of Master Chung 173
 transmission of 145–146
sorichaek (scripts) 25–26, 146–148, 173
soripuri (oral recognition) 97
Sosang palgyeong (eulogy) 102–103
soseol-yeongeuk (novel drama) 122
Spry, Tami 169
square bar (notation) 26
ssitkimkut (cleansing ritual) 37–39
Stanislavskian 'method acting' 43, 116

subsidiary voices 49–52
Sugungga, Song of the Water Palace 10–11, 45, 157
Sugyeong nangja jeon (Tale of Miss Sugyeong) 90
Sukchong the Great, King 7
Sun Quan 12
Sung Uhyang 175
Sunjong, King 121
Survey of Vocal Music (Pak Heonbong) 149
Swallow Calling Song (Nolbo) 104
Symposia on Korean Kut and P'ansori 155

Tang dynasty 23
taryeong (ballads) 86, 122
Tiger Comes Down (*Beom naryo onda*) 167
Tokki barrack (hare protests) 45
Tokugawa Shogunate 128
Tongjeongdaebu Lordship 135
tongseong 50
'True River-Mountain Style' 106–107
ttomaksori (excerpt singing) 72
Ttorang Gwangdae Contest (2005) 159
ttorang gwangdae (singer in the gully) 159–160
Turner, Victor 188

ujo gyeongdeureum 50
ujo style 102
Ujo/Gyemyeoncho 46–49
UNESCO Intangible Cultural Heritage of Humanity status 143
Unhyeon Palace, Seoul 92, 95

Universal Ballet 31
Urigeoseun joeungeosiyeo (catchphrase) 156

van Gennep, Arnold 188

Walcha taryeong see Musugi taryeong (Ballad of the Philanderer Musugi)
wanchang (entire narrative singing) 72
warm-up 32–33, 35–36
Watt, Ian 12
weonbakdaero (basic beat) 77
Weongaksa Theatre 119, 121, 135–136
Weongudan prayer hall 117
weonhyeong (archetypes) 24, 140
When Tiger Smoked Its Pipe (play) 181
Why Did Shim Cheong Plungeinto the Sea Twice? (Oh Taeseok) 156
Willoughby, Heather 158
World Cup (2002) 158
Wu Chundae 2
Wüllner, Frantz 170

yangban (ruling class)
  and *bigabi* 102
  and Gweon Samdeuk 103
  introduction 5–6, 14, 18
  and Jindo islands 97
  and *jungin* 93
  and new dramatic intellectualism 133
  paintings of Shin Yunbok 82–83
  and Song Mangap 136
Yangju, Gyeonggi Province 93

Yates-Lu, Anna 160
Yeolsaga (Songs of the Patriots) 163–164
Yeom Gyedal 50, 97, 148
yeonchang (consecutive singing) 72
Yeongeuk (theatre/play/drama) 133
yeonhui (playful talent display) 133–134
Yeoseong gukkeuk (all-women *changgeuk*) 170
   see also *changgeuk* (operatic pansori)
yeoseong gukkeuk-dan (all-women companies) 139
Yi Bohyeong 99–100
Yi Cheongjun 135
Yi Dongbaek 47, 119, 121–122, 135
Yi Haejo 128–129
Yi Hwajungseon 137

Yi Injik 119, 121–125, 128
Yi Jaegak, Governor 135–136
Yi Jaram 161, 165
Yi Jun 163–164
Yi Mongnyong 50
Yi Nalchi 55, 97, 167
Yi Sunshin, Admiral 163
Yi Wanyong 119, 128
Yoo Yeongdae 163
Yu Chinhan 85
Yu Geum 85
Yu Gilchun 116–117
Yu Giryong 55
yuga event 82–83
yukchabaegi-tori 38–40, 194.12
yukpo 26
yulchabo 26
Yun Bonggil 164
Yushin Constitutional Reformation (1972) 164

Zeami Motokiyo 43

Printed in the USA
CPSIA information can be obtained
at www.ICGtesting.com
LVHW020054280124
770066LV00003B/175